STATE HOUSES

AMERICA'S 50 STATE CAPITOL BUILDINGS

Susan W. Thrane
Tom Patterson

The BOSTON
MILLS PRESS

A Boston Mills Press Book

Copyright © 2005 Susan W. Thrane & Tom Patterson

First printing

Publisher Cataloging-in-Publication Data (U.S.)

Thrane, Susan W.

State houses : America's 50 state capitol buildings / Susan W. Thrane ; Tom Patterson.

[336] p. : col. photos. ; cm.

 Includes bibliographical references and index.

Summary: American state capitol buildings – exterior and interior photographs
and essays reveal the history, architecture, design, and art of the buildings
and their symbolic and practical roles as homes of the state legislatures.

ISBN 1-55046-457-4

1. Capitols–United States—Guidebooks. I. Patterson, Tom, 1958- II. Title.
973 dc22   NA4410.7 .T57 2005

Library and Archives Canada Cataloguing in Publication

Thrane, Susan W.
      State houses : America's 50 state capitol buildings / Susan W.
Thrane and Tom Patterson.

Includes bibliographical references and index.
ISBN 1-55046-457-4

      1. Capitols--United States--Guidebooks. I. Patterson, Tom, 1958-
II. Title.

NA4410.7.T48 2005   973C2005-901646-9

Published by Boston Mills Press, 2005

132 Main Street, Erin, Ontario N0B 1T0
Tel: 519-833-2407 Fax: 519-833-2195
e-mail: books@bostonmillspress.com
www.bostonmillspress.com

In Canada:
Distributed by Firefly Books Ltd.
66 Leek Crescent
Richmond Hill, Ontario, Canada L4B 1H1

In the United States:
Distributed by Firefly Books (U.S.) Inc.
P.O. Box 1338, Ellicott Station
Buffalo, New York 14205

The publisher gratefully acknowledges the financial support for our publishing
program by the Canada Council for the Arts, the Ontario Arts Council and the
Government of Canada through the Book Publishing Industry Development Program.

Design by Tom Patterson
Texas Capitol photographs by Tom Patterson, courtesy State Preservation Board; Austin, Texas

Printed in Singapore

Cover–The Great Western Staircase, New York State Capitol
Half-title page–The West Virginia State Capitol
Page 2–Hall of Flags, Massachusetts State House
Page 6–Rotunda detail, Missouri State Capitol

In memory of my parents
J. C. Nelson Waddell
1906–1955
Bernice Marguerite Wilhelmina Englehardt Waddell
1911–1994

For Ray Monsalvatge
who looked at my brothers and me and said,
"What hath Bill and Jane wrought?"

CONTENTS

PREFACE

My interest in state capitols can be traced back to my childhood in rural Iowa, not far from Iowa City, the state's first capital. There, amid the University of Iowa buildings and overlooking the Iowa River, stood the old stone Greek Revival capitol. To me it was the largest and most handsome building in the world.

My father knew its history: it was the territorial capitol (1842–1846) where Iowa inaugurated its first governor; home to the first six General Assemblies from 1846 to 1857; the site where the state constitution was drafted and where the state university was chartered in 1847. In fact, the capitol was the university's first permanent structure, and it housed the University of Iowa's administrative offices for over 113 years as the university built around and enveloped it. When my family traveled throughout the United States (most memorably in a 1948 Ford), we looked for state capitols, often recognizable by their Renaissance-style golden domes.

While preparing this book, I discovered that we were not alone in our interest. The admiration, even veneration, of people toward their civic temples became increasingly evident. This was especially clear to me the day I was visiting Des Moines and working in the elegant law library of the present Iowa State Capitol. I was interrupted by news from Iowa City that the first capitol, now a landmark, was burning. As the tragedy unfolded, I joined the librarians watching the collapse of its cupola on the Internet. Simultaneously, throughout the building and the state, distraught Iowans wept at their loss.

This respect and devotion are not surprising. Capitols are symbols of democracy. They are homes of history, where leaders are elected and laws are passed. Moreover, capitols reflect the unique past and identity of each state and, collectively, of the United States. Architecturally, despite the fact that

Iowa's old capitol with its reconstructed cupola.

at least thirty-two states have capitols with externally visible domes, each is distinctive. They are also repositories of arts and crafts in the stained glass, carved wood, delicate ironwork, mosaic tiles and large murals that are no longer economically feasible to incorporate into new public buildings.

Significantly, in our increasingly rootless twenty-first-century society, the capitols bring continuity from our past to the future. And the business carried on within these historic structures has become increasingly relevant to the lives of each of us as states assume a growing role in the fluctuating federal system.

The buildings notwithstanding, differences in the legislation of the fifty states demonstrate their unique character. One vintage legislation, "An Act Directing what Fence shall be deemed lawful," was enacted by the Vermont General Assembly in 1780, before Vermont became a part of the United States, and remains on the books. In contrast, the Wisconsin legislature outlawed oleomargarine until 1967 and still restricts its use. Throughout the book, many of the chapters contain examples of other laws passed in the legislative chambers of these buildings.

And along the way, what history and stories were discovered! During 1807, in the old house of the Virginia Capitol, Aaron Burr was tried for treason and acquitted, with John Marshall, chief justice of the United States Supreme Court, presiding. Angelina Grimke, the first woman known to address a state legislative body, gave a speech advocating the abolition of slavery in the old Massachusetts House of Representatives in 1838. In Ohio, in order to save money, the General Assembly drafted prisoners to build its state house. Jefferson Davis proclaimed independence and the birth of the Confederacy from Alabama's old state capitol, where later, in 1963, civil-

Kansas House of Representatives chamber.

rights activists protested Alabama's newly inaugurated governor, George Wallace. Wallace promised loyalty to segregation while standing on the capitol steps, within view of Martin Luther King's Dexter Avenue Baptist church. In Kansas, semi-nude women in frescoes commissioned by the Populist Party were replaced with fully clothed figures when the Republican Party took control.

While these are special, singular events, one in particular that tied many of the state capitols together and focused national attention on them occurred following Lincoln's assassination. His body was transported from Washington, D.C., to Springfield, Illinois, by train, befitting his strong support of railroads, first as an attorney and then as president.

During a three-week period, the cortège stopped at Pennsylvania's capitol, in Harrisburg, and at New York's state capitol, in Albany, before his body was brought through the front doors of the state house in Columbus, Ohio, and lay in state for eight hours. Thousands of grieving Hoosiers later filed through the first Indianapolis State House, when for eighteen hours his body lay in state in its rotunda. For two days in Representatives Hall of the Illinois old capitol, seventy-five thousand mourners passed before his casket before the burial in his hometown of Springfield. This mourning did not take place in churches or business auditoriums but in state capitols, or as some call them, civic churches, symbolic of state government and American democracy.

Events such as these indicate that state capitols represent history, as well as being repositories of legislation, architectural design, and especially interior design and artwork. The art is more than decoration — it conveys the state's history, by emphasizing public figures and events and by promoting government. Thomas Hart Benton and N. C. Wyeth created murals with westward expansion themes for Missouri's capitol in Jefferson City. The New Mexico State Capitol is considered an art museum, with changing displays of works by living New Mexican artists, reflecting the state's unique heritage. Charles M. Russell's painting of Lewis and Clark meeting Native Americans in 1805 dominates the Montana House chamber, while above the grand staircase is

a mural depicting the driving of the golden spike commemorating the completion of the transcontinental Northern Pacific Railroad at Gold Creek, Montana. Also noteworthy are John Steuart Curry's mural of John Brown in Kansas, Gilbert Stuart's portrait of George Washington in Rhode Island, and Virginia's life-size statue of one of its favorite sons, George Washington. War memorials and statuary placed on the buildings and grounds include a statue of Sergeant Alvin C. York, a hero of the First World War, on the grounds of Tennessee's capitol and Daniel Chester French's sculpture of the gilded quadriga above the entrance portico of the Minnesota Capitol. Moreover, after the Civil War, installing such public art as Confederate memorials preserved the culture of the South.

Eager to absorb and connect with the fifty capitols, my journey began in New England, followed by the Mid-Atlantic states and the Midwest, then on to the remaining states. While Atlanta, Boston, Honolulu and Denver are major metropolitan centers, others exist and are primarily known because they are state capitols. Juneau, for example, has only about thirty-one thousand inhabitants. Helena, Frankfort, Augusta and Pierre are even smaller than Juneau, but Vermont's Montpelier is the smallest, with less than one third the population of Juneau.

Throughout this long project I came into contact with too many men and women to acknowledge individually their gracious and enthusiastic assistance. They include state archivists and librarians, state historical preservation officers, capitol curators and historians, legislative council attorneys and staff, capitol tour guides, state legislators and officials. I am, however, particularly indebted to my children, John Wilfong and Sara Wilfong, and my husband, Bill Thrane, for their ongoing encouragement, support and good humor. After a hiking accident that had a significant impact on my ability to proceed, they rearranged schedules, became my drivers and travel companions, took on additional domestic responsibilities, and overall contributed to making life easier so that my work could be completed. Thank you.

Susan Waddell Thrane

INTRODUCTION

In the United States, with over 282 million people in fifty states with fifty capitols,* each state capitol bears some similarity to the others, yet individually reflects its state architecturally, culturally and historically. Each one is a noteworthy example of public-building architecture, constructed with a belief that the seat of government should be something significant — a monument located in a prominent position, constructed with the best available materials, surrounded by a park, and also more likely than not with a dome, rotunda, temple front and legislative wings.

The development of the architectural style of the American state capitol rose from the eastern seaboard, a region that also played a prominent role in the early growth of the United States. It was influential in the separation from England, and home to many early leaders, including Thomas Jefferson and Boston official Charles Bulfinch, architects of two of the earliest capitols.

Virginia's capitol, attributed to Jefferson, represented the first time an ancient temple form was adapted for use as a modern public building in either the United States or Europe. It set a precedent for incorporating Classical forms into American capitols and other public buildings. The design reflected Jefferson's belief in the power of architecture to influence democracy as practiced in ancient Greece and to distinguish it from the architecture associated with English royalty, as had been earlier constructed in Williamsburg, Virginia.

Following the addition of a dome to the Maryland State House around 1790, the Massachusetts State House, designed by Bulfinch, advanced the concept of this structure. Domes, particularly Bulfinch's hemispherical dome and its successor, a dome done in the popular Renaissance style, became the most prominent architectural symbol of American democracy and government authority. Inside, Doric Hall became a commemorative and ceremo-

Virginia State Capitol.

nial meeting place and predecessor to the central rotunda, which was later located below the dome. Bulfinch's Boston State House also set a precedent by following the lead of the Massachusetts Old State House in placing all governmental functions in a single building. Consequently, Bulfinch's state house is often referred to as the "Mother of the Capitols."

The towns in New England set a further precedent by fiercely competing to become their state's capital and thus, or so they believed, assuring their future growth and prosperity. As the states settled, early capitals were often located at a convenient site until a more central location was chosen. A larger and more impressive capital followed. Boston and Hartford were obvious choices for capitals in Massachusetts and Connecticut because of their colonial prominence. Boston, perhaps because of its prized Bulfinch-designed state house, persevered and overturned a bid to remove the capital to the more centrally located Worcester. Connecticut's General Assembly met in both New Haven and Hartford until the present capitol in Hartford was constructed.

By the nineteenth century, as the population of the United States increased and state governments started to expand, inadequate capitols or those destroyed by fire were replaced by larger buildings. Influenced by Jefferson's Virginia Capitol and the studies of Greek antiquities, many states adopted the Greek Revival architectural style for their capitols. The symmetry and orderly forms symbolized their own freedom and democracy. An added advantage to the adoption of this style was that the buildings were often designed from pattern books and constructed by unskilled workers, who were capable of working with the style's uncomplicated form of rectangular shapes, simple columns, plain pilasters and pedimented gables.

Because capitol *and* capital *are pronounced similarly, they are sometimes confused.* Capitol *is the building where legislatures convene, while* capital *refers to the city in which the government is located.*

The Illinois State Capitol.

It was also the period of the construction of the national Capitol. President James Monroe, impressed with the Massachusetts State House and Bulfinch's work, appointed him the architect of the federal Capitol in 1817. Bulfinch subsequently spent twelve years supervising its completion, designing the west front before completing his last building, the Maine State House. He designed the wooden dome of the federal Capitol, similar to the one he planned for the Boston State House. Later, during the Civil War, Thomas Walter, inspired by the domes of St. Peter's Basilica in Rome, St. Paul's Cathedral in London, and the Hotel des Invalides in Paris, replaced the Bulfinch dome with a larger, higher and more pointed cast-iron one.

Following the completion of the federal Capitol, a building boom started in state capitols and for the most part followed a pattern similar to the national one. They incorporated Bulfinch's three-part design, which Walter expanded, with its remodeled dome, rotunda, temple portico and wings, along with the now-priceless mosaics, statuary, murals and stained glass. One of the earliest was California, even though, prior to the transcontinental railroad, it was effectively cut off from the east coast due to the difficult transportation options of shipping over land or around South America. Old capitols needed to be enlarged to create more space, although many states wanted new, larger and more ornate buildings. This was especially apparent during the Gilded Age, those decades following the Civil War that were marked by prosperity and often excess. Economic growth and affluence facilitated these costly architectural projects.

Other influences on design included accelerating technological change with, among other things, the availability of cast iron to build larger domes and more intricate architectural ornamentation. There was also the influence of the École des Beaux-Arts, a late nineteenth-century French institution where leading architects trained in the classical styles. Large and grandiose buildings with an abundance of detail and finishes characterize the Beaux Arts style. Adding equal wings, the usual location of the richly decorated legislative chambers, reflected the power and importance of the Senate and House of Representatives as equally responsible for making states' laws, along with the removal of the governors to a separate area or floor, resulting in the strengthening of the concept of the Doctrine of Separation of Powers.

The capitols not only became monuments to governmental authority but to state pride, with many states competing to outshine neighboring and other states. New York's capitol, built to impress the world and last forever, was the most expensive building at that time. In 1898, during the construction

A model of the Georgia State Capitol's dome displayed in its capitol museum.

of its capitol, Rhode Island enlarged the diameter of its dome by five feet, purportedly so it would be larger than Minnesota's dome (also under construction). Wisconsin, a mostly rural state widely known for its progressive thinking and a pioneer in social legislation, constructed an elaborate Beaux Arts building with a lavish interior incorporating over forty different types of marble and precious stones imported from around the world.

Many architects working during this time were acquainted with each other's work. They often entered the same competitions or collaborated on projects that resulted in the incorporation of similar ideas and styles into the capitols. Elijah Myers, chosen as architect in Michigan,

The Wisconsin State Capitol in downtown Madison.

wings. Its style, American Classicism, is a form of public architecture that incorporates historical elements from the architecture of fifteenth- and sixteenth-century Renaissance Italy, reflecting the government buildings of ancient Greece and Rome. These buildings express order, symmetry and ceremony. The style also merged contemporary technological innovations with detailed masonry, hung on a steel-frame skeleton. The Rhode Island State House influenced other capitol designs such as the larger and more decorative Minnesota State Capitol, designed by Cass Gilbert, a former draftsman for McKim, Mead & White. Other capitols built in the American Classicism style include Utah, Kentucky, Montana, Arkansas,

Texas and Colorado, lost in other competitions, such as Wyoming and Georgia. Cass Gilbert, architect in Minnesota, Arkansas and West Virginia, lost in the Missouri, Montana and Wisconsin competitions. Charles Emlen Bell modeled South Dakota's capitol after his Montana Capitol design, while later in the twentieth century, North Carolina and Florida selected Edward Durell Stone to create their buildings.

Another influence was the World's Columbian Exposition, held in Chicago during 1893. The exposition, timed to celebrate the four hundredth anniversary of Christopher Columbus's voyage to the Americas, displayed technological, scientific, and cultural advances. It influenced architecture by elevating the Classical style for public buildings while displacing heavier forms such as the Romanesque and the elaborate Victorian style. The long stretches of columns, pilasters and arches of the pure white exhibition halls inspired the Rhode Island State House, designed by the architectural firm of McKim, Mead & White.

Rhode Island's State House features a colonnaded dome over a central block, a portico and matching

Idaho, Wisconsin, West Virginia, Missouri and Washington.

Washington's was the next to last of the domed American Classicism capitols; this building tradition ended with the West Virginia Capitol, completed in 1932. Rhode Island's influence on the design of Washington's capitol probably resulted from its architects, Wilder & White, who worked for McKim, Mead & White during the period in which the firm designed the Rhode Island State House. Certain features are similar, such as the rotundas, and both have the state seal embedded in their floor. The Rhode Island exterior incorporates four small domes, or tourelles, supported by columns at the base of the central dome. The original plans for Washington's capitol called for these features too, but in the end the columns were eliminated. Another similarity is that they both have solid masonry domes, an unusual feature in modern construction.

Unfortunately, during this period of enthusiastic capitol construction, many rumors of fraud and graft also surfaced. For example, an inquiry into charges of graft and corruption in the 1891 construction of the New Jersey Assembly chamber yielded a report

The Nebraska State Capitol.

detailing a committee's findings that included the following: "In the rebuilding of the Assembly chamber, which cost $232,000, an architect was employed who had never designed or erected a building. Of much of the work he appeared to have no control, it being under the supervision of the Governor. No plans of this work appear to be in the possession of the State except certain blueprints found among rubbish in the cellar of the State House. While much of the State House is said to have been done by contract after competitive bidding, the evidence of that fact is missing from the public files."

Not far away, in Pennsylvania, state officials and contractors were imprisoned along with the architect of the capitol, Joseph M. Huston. Huston served six months and twenty days in the state's eastern penitentiary following his conviction of conspiracy to defraud Pennsylvania by accepting bribes for work on the nearly $13 million building and charging more than $5 million for fraudulent overpayments to suppliers. The public was particularly outraged by the cost of a bootblack stand, located in the Senate men's room, that a supplier bought for $125 then subsequently charged the state $1,619.20.

Determining the chronological date of the fifty state capitols is difficult and clearly subjective. Complicating matters, many states boast about their status and right to be considered the oldest this or that. Convening its first legislative session during the fall of 1779, the Maryland State House, with its 1905 attached addition, is considered the oldest building in continuous legislative use in the United States. New Hampshire (1819) claims to be the oldest state house still in use with the full legislature meeting in its original chambers. Massachusetts dates to 1796, but its House of Representatives moved to a new chamber and its Senate took its place in the original Bulfinch-designed building. Vermont (1859) claims its legislative chambers are the oldest in their original condition. The Virginia State Capitol maintains that it houses the oldest continuous legislative body in America, with the present legislature descending from the colonial House of Burgesses. It also claims to be the second-oldest working capitol, having been in continuous use since October 1788 when the Assembly held its first session in the not-yet-completed building. New Jersey considers its state house to be the second oldest one, although little visibly remains of the original 1792 structure, a tiny part of the governor's reception area buried within today's sprawling building.

During the years of the Depression, interest in state capitols and the activity in their legislative chambers declined in importance as the role of the federal government increased in power and influence. The Second World War further reduced state legislative activity, and states ceded more authority to the federal government. As interest shifted to Washington, D.C., capitols were often neglected, until the late 1950s, when the federal government slowly began distributing funds and more responsibility back to the states. By the 1960s, with population and state government growing, many aging capitols were threatened with deteriorating wiring and plumbing, space pressures or obsolescence. State functions were often moved to separate buildings such as state libraries, legislative office buildings or annexes.

Also during the 1960s and into the 1970s, renovating or replacing original material with contemporary "upgrading" took place in many capitols. Some changes destroyed the original beauty and integrity by, among other things, lowering ceilings and covering carved decorative details; replacing original railings, doors, and windows with stainless steel; adding layers of paint to conceal moldings; allowing artwork to deteriorate; and replacing original lighting fixtures with fluorescent fixtures. Many times, in order to gain or reallocate office space or to save heating costs, large legislative chambers or other rooms were divided and floors were added between floors and renovated without regard for the building's architectural integrity or history. When Ohio's state house was completed in 1861 it contained 53 rooms. Over time, the number of rooms increased to 371. After renovations in the 1990s, the number now stands at 90.

Later, during the Depression, federal aid and relief programs such as the Works Progress Administration (WPA) provided jobs for unemployed workers in government-subsidized building projects. During this period, Industrial Moderne, or Art Deco, evolved into a more streamlined look, characterized by solid masses with a clear delineation of parts, along with a sense of verticality, while incorporating materials based on new technologies. Form followed function and superficial decoration was eliminated.

The development of manufactured high-strength steel made large buildings easier to erect, and with the invention of the elevator, higher ones. Although Art Deco buildings were constructed throughout the United States, the style was most influential in New York City, where it was associated with the design of many skyscrapers, including the Chrysler Building (1930), the Empire State Building (1931), and the RCA Building (1933). Four Art Deco state capitols provide evidence of its popularity for public buildings: the Nebraska State Capitol (1932); the Louisiana State Capitol (1933); the North Dakota State Capitol (1934); and the only one constructed using WPA funds, the Oregon State Capitol (1938).

Following the 1976 Bicentennial of the American Revolution, tastes started to change, and there emerged a renewed interest in America's past. Complete demolition and rebuilding, wiping out all traces of the capitols' history, was no longer a popular option. In this new period of historic preservation, there was both public and state support for the conservation of heritage architecture. It began with an increased emphasis on returning the capitols to their original conditions, accompanied by plans for future preservation. Since it is often difficult and expensive to conserve and update old buildings, some states found they had simply reached the point where the

Restored chamber of the Georgia House of Representatives.

Within these new or old buildings, state governments share a common constitutional framework with their national counterpart — a system of separation of powers that is organized into three complementary branches: the executive, judicial, and, with the exception of Nebraska, bicameral legislatures composed of a Senate and a House of Representatives. Senate membership is smaller, and chosen from larger districts. The members of each are elected by voters in designated districts subject to redistricting and reapportionment on the basis of population after each decennial census. Qualifications for the lawmakers are fixed by state constitutional provisions and differ with age and length of terms. Although as many as seventeen states partially control reelection through term limits; if the citizens do not like the way their legislators vote on the issues, they select someone else at the next election.

Unlike the Congress, which has only those powers granted to it by the United States Constitution, state legislatures possess powers not denied them by the constitutions of the United States and the states. The job of the legislators is to solve the problems of the state by appropriating funds, to confirm or reject the governor's appointees, and to pass laws relating to, among other things, education, health care for low- and moderate-income people, highways and public transportation, the state and community college system, the environment, the regulation of marriage, and care for the mentally and physically challenged. These elements of government often have

need for technology and space had outgrown their original designs.

Moreover, as the twentieth century proceeded, the cost of labor and materials spiraled, along with insurance and professional fees. Every construction budget expanded relative to its interior environmental technology, such as heating, air conditioning, plumbing, electricity, internet and global communication connections. Prefabrication increased as old construction skills disappeared, reducing hand-fashioned details. North Carolina, leaving its governor behind in the old capitol, moved into a modern legislative building. Florida and Arizona built new legislative buildings, designating their historic capitols as museums.

By the 1990s, general prosperity and the increased importance of state government in the federal system caused many capitols to be restored to their original appearance while at the same time being equipped for the twenty-first century. Utah rehabilitated its capitol after a study indicated that it might collapse during an earthquake. While preserving its historical, cultural and architectural elements, updates included installation of wireless and fiber-optic technology, a seismic retrofit, replacement of the concrete in the dome, improved accessibility, and other safety measures to bring it to lawful federal compliance, as well as security enhancement and construction of new buildings surrounding a rear mall to house legislators, their staff, and state agencies. Other restored capitols include those in Mississippi, Vermont, Ohio, Maine, Michigan, Indiana, Illinois, Iowa, Wisconsin, Connecticut, Texas and Georgia.

The California Senate chamber restored to its circa 1900 appearance.

more impact on the everyday quality of life of people than do the activities of the federal government.

During the legislative session, committees, or small groups of senators and representatives, review proposed laws and study issues. They report their findings to the entire legislative body. Many bills introduced in the legislature receive a public hearing, where citizens have an opportunity to present their opinions about proposed laws. The legislators vote on each bill, and those that pass both Houses become the laws of the state unless the governor vetoes them. Once implemented, the judiciary interprets laws.

In New Mexico, the constitution prohibits payment to the state's citizen legislators other than a per-diem and mileage allowance for attending legislative sessions and interim committee meetings. New Hampshire lawmakers work part-time for low pay ($100 annual salary plus travel expenses). With little staff, no offices and no desks, only lockers in the basement, it is sometimes difficult to recruit legislators because they must take time off from their regular jobs to attend legislative sessions. But these conditions reflect the will of the state, and ensure that New Hampshire continues to be governed by a volunteer citizen legislature.

By comparison, New York and four other states have full-time legislatures, with large staffs and annual pay surpassing $100,000. The remaining states fall somewhere in between part-time and full-time, although because of increasing demands and constituents' rising expectations, lawmakers devote more and more of their time to state business.

The lawmakers' proximity to the legislative chambers, usually the finest and largest rooms in the capitol, can affect legislative behavior. Connecticut lawmakers, with offices in a building separate from the chambers, tend to consider legislation in meetings outside the capitol, and the chambers are increasingly used primarily for electronic voting, not for debate. By contrast, the only working space for Vermont lawmakers is their desks in the legislative chamber, so that is where they tend to gather, discuss and deliberate.

In addition, state legislative traditions and practices continue to evolve. Technological advances not only assist elected representatives but, through the internet, make lawmaking more accessible to citizens, who can contact representatives and follow the legislative process more easily. This is especially significant for Alaska and Hawaii, where travel to their capital cities may be difficult due to location.

Electronic voting was introduced in order to expedite what had been a cumbersome and time-consuming procedure, but it now affects procedures and lawmaking. In the past, votes in New Hampshire's House of Representatives were taken by calling the roll, a procedure that took nearly an hour because its four hundred members comprise one of the largest legislative bodies in the world. Because roll calls were so long and tedious, with the name of each member called in alphabetical order, each member responding, and the clerk hand recording each vote, there were few. Now that members simply push the red or green button with the result immediately flashed next to their name on a board above the podium, the House votes nearly one hundred times a year.

Meanwhile, American federalism continues to reconfigure itself, the necessity for a strong federal government being relative to defense and international affairs. Following the tragic events of September 11, 2001, with the foreign-policy crisis and national security threats, there came an increased reliance on the role of the federal government in assisting the airline and insurance industries, providing disaster aid, extending unemployment benefits, and increasing airport security. On the other hand, some issues remain better suited to government at the state level, and the legislatures have continued to be laboratories for social and political experimentation. States often dominate policy initiatives in such diverse areas as education, health care, welfare reform and economic development.

Sometimes states tackle issues because the federal government has failed to do so. For example, during an ongoing deregulatory movement in Washington, D.C., states fill voids in such areas as anti-trust, environmental law, consumer safety, banking, health care, energy and telecommunications. Before the Federal Trade Commission established a national registry to curtail the growth and abuse of telemarketing, over half the states adopted laws to require telephone solicitors to avoid calling consumers who listed their objections to such calls on a registry. Other states outlawed what consumer groups call predatory lending, or loans with excessive or hidden fees, when Washington was reluctant to act, and some states have passed stricter consumer laws, such as those setting higher standards for baby cribs or non-flammable mattresses.

The judiciary also plays a significant lawmaking role with its interpretation of laws and rulings in tort reform, school finance, civil liberties, criminal law and other areas, showing the courts' willingness and ability to assert their policymaking role. Although those rulings have often generated considerable controversy and resistance (courts should interpret not legislate) many of the decisions fill a vacuum created by the inaction of the state legislators. For example, school finance decisions in a number of states provided the impetus for educational reforms. It was a Vermont Supreme Court directive that gave momentum to the Civil Unions Law.

Within this fluctuating system, the importance of state capitols continues. But they are not only legislative, executive and sometime judicial workplaces, they are about the people, and in examining them we see America's history unfold. Determining the chronological date of the fifty state capitols is difficult and clearly subjective, yet the book starts with the oldest building housing a legislature or attached to where it convenes, and then moves chronologically to the most recent, measured by the completion date, to roughly show the evolution of state capitol architecture. In spite of this, the intention of this book is not to attempt to write a history of capitol architecture, but rather to provide a context for giving our state capitols a larger meaning.

Interior dome of Montana's state capitol.

MARYLAND

MARYLAND STATE HOUSE
ORIGIN OF NAME: Named by Lord Baltimore for
    Queen Henrietta Maria, wife of King Charles I of England.
CAPITAL: Annapolis
CONSTRUCTED: 1772–1779
ARCHITECT: Joseph Horatio Anderson
ADMITTED TO THE UNION: April 28, 1788 (seventh)
SENATE: 47 members
HOUSE OF DELEGATES: 141 members

Maryland was established under a charter granted on June 20, 1632, by the English King Charles I when he sliced a section out of northern Virginia and gave millions of acres of wilderness to his friend George Calvert, Lord Baltimore. Calvert, a Roman Catholic convert, wanted to establish a place where Catholics could worship freely. Colonization began in 1634 on Saint Clement's Island, in the Potomac River. Here Catholic and Protestant settlers would practice religious tolerance. In 1649, the General Assembly, meeting in the first capital, St. Mary's City, passed one of the earliest laws concerning religious freedom, "An Act Concerning Religion."

The statute was repealed in 1692 when the English royal governor, Francis Nicholson, arrived. He established the Church of England as the official church and persuaded the official governing body to move the capital from the Catholic-dominated St. Mary's City to the town of Anne Arundel, later renamed Annapolis, farther up Chesapeake Bay.

Even before Maryland became a state, colonial laws, passed at the direction of the Crown, designated sites for towns and established the method of land acquisition, land valuation, layout and disposition of lots. While many of the laws were later repealed, Nicholson's town plan for Annapolis was enacted, and it is only fitting that as a result of this early legislation the oldest state house in the nation sits on Public Circle, land specifically set aside for public use.

This town-planning legislation evolved from the English and European tradition of integrating public and private places. The colonial commissioners appointed to oversee each town's establishment were directed to have the site "marcked staked out and devided into Convenient streets, Laines & allies, with Open Space places to be left On which may be Erected Church or Chappell, & Marckett house, or other publick buildings, & the remaining

Part of the said One hundred acress of Land as neare as may be into One hundred equall Lotts."

Nicholson, who at other times served as the royal governor of New York and Virginia, designed Annapolis and later Williamsburg. He promoted town layouts such as the Annapolis plan that provided two great circles, a square, and radiating diagonal streets. The state house and church were constructed on the highest and most commanding sites, Public Circle (about 500 feet in diameter) and Church Circle (about 300 feet). The other open space, Bloomsbury Square, measured about 350 feet square. The proportions of these three spaces are such that the square fits inside the larger circle, while the smaller circle can be contained in the square.

A statue of Revolutionary War hero Baron Johann De Kalb.

The lobby of Maryland's state house.

Nicholson's plan was generally maintained when the Maryland legislature passed an act to build the state house in the larger circle, where it remains today. Despite traffic congestion on the narrow diagonal streets dating from the plan, the circle is still clearly apparent. The state house, not the church (as was so often the case in England and New England), retains its preeminent public position.

The Maryland State House is unique because it is the only state house designed in the Georgian style in the United States, located in a city known for its many Georgian buildings. It is also the only state house to have served as the Capitol of the United States, from November 26, 1783, to August 13, 1784. In the old Senate chamber, during a session of the Continental Congress on December 23, 1783, George Washington resigned his commission as commander in chief of the Revolutionary Army after he reportedly declined an offer to become king. It was also here, on January 14, 1784, that the Treaty of Paris was ratified, officially recognizing peace with Great Britain and establishing the United States as an independent nation.

On September 11, 1786, the Annapolis Convention, composed of delegates from New York, New Jersey, Delaware, Pennsylvania and Virginia, met in the state house to consider the possibility of a closer union. This meeting led to the constitutional convention in Philadelphia, where the separate states formed one nation under the Constitution.

The oversized wooden dome was added to the building between 1785 and 1789. Dominating the exterior, the octagonal dome replaced a small and poorly constructed cupola. It is the largest wooden dome in the United States constructed with wooden pegs, perhaps because nails were taxable commodities and considered too expensive. Steel was used to reinforce the dome in 1947.

The dome rises from a central platform set on the building's hipped roof. The first stage incorporates long, arched windows on the eight surfaces. The second stage features elliptical windows. A concave roof curves upward to the third section, containing a balcony with balustrade entirely surrounding this smaller octagonal section, which includes doors and small square windows. The fourth and last stage culminates in the dome. The dome incorporates an inner and outer shell. At one time, access between the walls was used by visitors, including Thomas Jefferson, to climb up to the doors and step outside in order to enjoy the view of the landscape and water.

Symmetry is emphasized in the red-brick state house. Its central main entrance, facing the harbor, is covered by a pedimented Corinthian portico with columns, iron capitals, and cast-iron railing. The twenty-four-paneled sash windows are evenly spaced. Between 1902 and 1905, a rear wing with a pedimented portico replaced an earlier Colonial Revival addition. Since then there have been no changes in the exterior appearance, though there have been interior alterations and redecorations.

The main entrance opens to the light-filled lobby with its black-and-white marble floor. To the right is the old Senate chamber, restored in 1940 to its 1783 and 1784 appearance. Not only were the draperies replaced and the room repainted and refurbished, but chairs and desks were added to a total of sixteen, the number that originally furnished the room. In 1950, two original desks and a chair were added to the others. The president's desk is one of the original pieces made for the state house in 1797 by Annapolis cabinetmaker John Shaw. Shaw, who lived across the street, also maintained the state house and supervised the finishing touches of the plasterwork, including the work inside the dome.

The old historic Maryland State House Senate chamber with its mannequin of George Washington.

The working chamber of the Maryland Senate.

The Senate chamber served as the meeting place for the Maryland Senate from the building's completion until the erection of the annex. It features a mannequin of George Washington with a head that is a copy of the head of a full-length statue sculpted by Jean Antoine Houdon in 1785, and stands in the Virginia Capitol rotunda. The uniform is a replica of one worn by Washington that is in the Smithsonian Institution in Washington, D.C. On the wall hangs a 1784 painting by Charles Willson Peale depicting Washington with his aide-de-camp and secretary, Colonel Tench Tilghman, and Marquis de Lafayette. Tilghman, a Marylander, delivered the news of the British surrender at Yorktown to the Continental Congress in Philadelphia. Today, receptions and gatherings are held here, including meetings of the Maryland presidential electors. Across the lobby is the old House of Delegates, divided into a meeting room and a museum.

A large black marble line separates the original section of the state house from the new wing, or annex, where the Senate and the House of Representatives' chambers are located. Images from Maryland's past continue in

Maryland's state house is located in Annapolis's Public Square.

the Senate. Two statues flank the podium, those of John Hanson, a Marylander and the first president under the Articles of Confederation in 1781; and Charles Carroll of Carrollton, one of Maryland's four signatories of the Declaration of Independence and member of the Maryland Senate and the United States Senate. In addition, four paintings depict the Maryland four who signed the Declaration of Independence: William Paca, governor of Maryland for three terms; Thomas Stone, state legislator; Samuel Chase, associate justice of the U.S. Supreme Court; and Carroll. The full-length portrait of Carroll is attributed to Thomas Sully, one of the foremost portrait painters of the time. In 1834, the Sully painting cost $1,200. The room is lighted by a Tiffany-designed skylight, and Ionic columns support the spectators' gallery. The Italian marble on the walls is of rust and black colors, possibly chosen to approximate the gold and black of the Maryland state flag. The House also integrates the rust-and-black-colored Italian marble on its walls and features a Tiffany skylight. Paintings of former speakers of the House line its walls.

Above the grand staircase leading to the second floor hangs the painting *Washington Resigning His Commission*, completed in 1859. The second floor of the original section contains the offices of the governor and the lieutenant governor. Since 1779, every Maryland governor has maintained an office above the old Senate chamber. Governors also work from a suite on the top floor of an office tower in Baltimore.

The Maryland House of Representatives chamber.

VIRGINIA

VIRGINIA STATE CAPITOL
ORIGIN OF NAME: Named for Queen Elizabeth I, the "Virgin Queen."
CAPITAL: Richmond
CONSTRUCTED: 1785–1789
ARCHITECT: Thomas Jefferson
ADMITTED TO THE UNION: June 25, 1788 (tenth)
SENATE: 40 members
HOUSE OF DELEGATES: 100 members

The location of Virginia's seat of government and the design of its capitol are attributed to Thomas Jefferson. As governor of Virginia from 1779 to 1781, he influenced the removal of the capital from Williamsburg (1699–1780) to Richmond because he considered Williamsburg and its architecture too closely associated with England and colonial rule. Richmond was also more centrally located and more accessible to Virginia's western regions. In support of Jefferson, the General Assembly passed an act in May of 1779 ordering the move to Richmond. One year later, the lawmakers held their first session in a small frame building in the new capital.

A prominent site, Shockoe Hill, was chosen for the capitol, and Jefferson, a self-taught architect, presented his idea to construct separate buildings to house the three branches of government. The building committee rejected his plan because of its expense and decided to construct just one building. Later in 1785 it contacted Jefferson, while he was serving as the American minister to the Court of France, and asked him to "consult an able Architect on a plan fit for a Capitol" combining "economy with elegance and utility."

Jefferson knew Charles-Louis Clerisseau, prominent in the French Neoclassic architectural movement, and sought his assistance. But it was apparently Jefferson, and not Clerisseau, who suggested a Classical temple similar to the ancient Roman Maison Carree at Nimes, in southern France, as a model for the Virginia capitol. He described the old temple, built for Augustus Caesar, as "one of the most beautiful, if not the most beautiful and precious morsel of architecture left us by antiquity…it is very simple, but is noble beyond expression, and would have done honor to any country."

And it was Jefferson who furnished the design that remains the central core of today's capitol. Although he kept the form and proportions of the Roman temple, he adapted and simplified it to meet the requirements of the Virginia government by enlarging it (adding two main stories and elevating the basement for additional office space), changing the Corinthian order to Ionic, and reducing the depth of the porch from three to two columns. The columns and pilasters support an entablature with a dentil (tooth-like blocks) cornice. He also added windows framed by Ionic pilasters to the seven bays on the side elevations. Panels, left undecorated, separate the first- and second-floor windows. In order to assist in the construction, Jefferson, with the help of Clerisseau, prepared drawings and sent them along with a plaster model to Richmond.

Even before the capitol was completed, the Assembly held its first session there in October 1788. The south portico was added in 1790, and in 1800 stucco was added to the 3-to-5-feet-thick handmade-brick walls. The building was designed to include a broad flight of stairs ascending to the portico, but the stairs were not completed until 1906. At the same time the capitol was enlarged to accommodate modern use, though it changed the character of the building. Two-story porticoed wings were added to house larger chambers for the Senate and the House of Delegates. The areas connecting the wings to the original building were further widened in a 1962 renovation, causing even more of the original side elevations to be hidden.

The old Senate chamber.

The Virginia State Capitol.

The interior of the building was also altered. To make the south portico the main entrance, the old Senate chamber, originally extending across the entire front, was divided by a center hall leading from the entrance to the redesigned rotunda. The remains of the old Senate, with its eighteenth-century woodwork, now function as a meeting and committee room. Among the paintings is one showing the arrival of the first Englishmen in three small ships at Jamestown in the early seventeenth century. Jamestown not only became the first permanent English settlement in the Western Hemisphere, but it also served as Virginia's first capital. Another canvas depicts the raising of the American flag at Yorktown during the Revolutionary War. A portrait of John D. Rockefeller II, named an honorary citizen of Virginia because of his financial role in restoring Williamsburg, hangs on the south wall.

Other reminders of Virginia's role in the history of the United States occupy the rotunda. Jefferson wanted the look of a plain temple roof from the exterior so that the dome of the capitol is only visible from the inside. The decoratively painted dome, 20 feet below the roof, measures 57 feet 3 inches from the top of the dome to the floor. Skylights illuminate the marble sculptures filling the space below, including the precious life-sized statue of George Washington.

In 1784, before the capitol was constructed, the Virginia legislature voted to honor its favorite son, George Washington. Through Jefferson, it offered a commission to Jean-Antoine Houdon, a French sculptor. Accompanied by Benjamin Franklin, Houdon came to the United States in 1785 to meet the President. Houdon completed a life mask of Washington before returning to Paris, where, after three years, he finished the work. The Italian Carrara marble statue showing Washington at fifty-three years old, when he was 6 feet 2 inches tall and weighed 210 pounds, was displayed in the Louvre for eight years before being installed in the rotunda in 1796. The head was considered by his friend the Marquis de Lafayette as the most realistic likeness of Washington.

Houdon also completed a bust of Lafayette, an honorary citizen of Virginia, which stands in a niche opposite Washington. In 1931, marble busts of the seven other Virginia-born presidents were added to the rotunda: Thomas Jefferson (1801–09), James Madison (1809–17), James Monroe (1817–25), William Henry Harrison (1841), John Tyler (1841–45), Zachary Taylor (1849–50), and Woodrow Wilson (1913–21).

On the other side of the rotunda, unlike the Senate, the basic form of the Classical House of Delegates chamber survives. After Virginia joined the Confederacy, its government moved from Montgomery, Alabama, to Richmond, where it simultaneously became the Confederacy's and the state's seat of government. Today, appearing as Jefferson designed it, with a coved ceiling, wooden balconies and curved stairways, niches, pilasters and columns supporting the balconies, the room serves as a museum. Statues and busts of famous sons are numerous: Henry Clay, the orator born not far from Richmond; George Mason, author of the Bill of Rights; Cyrus H. McCormick, inventor of the reaper; Sam Houston, born in Virginia, first governor of Tennessee, president of Texas, governor of Texas, and United States senator from Texas; John Marshall, United States Supreme Court chief justice, clad in a Roman toga (considered to be a sign of respect at that time); Jefferson Davis, the only president of the Confederacy; and Patrick Henry, who made his famous speech ending with "Give me

Statue of George Washington inside the dome.

The old Virginia House of Delegates chamber with its statue of General Robert E. Lee.

The Virginia Senate chamber.

liberty or give me death," in Richmond. A statue of General Robert E. Lee stands where he accepted command of the Confederate forces in Virginia on April 23, 1861.

The desks and chairs are copies of those designed by Jefferson, which were nearly all destroyed on April 27, 1870, when the floor of a courtroom above the chamber collapsed under the weight of spectators witnessing a Reconstruction-era trial. Sixty-two people were killed and as many as 251 others were injured.

In contrast to the old Senate and House of Delegates, the new ones are similar in design. The House is semicircular and features a coffered ceiling with skylights. Iron columns support the curved balcony, while gilded and painted Ionic pilasters line the wall. Members sit at wooden desks on leather-and-fabric chairs, complete with the seal of Virginia on the seat backs.

Winston Churchill spoke from the marble-backed podium of the House in 1946. The Virginia Capitol was apparently selected because it provided him with the opportunity to address the oldest continuous English-speaking legislative body in the world, with the present one descending from the House of Burgesses. Parliament was dissolved by Oliver Cromwell for about twelve years. Accompanying Churchill was General Dwight D. Eisenhower, who also spoke.

In the Senate, red predominates. On the rostrum hangs the seal of Virginia, and behind it the "Signer's Tablet," honoring Virginia's signatories of the Declaration of Independence. Above the chambers, on the third floor, is the governor's office and reception room, with a bust of Jefferson prominently displayed. Covering the walls that encircle the open well of the rotunda are portraits of the sixteen most recent governors.

The Virginia House of Delegates chamber.

MASSACHUSETTS

MASSACHUSETTS STATE HOUSE

ORIGIN OF NAME: From a Native American word meaning "near the great hill," referring to the Great Blue Hill region, near Milton.

CAPITAL: Boston

CONSTRUCTED: 1795–1798

ARCHITECT: Charles Bulfinch

ADMITTED TO THE UNION: February 6, 1778 (sixth)

SENATE: 40 members

HOUSE OF REPRESENTATIVES: 160 members

The frugal Yankee influence is apparent in northern New England state houses, and their fiscal prudence protected these early buildings from destruction. Two of them, Massachusetts and Maine, highlight the work of architect Charles Bulfinch. Bulfinch's influence in shaping Boston's architectural history is reflected in his designs of more than forty churches, residences and public buildings, including the Massachusetts State House. Planned and drawn when he was twenty-four years old, the state house was constructed on a cow pasture that belonged to John Hancock. With its hemispheric dome, Bulfinch's design was probably influenced by his impressions during travels in England following his graduation from Harvard, especially London's Somerset House, with its similarly styled dome and central pavilion.

Located at the summit of Beacon Hill and overlooking the Boston Common, the Bulfinch front measures just over 60 feet wide. The central facade is flanked by two wings with rectangular and Palladian windows and features a ground-level arcade of brick arches surmounted by a projecting portico with a colonnade of Corinthian columns. The pine tree trunks used for the columns originated from Maine (then part of Massachusetts) and were hand-carved on the front lawn. In 1960, cast-iron reproductions replaced the wooden columns.

The 35-foot-high wooden dome and its drum rest upon the brick walls of an above-the-roofline pediment, which is supported by brick walls with pilasters. Covered in whitewashed wood shingles, the dome began to leak almost immediately. In 1802, Paul Revere protected it with copper, painted gray. During the Civil War, the copper was repainted gold, before being further enhanced with gold leaf in 1874. A lantern with a gilded pine-cone finial, symbolizing the importance of the lumber industry in the state's early economy, tops the dome. Although the dome

was rebuilt in 1859 and 1897, an effort was made to reproduce its original form.

The brick for the state house came from nearby Charlestown. At that time, if granite and marble were not used, brick was often painted. The red brick was painted white in 1835, thirty years later yellow, and then white again in 1918 to match the new marble wings. Finally, in 1928 the paint was removed, once again exposing red brick. Today, the red contrasts with the white marble lintels and keystones, as well as its columns and trim.

The Senate reception room once served as the Senate chamber.

The Massachusetts State House with its Bulfinch-designed front.

During the Gilded Age, with Massachusetts' growth and prosperity, the state house became too small for its state government. A proposal to build a new one in the geographic center of the state was defeated by the legislature, which voted instead to expand the existing one. A rear addition extended its size by six times, though its height left the Bulfinch dome dominant. Constructed of yellow brick with gray trim, in order to match the then-yellow-painted brick of the Bulfinch front, the Brigham addition incorporated classical architectural motifs in stone. Between 1896 and 1898, a preservation effort saved the front and it was strengthened with steel beams. In 1917, white marble wings containing legislative offices were added to the original section.

Across Beacon Street, facing the state house and its grounds, stands the Robert Gould Shaw Memorial by Augustus St. Gaudens. From the state house grounds and behind an 1859 statue of Daniel Webster by Hiram Powers, the main entrance leads directly into Doric Hall. Today, the entrance doors open only for ceremonial purposes: official visits from the President of the United States (last in 1912 by President William Howard Taft); the departure of the governor at the end of the elected term, exiting toward the Boston Common, symbolically fulfilling the founding fathers' ideal of returning to the plow after leaving public life; and the return of the Massachusetts regimental flags to the state's custody.

Inside the hall, with its double row of Doric columns, works on display include the first statue added to the state house — George Washington wearing a toga (or as many prefer to call it, a Revolutionary War blanket); a bronze bust of John Hancock, first governor and signatory of the Declaration of Independence; John Andrew, Massachusetts governor during the Civil War;

The old Massachusetts State House.

and a rare full-length portrait of sixteenth president Abraham Lincoln.

Above Doric Hall and immediately behind the portico, Bulfinch placed the House of Representatives. Set beneath the dome, it is the heart of the oldest part of the state house. On January 11, 1798, the 189 lawmakers, elected from the towns of Massachusetts and the District of Maine, assembled for the last time in the old state house on State Street and at noon marched to the new building on Beacon Hill. They brought to it a tradition of representative government that started in 1644 when the Massachusetts legislature, or General Court, was established.

After the procession, the representatives assembled in the nearly 55-square-foot room. Today, white marble busts of state and national figures, including Benjamin Franklin, Charles Sumner, George Washington and Abraham Lincoln, line the blue-painted walls and fill niches in the corners. White plaster symbols of Commerce, Agriculture, Peace and War ornament the pendentives, while a plaster sunburst fills the ceiling. House sessions were held here for ninety-seven years, until January 2, 1895, when the representatives moved to the present chamber in the addition.

Simultaneously, the Senate moved into the old House chamber and the old Senate chamber became the Senate reception room. Restored, the reception room incorporates a barrel-vaulted ceiling supported by four wooden Ionic columns (each carved from a single pine tree) and original stucco ornamentation. Three high-arched windows separated by pilasters at one time overlooked the harbor, while others overlook the Boston Common. Oil portraits of men who served as president of the Massachusetts Senate, such as Calvin Coolidge, further adorn the room.

The Massachusetts House of Representatives dates back to the late nineteenth century.

Portraits of the state's governors line the walls of the hallways leading to the current House of Representatives, including one of Elbridge Gerry. Gerry, governor from 1810 to 1812, is notorious for rearranging voting districts to favor his own political party. His opponents called the practice "gerrymandering."

Unlike the painted walls in the Bulfinch front part of the state house,

Honduras mahogany walls line the two-story House chamber. At the second-story level, ten plaster-fluted Corinthian columns support the ceiling of the public and press galleries. A frieze incorporates the names of fifty-three Massachusetts men who contributed to the founding and preservation of the state and the nation. Representing government, science and literature, they include William Bradford, John Adams, Henry Knox, Alexander

Graham Bell, Oliver Wendell Holmes, Charles Sumner, Horace Mann, Bulfinch, Ralph Waldo Emerson, Nathaniel Hawthorne, Henry Wadsworth Longfellow and John Singleton Copley. At one time there was an elliptical skylight above the frieze. Now covered, it contains additional electrical lighting for the chamber.

On December 16, 1942, five murals, placed between pilasters, were unveiled in the house. Entitled *Milestones on the Road to Freedom in Massachusetts*, they were painted by Albert Herter and his son, Christian A. Herter, at that time speaker of the House of Representatives. The murals fill the space above the speaker's desk and are entitled *1630 Governor Winthrop at Salem Bringing the Charter of the Bay Colony to Massachusetts*; *1697 Dawn of Tolerance in Massachusetts*; *Public Repentance of Judge Samuel Sewall for his Action in the Witchcraft Trials*; *1788 John Hancock Proposing the Addition of the Bill of Rights to the Federal Constitution*; *1779 John Adams, Samuel Adams and James Bowdoin drafting the Massachusetts Constitution of 1780*; and *1689 Revolt Against Autocratic Government in Massachusetts*.

Historical references continue elsewhere in the building. A memorial statue to the nurses of the Civil War is exhibited in Nurses Hall, along with paintings depicting the midnight ride of Paul Revere, James Otis arguing against the Writs of Assistance, and the Boston Tea Party. In the Hall of Flags, arches and glass shelter ancient battle flags, reproduced in photographs for the sake of preservation. They are further protected by brass railings decorated with iron griffins that rest on a marble mosaic floor. Above, murals entitled *The Pilgrims with the Mayflower*, *The Return of Colors at the end of the Civil War to the Custody of the Commonwealth*, *John Eliot Preaching to the Indians*, and *The Battle of Concord Bridge* are displayed. An art-glass skylight in the coffered ceiling includes the central Massachusetts state seal and surrounding it the seals of the other twelve original states.

The state house itself has been the forum of many achievements, from a child-labor law passed in 1837 to approval of a statewide smoking ban in 2003. During 1891, lawmakers created a commission that led, in 1897, to the building of the first American subway along Boston's Tremont Street. Originally, the subway ran just one stop to Boylston Station, its purpose to relieve pedestrian and traffic congestion in the heart of the city.

A century later, still struggling to relieve Boston's traffic congestion, the legislature joined the Federal Highway Administration to undertake the most expensive public-works project in American history. The Central Artery/Third Harbor Tunnel Project, also known as the "Big Dig," consisted of a nearly $15 billion highway, bridge and tunnel effort instigated not only to relieve traffic problems and congestion along Boston's urban corridor but to ensure the city's long-term viability by opening up valuable downtown property, reconnecting Boston's waterfront with its downtown, generating employment, and beautifying the city by replacing the elevated highway with parks and landscaped plazas. Although Boston was severely disrupted, the complex and often controversial project was completed without shutting down the city.

The Big Dig extended the Mass Pike through downtown Boston directly to Logan International Airport with a new four-lane harbor tunnel. Named the Ted Williams Tunnel, it incorporates a sophisticated system of emergency detection equipment, including video cameras and strobe lights. A system of wires underneath the roadway can determine the flow of traffic inside the tunnel by measuring its surface weight at any given time. This connector, covering 3.5 miles, cost $6.5 billion, making it one of the nation's most expensive stretches of roadway.

Finally, the world's widest cable-stayed bridge, Leonard P. Zakim Bunker Hill Bridge, replaced an obsolete double-decked viaduct over the Charles River. It is the first cable-stayed bridge in the United States to use both steel and concrete in its frame. The towers, at 295 and 330 feet, reflect the Bunker Hill Monument in Charlestown and Boston Harbor.

At the rear of the House of Representatives, directly opposite the speaker's desk, hangs the sacred codfish. Carved from a solid piece of pine, it measures nearly 5 feet long and about 10 inches wide. Symbolizing the source of Massachusetts's early wealth, a local merchant gave the fish to the House in 1784, where it hung in the old state house. Since then, it is considered to be a good luck charm and hangs whenever the House is in session.

In 1798, the codfish was transferred to the new state house, where it was seen by one of the many famous visitors to the building, Davy Crockett. In 1834, he wrote, "From the top of the State-house I had a fine view of the city, and was quite amused to see the representation of a large codfish hung up in the House of Assembly, or General Court, as they call it — to remind them either that they depended a good deal on it for food, or made money by the fisheries. This is quite natural to me, for at home I have on one end of my house the antlers of a noble buck, and the heavy paws of a bear."

On March 7, 1895, the sergeant-at-arms and a committee of fifteen men lowered the symbol, wrapped it in an American flag and carried it to the new House chamber, where it was set upon a table in front of the speaker's desk. After being repaired and repainted, the codfish was hung where it was accessible to Harvard fraternity pranksters. After taking the cod, the men finally returned it when lawmakers refused to convene until it was suspended in its present high spot, facing in the direction of the party in political control.

The Grand Staircase leads to a stained-glass window that depicts the history of the state seal.

New Hampshire

New Hampshire State House
Origin of Name: The English county of Hampshire.
Capital: Concord
Constructed: 1816–1819
Architect: Stuart James Park
Admitted to the Union: June 21, 1788 (ninth)
Senate: 24 members
House of Representatives: 400 members

The New Hampshire General Court, as the House and Senate together are formally known, first met in a small house constructed for it by the town of Concord in 1790. The legislature soon outgrew that building, and in 1814, with the financial support of Concord, decided to construct a state house according to the plan of a master builder.

The result was a granite building consisting of two stories, three entrances, four corner fireplace chimneys and a wooden cupola topped with a wooden eagle centered on its roof. The center door led into the first floor to Doric Hall, probably modeled after the Doric Hall of Bulfinch's Boston state house and named for its columns. Renamed the Hall of Flags, it contains cases holding 107 New Hampshire battle flags representing regiments and batteries from the Civil War, Spanish American War, the First and Second World Wars, and Vietnam.

The other entrances led to stairways to the second-floor legislative chambers — the Senate to the north, and the Hall of Representatives in the center, over Doric Hall. But by 1863 the state house was considered inadequate. Although Manchester sought to become the capital, Concord prevailed after it offered to build what is now Capitol Street and to pay for the state house's improvements. During the remodeling, the building lost most of its earlier identity, with a wing added to the rear and a hemispherical dome on an octagonal base replacing the cupola. The two doors leading into the north and south wings were removed, and a two-story portico was added to cover the main entrance.

As a result of the construction, Doric columns support the upper portico while Corinthian columns support the pediment. A balustrade encircles the flat roof from which a golden dome protrudes. The bull's-eye-windowed dome is topped by a lantern with the traditional golden eagle (an eagle has capped the building since 1819). The first was a 78-inch wooden "war" eagle with its head cocked to the left. After the 1865 remodeling, the eagle returned to its perch on a new, larger dome; however, by 1957, its tail feathers became so worn that it was replaced by a metal "peace" eagle with its beak poised to the right.

The eagle looks down upon the statues of famous sons of New Hampshire erected on the 2.6-acre lawn, including Daniel Webster, orator, U.S. congressman and senator from New Hampshire, and U.S. secretary of state for three presidents; General John Stark, Revolutionary War hero and author of New Hampshire's motto "Live Free or Die"; John P. Hale, former speaker of the New Hampshire House, anti-slavery advocate, U.S. senator and minister to Spain; and Franklin Pierce, fourteenth and only President of the United States from New Hampshire.

By 1909, another addition was necessary. Manchester, by then a thriving textile center, offered a million dollars to replace Concord as the capital. The legislature decided to stay in Concord, primarily because of its substantial sacrifice in cash and land to construct the state prison and state hospital and its agreement to construct the state library. This time, the General Court financed the entire cost of the project.

Once again, the state house doubled in size with an addition to the rear. And yet the House of Representatives, the largest legislative body in the United States, consisting of four hundred members, each representing fewer than three thousand constituents, still meets in the space originally assigned to it. The 1909 addition somewhat enlarged the chamber and also provided pilasters and a cove ceiling with medallions containing 4-foot-wide loops of plaster leaves and flowers. Five large portraits hang on the wall behind the rostrum: John P. Hale; Abraham Lincoln; George Washington (copy from Gilbert Stuart and the first portrait hung in the state house, in 1835); Franklin Pierce; and Daniel Webster.

Next door to the House of Representatives, in the northeast corner of the building, is the Senate, with one of the smallest memberships in the nation, just twenty-four senators. Arched windows light the chamber. The furniture, especially the curved tables, or desks, is a copy of surviving pieces in private and museum collections, or based on the 1819 cabinetmaker's drawings. On the inside wall behind the rostrum are murals by Barry Faulkner, completed in 1942, depicting events in the state's history. The painting on the left shows the first commencement at Dartmouth College, signifying New Hampshire's contribution to education. Next is Daniel Webster as a boy, reading a copy of the U.S. Constitution on the floor of his parents'

The Senate chamber of the New Hampshire State House.

store in Salisbury. He reportedly always carried the Constitution with him, printed on a handkerchief. This mural signifies New Hampshire's contribution to government and politics. Next, an art class led by painter and scientist Abbott Thayer, who taught the young Faulkner about protective coloration in the animal kingdom. The fourth painting depicts John Stark preparing for the Revolutionary War, where he fought at the battles of Bennington and Bunker Hill.

The 1909 addition also integrated into the building the present executive offices, composed of the governor's office and the Council chamber. The Executive Council, or Governor's Council, dates to 1680, when a royal decree established New Hampshire as a separate colony to be ruled by a governor and council with a veto power over a small elected legislature. The five councilors, elected every two years from equally populated districts, serve as advisors and approve the governor's appointments, pardons and state contracts in excess of $5,000. Massachusetts is the only other state with a council, but its singular role is to approve judicial appointments. Today, the council is con-

The four hundred seats of New Hampshire's Representatives Hall.

sidered an additional check and balance for New Hampshire government, limiting the possibility of an excessively strong governor.

Down the hallway from the executive offices is the secretary of state's office. This is where candidates can pay $1,000 and register for the first-in-the-nation presidential primary on a cherished bird's-eye maple desk. The desk, made for the Senate clerk, stands beneath the east windows in the Senate. Every four years, however, it is removed to the secretary of state's office for the presidential primary season. It was part of the 1818–1819 order for furnishings for the state house from Porter Blanchard, a local furniture maker, and delivered on the opening of the state house.

One of New Hampshire's most famous laws makes it the first state in the nation to hold a presidential primary every four years. New Hampshire held its first presidential primary in 1916 on Town Meeting Day, the second Tuesday in March. In keeping with the New England tradition of frugality, taxpayer money was saved. Although Indiana competed by also holding an early presidential primary, four years later Indiana moved its primary date forward, making New Hampshire, by default, the earliest.

The progressive reform of a primary, with voters choosing a delegate pledged to a particular presidential candidate, was initiated as an alternative to the party caucus and convention in the nominating process, replacing the back-room cronyism of political party bosses who were often corrupted by moneyed interests. Initially, the people voted for delegates pledged to specific presidential nominees, but in 1949 the General Court passed a law making the 1952 primary the first to provide the voter with the opportunity to directly cast a vote for a presidential candidate. This was significant because the candidates could no longer depend on delegates to obtain support but were required to go to New Hampshire and convince voters to vote for them.

Over the years, the legislature passed a number of amendments to the law in order to ensure that the New Hampshire presidential primary remains the first in the nation. In 1996, it provided that the primary

An 1819 desk original to the state house.

A second-floor corridor, lined with portraits.

The Executive Council meeting room located adjacent to New Hampshire's governor's office.

be held "on the Tuesday at least seven days immediately preceding the date on which any other state shall hold a similar election." At that time, lawmakers also allowed election-day registration for the first time. This not only stimulated voter participation but also helped to solidify New Hampshire's lead in voter turnout.

New Hampshire voters take their responsibility seriously, and the retail or personal politics, where voters listen and question contenders during the cold and snowy months leading to the primary, is considered to be a valuable part of the political process, where such debate and discussion are not possible in larger states or during multiple elections. The voters usually favor the candidate who ultimately wins the presidency (there are exceptions, such as Senator John McCain, who won the Republican primary in 2000 but lost the nomination). Not inconsequentially, New Hampshire's economy benefits, as the campaigns and media add millions of dollars to it, and the primary gives the state political power shared by few others.

The New Hampshire State House.

MAINE

Maine State House

Origin of Name: The Old French province of Maine or the word "mainland."

Capital: Augusta

Constructed: 1829–1832

Architect: Charles Bulfinch

Admitted to the Union: March 15, 1820 (twenty-third)

Senate: 35 members

House of Representatives: 151 members

Maine separated from Massachusetts and became a state as a part of the Missouri Compromise in 1820. A small, temporary state house, located in Portland, served as the site of the constitutional convention. Soon the search for a permanent capital began, with Portland, Brunswick, Hallowell, Waterville, Belfast, Wiscasset and Augusta as contenders. Surprisingly, the legislature chose the small town of Augusta, located in a sparsely settled wilderness. In 1827, it selected a 34-acre site on Weston's Hill, above the Kennebec River, for construction of the state house. Portland continued to fight to recapture the capital throughout the remainder of the nineteenth century by unsuccessfully offering buildings and cash.

After selecting the site, the legislature chose Charles Bulfinch, then serving as architect for the United States Capitol in Washington, D.C., to design its state house. He created a small Greek Revival building that was a transformation of his Federal brick Boston state house constructed thirty years earlier. As an economy measure, Maine borrowed an idea from New Hampshire and incorporated local granite for its exterior from the nearby Hallowell quarry and Maine pine for the interior woodwork. The four-story building measured 146 feet long by 50 feet wide, with an 80-by-15-foot protruding central portico containing seven arches leading to the ground entrance and topped with a Doric colonnade supporting an unadorned pediment. Unlike the one in Boston, this pediment spans the full width of the portico and rests directly upon it. Above the central section, Bulfinch added a low dome and lantern.

The Maine State House was the last of Bulfinch's designs to be executed. One of his letters, dated June 30, 1830, suggested a revision to his building plan:

The Maine State House with its Bulfinch front.

To the Governor & Council of the State of Maine.

I have had the honor to prepare plans for a State House to be erected at Augusta, which have been accepted, and the building is now in a state of progression. This plan was designed with a platform over the East Colonnade & an Attic story & Cupola. Upon revising the plan, I take the liberty to suggest, that it would be more conformable to the simplicity of good models of Antique buildings, to crown the Colonnade with a pediment, & to terminate the building with a Dome of about fourteen feet elevation, & a Cupola as first proposed. Being now on a visit to Augusta, I have the opportunity of viewing the site of the building, & am confirmed in my opinion of the advantage of this proposed alteration.

I have the honor to be,
with much respect
Your obedient Servant
Charles Bulfinch (signed)

Just twenty years after its completion, alterations to the interior of the state house began in an effort to correct some structural problems and to provide additional office space. During 1890–1891, an addition designed by Boston architect John C. Spofford included a three-story wing also con-

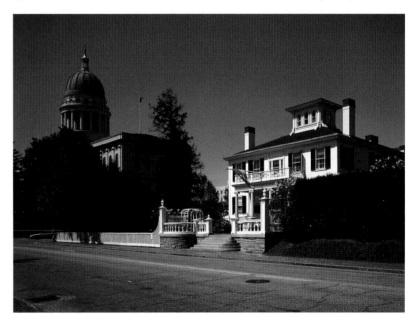

Blaine House, the governor's mansion, located next to Maine's state house.

structed out of local granite, to the rear of the building, terminating with a round bay. Spofford designed its Neo-Greek Revival lines to harmonize with the original building.

Another competition was held to choose an architect for the purpose of enlarging the state house in 1907. G. Henri Desmond was named the winning architect. His design altered the building on both the exterior and the interior, though once again the granite for the additions came from the Hallowell quarry, close to where the stone in the original building had been excavated. The state house doubled its length by adding 75-foot wings to the north and south sides at a cost of $350,000.

To compensate for the increase in size, Desmond replaced Bulfinch's low saucer dome with one rising 185 feet from the ground. Doric columns support the drum and an exterior balcony with a granite balustrade encircling it. Covered with copper, the dome is constructed of steel and concrete and crowned by a golden 12-foot female figure representing Wisdom. The draped statue, with her right arm stretched upward, holds a pine bough in the form of a torch.

On the flat roof below, smaller domes protrude slightly from the wings, one over the House of Representatives and the other covering the Senate. The windows are rectangular except for those on the third and fourth floor, which are arched. The only recognizable Bulfinch features remaining are the portico at the center of the facade and the wall immediately behind and adjacent to it.

Unlike the Bulfinch section, with its interior wooden construction, the enlargement made the entire building fireproof. All corridor floors above the lower one consist of white marble with a colored border. The floor plan is uniform throughout. From a central chamber under the dome the corridors lead into the wings, while a broad hall extends into the west wing. The old rotunda on the second floor, transformed into Doric Hall, includes eight Doric columns. A floor above, the Octagonal Hall or rotunda rises into a dome that can be reached via an exposed black iron staircase.

Off the rotunda, the House of Representatives, the largest room in the building, with more than 4,000 square feet, occupies the third and fourth stories of the north wing. Along three walls, a double tier of arched windows, set between Corinthian pilasters, contributes to the brightness of the room. It also features new bench desks with electronic voting capability.

In the south wing, the smaller Senate and executive offices share a space. The Senate is lighted by large arched windows below smaller paired rectangular ones along two walls.

At the end of the twentieth century, the legislature undertook a $32-million renovation of the state house and the 1950s-era state office building connected to it by an underground tunnel. After years of benign neglect resulting in peeling paint, chipped plaster, code violations and a generally run-down appearance, the state house was restored to its historic 1910 look, with technological upgrades in both buildings. This required that the buildings be vacated for nearly five years, but the results include improved security, the removal of lead and asbestos, an upgraded electrical system, improved graphics and signage, roof replacement, restored chambers, installation of a fiber-optic network, and other technological advancements.

For this renovation, however, no Hallowell quarry existed to provide the granite for exterior repairs. The quarry closed in the 1930s and Maine's only

The tunnel connecting Maine's state house and the state office building.

Doric Hall with its columns supporting the rotunda above.

active granite quarry, on Deer Isle, produces granite with a pinkish red cast, not the light gray required for the state house. State officials reluctantly authorized construction workers to incorporate a small amount of Vermont granite where necessary, because it was the best color match and cheaper to obtain than reopening the Hallowell quarry.

Decisions taking place in this state house include legislation concerning the state's longest residents, Native Americans. Over the years, legislative efforts to provide restitution for past wrongs have included the 1999 passing of a law banning the word "squaw" from two dozen place names and the state-required ratification of the federal 1980 Maine Indian Claims Settlement Act.

The settlement provided compensation to the small and impoverished Passamaquoddy and Penobscot tribes for land taken from them by the state (then part of Massachusetts) in 1794 in violation of the federal 1790 Indian Non-Intercourse Act. The act was passed by the first Congress and signed into law by George Washington in order to protect Native Americans from

The Senate chamber.

land grabbers. It stipulated that tribal rights to land could only be conveyed or extinguished by the federal government, prohibiting states from entering into treaties with Native Americans.

A controversy arose when Native Americans claimed that large areas of Maine, based on original Native American title, were deeded to the state by a treaty in which the federal government did not participate and which it did not ratify or approve. In exchange the tribes received, among other things, 150 yards of blue cloth for blankets, 400 pounds of shot, 100 pounds of powder, 100 bushels of corn, 13 bushels of salt, 36 hats, a barrel of rum, and the promise of an annual stipend consisting of similar items.

In the mid-1950s, a Passamaquoddy member discovered a copy of the 1794 treaty in an attic. An attempt to determine what had happened to Native American land led to an eventual settlement involving tracts of ancestral land covering 12.5 million acres, or nearly two-thirds of the state. The size of the claim made it tactically difficult to pursue because the option is available

to the federal government to extinguish without compensation the original Native American title upon which the claims were based. While such an action would have been a drastic method of defeating tribal claims, fear of the possibility apparently created an incentive for settlement rather than the pursuit of total recovery in the courts, as some preferred to do. At the same time, however, many property owners were anxious about the cloud over the title to their land and afraid of economic chaos if the tribes prevailed in their estimated $25-billion land claim.

In the state-ratified final settlement, the United States government paid the Penobscots and Passamaquoddies $81.5 million to give up their claim to the land and recognized them as Native tribes under United States law. With the money, the tribes purchased 300,000 acres of land, invested in a variety of business ventures, including sawmills, a cement-manufacturing plant, a radio station and a blueberry farm near Machias, and deposited the balance in a trust fund.

Maine's state house rotunda.

1796

In 1795, a census revealed
that the territory exceeded
the required 60,000 population
to petition Congress for
Tennessee statehood.

In 1794, an elected Territorial Assembly
held its first session.

Defeat of Chickamauga,
Creek, and Shawnee
Indian warfare by 1794.

Tennessee

Tennesee State Capitol

Origin of Name: The Cherokee word *tanasi*, referring to a village and a river of the same name.

Capital: Nashville

Constructed: 1845–1859

Architect: William F. Strickland

Admitted to the Union: June 1, 1796 (sixteenth)

Senate: 33 members

House of Representatives: 99 members

Tennessee's first General Assemblies convened in a log cabin, then in houses, schools, churches and a Masonic hall located in the towns of Knoxville, Kingston, Murfreesboro and Nashville. Nashville finally became the official capital in 1843, after it donated land to the state for the site of the capitol building. The next year the legislature created a building commission with the mandate to choose an architect and construct a stone capitol building.

The commission selected William Strickland as architect over applicants such as Gideon Shryock of Kentucky and James H. Dakin from Louisiana. A protégé of architect Benjamin Latrobe, who was trained in the Classical style, Strickland assisted Latrobe on the United States Capitol. Later, Strickland became well known for his carefully proportioned Greek Revival buildings, such as the Second Bank of the United States (1824); the reconstructed tower of Independence Hall (1828); the Merchants Exchange (1837) in Philadelphia; and the United States mints in Charlotte, North Carolina (1835) and in New Orleans, Louisiana (1836).

But Strickland died five years before the completion of his Greek Revival Tennessee Capitol. Like Christopher Wren in St. Paul's Cathedral in London, Strickland is interred in a cavity in the capitol's portico. After Strickland's death, his son, who worked closely with him, completed the building.

Constructed upon the bedrock of Nashville's highest point, Strickland's capitol incorporated a rusticated base with pedimented Ionic porticoes of eight columns at each end, and on the longer east and west side walls, porticoes with six columns each, lacking pediments. The twenty-eight hand-carved columns, along with Corinthian columns on the tower, have the capitol's only carved decoration.

Originally, the load-bearing walls, pierced by tall, narrow, paired windows, consisted of smooth local limestone. As a controversial cost-cutting measure, especially offensive to local laborers, the limestone was excavated, shaped and transported to the site by slave and convict labor. Many of the stones weighed between six and ten tons. Iron was used for the roof trusses and ornamental work, wood for windows and doors, and copper for the roof.

In addition to its uniqueness as a solid-stone building, another unusual feature of the capitol is the slim tower centered on the top of the roof. It was modeled after the Choragic monument to Lysicrates, erected in Athens in 335 BC. The Greeks did not incorporate domes on their structures, so Strickland, carefully adapting Greek designs for his Classical Revival buildings, used the same Choragic monument model that he had earlier added to the commercial Merchants Exchange building in Philadelphia. Completed in July 1855 by Strickland's son, the 42-foot tower supports a 37-foot lantern. Eight Corinthian columns are partly embedded into its wall, and it is crowned with an iron finial surmounted by a flagpole.

After the capitol was completed, landscaping the rocky grounds became a priority. However, its completion was interrupted by the Civil War. On February 1862, the people of Nashville, along with the governor, lawmakers and the Confederate Army, evacuated the city prior to the arrival of the Union Army. The Tennessee State Capitol became the first in the South to fall to the Union Army. Afterwards, President Abraham Lincoln appointed Andrew Johnson as military governor, and the fortified capitol, renamed Fort Johnson, became the seat of government during the Union occupation, as well as quarters for its soldiers. Johnson watched the Battle of Nashville from the tower during December of 1864. In July of the following year the occupation ended, without extensive damage to the building.

Time, weather and atmosphere were not so benevolent. The deteriorating exterior limestone, a safety concern for many years, became so badly weakened by the 1950s that it was a safety hazard, with large pieces breaking off and falling to the ground. In 1953, the General Assembly appropriated funds to repair and restore the capitol.

Between 1956 and 1958, 90,000 cubic feet of Indiana limestone replaced the original, softer Tennessee stone. This included the Ionic columns and the pediments and parapets above them, the entablature, projecting cornices, the upper and lower terraces, and the columns and entablature on the tower. Every piece to be replaced was carefully measured, and templates were made to ensure exact reproductions. Additional improvements included a new copper roof, bronze rails around the upper terrace and in the porticoes,

Tennessee's state capitol on a hill overlooking Nashville.

and new exterior doors and windows. Today, in spite of the extensive reconstruction, the exterior looks almost exactly as Strickland planned it.

Inside, the first and second floors are intersected by a long central hallway. The first-floor ceilings incorporate painted plaster over the brick vaults supporting the upper floor. The governor's office, the Tennessee Supreme Court, the federal court, the secretary of state and other governmental officials initially occupied this floor.

In the central hall, portraits hanging near the visitors' desk include one of Strickland and of the three presidents of the United States with strong Tennessee ties — Andrew Jackson, James Polk and Andrew Johnson. The surrounding ceiling is frescoed with westward expansion and justice themes, the Tennessee state seal, and a depiction of an American eagle surrounded by thirty-one stars, representing the states in the union at the time of the frescoes' completion. Over the years these frescoes were whitewashed, but since they were painted into wet plaster their designs survived. The ceiling of a hallway corner outside the governor's office was left as restored in the 1980s, while the remaining frescoes were repainted to their original appearance.

Throughout the long hallway and outside the governor's suite, portraits of Tennessee governors line the walls. In 1938, the Works Progress Administration remodeled the Governor's Reception Room to a Georgian Revival style, with six-panel doors set into painted wooden frames featuring Ionic pilasters and a broken pediment, stenciled ceilings, and mural canvases depicting scenes from Tennessee history. The paintings include images of Cherokee people, symbolizing early Native American presence in the region; Hernando de Soto, the first European to explore the area that is now Memphis; Fort Loudoun, the first British outpost, now part of Knoxville; the founding of Nashville; Nashville during construction of the capitol; the failed state of Franklin (preceding Tennessee); the Hermitage, home of Andrew Jackson; and laboring African Americans, who made up nearly a quarter of the state's population in 1860.

Tennessee's Senate chamber.

From the first floor, the main staircase leads to a landing then divides and continues to the second floor, with its steps formed from stone cantilevered from the walls of the central hall or lobby. The Tennessee red-marble balustrade contains chips in its handrail from bullets fired at former Confederate lawmakers in 1866. They were attempting to leave the building so there would not be a quorum present to vote on the 14th Amendment to the Constitution, giving African Americans equal rights. After guards fired warning shots, the lawmakers decided to stay and the amendment passed. As a result, Tennessee became the first Confederate state readmitted to the Union.

Next to the lobby and filling the southern and eastern end of the building is the large two-story House of Representatives. Along with its unpainted stone walls, it features a Tennessee marble screen behind the podium and sixteen 22-foot-high fluted columns of Nashville limestone fronting the side galleries that also support the roof. As on the exterior, all capitals are hand-carved. In 1889, the original forty-eight-burner gas chandelier with bronze Native Americans, buffaloes and cornstalks swayed so much that lawmakers feared it might fall, so it was removed. Today's light fixtures date from the 1950s.

Down the hall in the Senate, the original gasolier by Cornelius and Baker, manufacturers of ornamental lighting fixtures in Philadelphia, made specifically for Tennessee with native corn, elk heads, cotton blossoms, and tobacco

The House of Representatives chamber.

leaves, hangs from the ceiling, though it is now electrified with thirty round fixtures. The room is also illuminated through large windows on the east and north sides. Twelve columns of red variegated Tennessee marble with white Ionic capitals support the visitors' gallery, fronted by a wrought-iron railing in a spear-and-shield pattern. Eight Ionic pilasters line the walls, supporting an entablature. The ceiling is divided into radiating plaster panels. The speaker's dais, originally made of East Tennessee marble, was removed in a 1950s remodeling.

Across the hall is the former Tennessee state library, once filled with books and documents covering Tennessee law and legal precedent. Because of the heavy weight of the books and the stacks, library interiors such as this were among the first public spaces to make extensive use of cast-iron. The ironwork, including the stacks and the cast-iron spiral staircase with portrait medallions on it and on the balcony railing, was ordered from a Philadelphia company catalog. The portraits include figures from state and national political scenes as well as famous writers such as Dante and William

The restored Tennessee state library.

Interior hallway of the state capitol.

Shakespeare. Another 1855 gasolier chandelier from Cornelius and Baker and ceiling portraits of Tennessee notables such as the first state geologist are also featured. During the 1980s, restoration of the library brought it back to its mid-nineteenth-century appearance. Among other things, the modesty curtain added to the spiral staircase was removed.

One controversial bill with its history documented in the library overwhelmingly passed the Tennessee legislature on March 13, 1925. The law prohibited the teaching of evolution in any state-supported school or college. Although Governor Austin Peay signed the bill into law, he supposedly interpreted it as a protest against anti-religious tendencies in "modern America" and did not expect it to become an active statute. But it was a period of discontent. Many Tennesseans believed they were losing control of their lives, that the First World War had failed to live up to its promises, and that the anti-evolution laws were the answer for all the wrong brought about by changing times. It was a time of intense Christian fundamentalism with many states, both North and South, considering some form of anti-evolution law similar to Tennessee's. In addition to legislative efforts, resolutions and policies against evolution were adopted by boards of education. Even today, religion-based concepts of creation remain so widely held that a few states contain no references to evolution in their school science curricula.

It was in such a climate that a group of merchants in the small town of Dayton, ostensibly seeking publicity for their town, led the prosecution of its high-school football coach and science teacher for violating the law. This resulted in America's most famous confrontation over evolution, the Scopes Trial. It not only attracted nationwide attention to the strength of religious fundamentalism in Tennessee, but to its philosophical conflict with science, academic freedom and the rights of parents to control their schools.

The trial also involved well-known lawyers, including special prosecutor and three-time presidential candidate William Jennings Bryan, who argued that the law was a legitimate effort by the legislature to control the public-school curriculum. Opposing him, the famous defense attorney Clarence Darrow argued that the law was an attempt to establish the religion of Protestant Fundamentalism, a violation of the 1st Amendment to the U. S. Constitution. In the end, Scopes was convicted and fined $100, but on appeal the conviction was reversed on the technical ground that the fine was excessive. No other cases were tried under the statute, and the Tennessee legislature revoked it on May 16, 1967.

The Tennessee State Capitol.

VERMONT

VERMONT STATE HOUSE

ORIGIN OF NAME: From the French words *vert* and *mont*,
   meaning "green mountain."

CAPITAL: Montpelier

CONSTRUCTED: 1857–1859

ARCHITECTS: Ammi B. Young, Thomas W. Silloway

ADMITTED TO THE UNION: March 4, 1791 (fourteenth)

SENATE: 30 members

HOUSE OF REPRESENTATIVES: 150 members

Vermont was an independent republic for fourteen years before it became the first state admitted to the Union after the ratification of the United States Constitution. It sought statehood from the time of the American Revolution, but a longstanding territorial disagreement with New York needed to be settled first. After New York accepted $30,000 for the land in dispute, it dropped its objection to Vermont joining the Union.

The General Assembly met in towns throughout Vermont until 1805, when it designated Montpelier as the capital. A wooden three-story meeting house, built circa 1808 on land donated by the town and close to the site of the present Vermont Supreme Court building, became the first state house. The second, a Greek Revival building designed by architect Ammi Burnham Young, was constructed of local granite with a wooden dome and wooden interior. It sat on a ledge blasted from the rocky hillside rising behind it.

When the interior and the dome burned on January 6, 1857, William Silloway was chosen as the architect and Thomas E. Powers as the superintendent to rebuild the popular building. It was soon determined, however, that only the foundation and portico were salvageable. So although the present state house dates from 1859, it incorporated the Doric portico of the 1838 state house, including its fluted columns, six feet in diameter and made up of six pieces. Silloway enlarged the building by adding one bay to each end and two bays to the rear, but kept the pedimented portico to provide continuity from the old to the new.

Other features include first-story windows that incorporate cornices, while triangular pediments top those on the second floor. Silloway also replaced the low dome with a taller one, about 57 feet high, mounted on a twelve-sided pilastered drum with windows.

The dome, an exterior feature only, is sheathed in copper and was first covered with gold leaf in 1907. Crowning it stands a 14-foot wooden stat-ue of Ceres, the goddess of agriculture, originally hand-carved in 1859 by Vermonter Larkin Goldsmith Mead. In 1938, when the statue became so rotten that it was a safety concern, an 87-year-old sergeant-at-arms, assisted by state-house custodians, replicated it. That the goddess of agriculture presides over Vermont's most important public building alludes to the significant role of agriculture in the state.

Silloway integrated the somewhat austere exterior with an equally restrained all-white interior decor. He ordered cast-iron columns with Ionic capitals for the lobby to support 18-foot ceilings consisting of molded sunken panels throughout the first floor. Stone quarried in Vermont was used for the black-and-white marble floors.

Second-floor House of Representatives vestibule.

The Vermont State House.

In the lobby is the bust of Abraham Lincoln, also by Mead, who created it as a study for his bronze statue at Lincoln's tomb in Springfield, Illinois. Joining Lincoln on the walls opposite the entrance are portraits of the two Vermont-born presidents of the United States: Calvin Coolidge and Chester A. Arthur. There 130 paintings in the state house's collection.

Semi-elliptical cast-iron stairways lead to the second floor, where to the west is the Cedar Creek Room or Governor's Reception Room, originally designed to house the state library. Because Vermont lacks a governor's mansion, the room is considered the governor's official reception room. When Governor Howard Dean shunned traditional inaugural balls for public open houses at the start of his five two-year terms, well-wishers were entertained by Vermont high-school musicians.

This room, decorated in an even later style than the rest of the state house, is dominated by a 10-by-20-foot oil painting entitled *The Battle of Cedar Creek*. The legislature paid artist Julian Scott $10,000 to paint this Civil War memorial work specifically for the state house. It depicts the Vermont Brigade leading a rally that resulted in reversing a Union retreat on October 19, 1864. Scott, who fought in the battle, brought Vermont veterans of the battle to his New York studio and painted their portraits into the work. Begun in 1871, it was not completed until 1879.

After the completion of the first floor, a design controversy with the building superintendent occurred, and Silloway was removed and replaced by Joseph R. Richards of Boston. Rather than continue with Silloway's integrated plan, Richards' design was in the more flamboyant Renaissance Revival style then fashionable.

The Vermont House of Representatives.

For the rest of the second floor, Richards chose elaborate plasterwork, decorative bronze sconces, bronze-and-gilt chandeliers, ornate ironwork, Corinthian columns, brightly colored carpets and hand-carved furniture, some of which is still in use today. This includes Representative Hall, restored to its original appearance. Fluted pilasters with Corinthian capitals flank the windows. In the ceiling, a plaster lotus measures 18 feet in diameter, with its blossom petals weighing approximately 500 pounds each. Hanging from the lotus is a chandelier, originally a gas fixture but electrified in 1898. Manufactured by Cornelius and Baker, it holds twenty-four lamps on two tiers and measures 10 feet in diameter and 14 feet high. Statues representing Prudence, Science, Commerce, and Eloquence are interspersed with four copies of the *Greek Slave* statue sculpted by Woodstock, Vermont, native Hiram Powers, a cousin of Thomas Powers.

Fifteen smaller bronze fixtures around the room incorporate such classic figures as Mercury, the Minuteman, Christopher Columbus, William Penn, Benjamin Franklin and George Washington. Washington's portrait by George Gassner, after Gilbert Stuart, hangs above the elevated speaker's rostrum. Rescued from the fire that destroyed the previous state house, this circa 1836 portrait hangs in the same location as it did then.

The elliptical Senate chamber occupies the east wing of the second floor. Corinthian fluted columns support the gallery. Custom-made carpet, based on an 1874 design, and heavy dark-green velvet drapes were added before lawmakers arrived January 3, 2001. Completion of the Senate ended a decade-long restoration of the state house, with most of the rooms returned to the way they looked when the building was constructed. A private group, Friends of the State

The Vermont State House's renovated Senate chamber.

House, helped raise some of the more than $2 million for the work, including the $50,000 for the new Senate carpeting.

The final phase of the restoration involved ripping out the floor of the Senate chamber in order to install new electrical and telephone wiring instead of hiding the modern technology in dropped ceilings, thus ensuring architectural integrity. Tunnels were excavated through bedrock beneath the building to allow rerouting of heating, ventilating and cooling systems, and computer cables. Workers used hand tools to break up rock close to the building's old brick foundation.

An annex on the rear west side was added to the state house in 1886 to house the state library and the supreme court. After both moved to a separate building next door in 1919, the annex became home to legislative committees. It is now a legislative lounge with computer terminals. Many of the lawmakers working there also participate in their local town meetings. It is often said that Vermonters bring their traditional New England town meeting mentality to legislative deliberations; they are known for their independence and commitment to the protection of individual rights Vermont was the first state with a no-slavery clause in its constitution,

The Cedar Creek room in the Vermont State House.

drafted when Vermont was still an independent republic. Vermont also claims to be the first state to constitutionally establish universal suffrage without requiring ownership of property or a specific income.

More recently, this independence is reflected in Vermont's environmental protection laws and efforts to regulate common interests, such as Act 250, enacted to preserve and protect land from development and exploitation. Educational reform legislation was passed as a response to a state supreme court decision that threw out the local property tax as the primary source of school funding because of its failure to offer equal opportunity to all students. The present law includes a complex statewide property tax.

In December 1999, the Vermont Supreme Court ruled that denying homosexual couples the benefits of marriage also amounted to unconstitutional discrimination. The court left it to the lawmakers to work out the details. After months of difficult debate, negotiation and compromise, the legislature created the nation's first law extending the rights, privileges and responsibilities of marriage to gay and lesbian couples by allowing them to enter into civil unions, effective April 26, 2000.

Although the legislation does not allow same-sex marriage with all its legal rights, a gay couple may apply for a licence and obtain a certificate of civil union. They are then treated like spouses with respect to the more than three hundred benefits that Vermont confers on married couples, including filing joint state tax returns, inheriting estates, health and pension benefits, making medical decisions, taking family leave, and ensuring protection from having to testify against one another. There are also responsibilities such as assuming the debt of one another and duties of child support. Couples that want to end a civil union must go to a Vermont family court to seek a dissolution, similar to a divorce.

Stairwell and dome.

OHIO

OHIO STATE HOUSE
ORIGIN OF NAME: The Iroquoian word for "great river."
CAPITAL: Columbus
CONSTRUCTED: 1839–1861
ARCHITECTS: Henry Walter, Alexander J. Davis, William R. West, Nathan B. Kelly, Isaiah Rogers
ADMITTED TO THE UNION: March 1, 1803 (seventeenth)
SENATE: 33 members
HOUSE OF REPRESENTATIVES: 99 members

Following the American Revolution, Congress passed the Ordinance of 1787 creating the Northwest Territory, consisting of the present states of Ohio, Illinois, Indiana, Michigan and Wisconsin. Among other things, the ordinance prohibited slavery and set out the requirements for statehood by allowing any area with sixty thousand people to organize and apply for admission to the Union.

After the Ohio Territory separated from the Northwest Territory in 1800, the small town of Chillicothe became its first capital. From 1809 to 1812, the General Assembly moved the capital back and forth between Chillicothe and Zanesville before finally settling on the more centrally located town of Columbus. There the first state house stood at the southwest corner of the ten-acre Public or Capitol Square. The small brick building with a hipped roof and centered belfry served as Ohio's capitol from 1816 until fire destroyed it in 1852.

Even before the fire, a campaign was underway to construct a larger building to better serve the growing state government. The State House Act of 1838 created a three-member commission to conduct a national competition to select a design for a new state house. From the nearly sixty submissions, first place was awarded to Cincinnati architect Henry Walter; second to New Yorker Martin E. Thompson, who was for a time an associate of the Ithiel Town and Alexander Jackson Davis architectural firm; and the third prize went to landscape painter Thomas Cole.

The three winning plans were similar, with balanced wings containing the legislative chambers, porticoes and domes. When the building commission could not make up its mind as to which one of the three to construct, it advised the legislature that any one of them was acceptable.

Meanwhile, the commission was under pressure to remove the capital from Columbus. In order to keep it there, they decided to start construction based on a composite design incorporating the best features of the three winners, drawn by architectural consultant Alexander Jackson Davis. His design emphasized Cole's colonnaded facade, though it lacked a pediment and dome. Soon a rectangular foundation that could serve as a foundation for any of the plans was completed, and on July 4, 1839, a cornerstone was laid.

From the beginning, the legislature intended to draft prisoners from the nearby Ohio Penitentiary to construct the state house, and it became an important financial incentive for keeping the capital in Columbus. But in 1840, after more than four hundred local workers angrily protested the use of prison labor, the General Assembly repealed the State House Act and ordered its construction shut down. All unused materials were sold. The

Hand-carved Senate dais with trompe l'oeil bracket.

The Ohio State House in the center of downtown Columbus.

foundation was covered with dirt, and cows and other animals grazed among the weeds and saplings growing on Capitol Square.

Not until the fire destroyed the first state house did the legislature finally approve another State House Act. Soon the walls and the drum-shaped cupola were constructed under the direction of W. Russell West. Starting in 1854, architect Nathan B. Kelly completed the roof and a large part of the interior, including the House chamber. Kelly incorporated a colorful and decorative interior design that contrasted with the building's plain exterior. In 1858, the building commission replaced Kelly, partly due to stylistic differences, and appointed Isaiah Rogers to finish the interior, terraces and landscaping. Rogers was also responsible for the finish of the rotunda, installing a low-pitched roof, and completing West's drum-shaped cupola.

Even though legislators met in the state house in 1857, it was not until 1861 that the building was considered complete. Surprisingly, after twenty-two years of intermittent construction, many design changes, conflicts between the legislature and the commissioners, conflicts between the commissioners and the architects, misunderstandings between the architects and public opinion, charges of fraud and mismanagement, use of free prison labor, and the fact that it was completed during a period of stylistic change, the intact building is generally considered well-proportioned and a fine example of Greek Revival architecture.

The entrance porches of the rectangular building are recessed behind screens of Doric columns, eight on the east and west, four on the north and south. Without a projecting portico, the entire facade is contained in a single plane unified by a continuous oversized entablature above both the columns and the weight-bearing pilasters lining the walls. The low pediments to the east and west appear to float over the cornice above the main entrances. The ends of the building are

The rotunda in the Ohio State House.

identical to the main facade except that they are narrower and lack the pediments. Centered on the roof is a cylindrical lantern, or cupola, two stories high, with Doric pilasters and a plain entablature.

The state house is made even more austere by a dome hidden inside the lantern, which was originally intended to be capped by a low saucer dome. Also, the use of prison labor may have necessitated a simpler design because the prisoners were probably not trained as stone carvers or artisans. Another contribution to the austerity is the incorporation of the stout, unfluted columns, weighing 10 to 12 tons each. They were carved from large-grained limestone taken from quarries located about three miles west of Capitol Square.

Internally, the plan of the state house resembles that of the national Capitol, with equal-sized legislative chambers on either side of the rotunda. The rotunda measures about 63 feet in diameter and rises 120 feet high. It features an interior dome and a mosaic-tiled floor. The floor consists of nearly five thousand pieces of hand-cut marble imported from around the world. The middle symbolizes the history of the United States as of 1860 when the floor was laid. The stones in the center represent the thirteen original colonies. Three marble bands represent the unorganized territories, the Louisiana Purchase, and the territories acquired during war with Mexico. The thirty-two-point starburst indicates the number of states in the Union at the time, and the last band represents the United States Constitution, uniting the nation.

The chambers of both the Senate and House feature a trompe l'oeil bracket recreated from historical photographs behind a white Italian marble dais. Only the House includes gallery balconies for spectators. In the Senate, visitors sit on sofas, original to the room, located to the left of the rostrum on the floor. In the rear of the Senate chamber stand white Pennsylvania marble columns topped with Corinthian capitals. Its electric chandelier was

The restored Ohio House of Representatives chamber.

reproduced from a gas light fixture design borrowed from the Vermont State House. It weighs 1,200 pounds and is 12 feet wide with twelve arms. The carpeting is a reproduction based on a photograph of the original flooring.

Although the House appears old-fashioned, it is technologically advanced. The mahogany speaker's chair dates from about 1879. Most of the woodwork is original, with the wood grain hand-painted to resemble oak. The Corinthian columns of white Pennsylvania marble support galleries for spectators. The carpeting is a reproduction of one used to cover the stone floor in 1858. The members' desks date from 1909 but are refinished and technologically upgraded with telephones, intercoms, microphones and jacks for computers. When the state house was first constructed, the lawmakers' desks served as their offices. Today, representatives have office suites in the modern high-rise building across the street from the state house.

By the late 1890s the General Assembly responded to Ohio's population growth and concomitant growth in government by building the Judiciary Annex (1899–1901) east of the state house to house the Ohio Supreme Court and the attorney general's office. An adaptive-use conversion of the annex and an atrium addition joining it to the original building were part of the largest preservation project in Ohio (1988–1996). The annex was renamed the Ohio Senate Building, and Senate hearings and caucus deliberations are held there. It also houses offices for Senate members.

The total cost of the restoration was $112.7 million, including the addition of such amenities as wiring for high-tech communication and computer-controlled heating and cooling systems. The rotunda's stained-glass skylight and interior-light court windows were uncovered and restored to allow natural light. The purpose of the effort was to ensure that the state

Atrium between the state house and the Senate building.

house continues to serve as the working seat of Ohio's state government and not as a museum.

Following the restoration, on March 27, 1997, the Ohio Supreme Court gave the General Assembly one year to make a "complete and systematic overhaul" of the way it funds primary and secondary education. The genesis of this mandate was a lawsuit filed in December 1991, in a southeastern Ohio county court. Parents of a student who, among other things, did not have books to take home because the school district provided too few, objected to Ohio's school financing system, claiming its dependence on property taxes favored more affluent districts. Eventually the suit expanded to include about 80 percent of the school districts throughout Ohio (the Coalition for Equity and Adequacy of School Funding). On July 1, 1994, the county judge ruled in their favor.

When the case, *DeRolph v. State of Ohio*, reached the Ohio Supreme Court, the justices upheld the county court judge's decision and concluded, largely in light of the terrible physical conditions present in many

Ohio schools, that the public-school financing system violated the Ohio constitution. A major thrust of the ruling agreed with the coalition that Ohio relied too heavily on local property taxes, unfair to low-wealth districts, and that a greater equality among its school districts must be achieved. The lower court where the case originated was given jurisdiction over the constitutionality and implementation of a new funding system.

After further hearings, the county judge found that the state legislature failed to meet the mandate. In *DeRolph II*, the supreme court agreed and stated that although local property taxes may be "part of the funding solution," they could "no longer be the primary means" of it.

In its September 6, 2001, *DeRolph III* ruling (with the legislature still unable to act), the court prescribed specific changes to make the system constitutional, including statewide academic standards, requirements that all school buildings be brought up to fire and building codes, elimination of over-reliance on local property taxes, and funding for all state mandates.

Carrara marble staircase in Ohio's Senate building.

CALIFORNIA

CALIFORNIA STATE CAPITOL

ORIGIN OF NAME: Named by Spanish explorers after a fictional land in a popular sixteenth-century novel by Garcia Ordóñez de Montalvo.

CAPITAL: Sacramento

CONSTRUCTED: 1860–1874

ARCHITECTS: Miner Frederick Butler and Reuben Clark

ADMITTED TO THE UNION: September 9, 1850 (thirty-first)

SENATE: 40 members

ASSEMBLY: 80 members

Spanish claims to what is now California began as far back as the sixteenth century. After Mexico gained independence from Spain in 1821, California came under Mexican rule, along with vast areas of what later became the western and southwestern United States. When the United States annexed Texas in 1845, it sought to purchase California and other southwestern areas, but Mexico refused, leading to a war between the United States and Mexico (1846–1848). On February 2, 1848, the Treaty of Guadalupe Hidalgo, which ended the war, ceded California to the United States. Following the discovery of gold and the resultant increase in population, a government became necessary. When Congress deadlocked over the issue of slavery under a territorial government, Californians bypassed territorial status and in 1849 adopted a state constitution prohibiting slavery. Statehood followed, and between 1849 and 1854 four cities served as state capitals — San Jose, Vallejo, Benicia, and finally Sacramento.

Located in a downtown Sacramento park, California's state capitol, the oldest capitol west of the Mississippi River, is surrounded by over four hundred varieties of trees and plants, and features spectacular flower gardens. The original four blocks, covering 40 acres, were planted in 1870 with eight hundred trees and flowering shrubs from all over the world. While not all survived, many California fan palms planted in 1882 continue to stand guard around the perimeter of the park.

Among the many cultural and historical monuments located throughout the park are a Civil War Memorial Grove with saplings from famous Civil War battlefields, planted in 1867; a life-sized statue of Father Junipero Serra, a Roman Catholic missionary sent by Spain to colonize California, along with a map of twenty-one missions built along the coast from San Diego to Sonoma; and numerous veterans' memorials.

California's state capitol sits amid its park-like grounds.

Facing the Sacramento River, the capitol's west facade has slightly projecting end bays and a central portico supported by seven granite archways, similar to Charles Bulfinch's earlier state houses. The portico's eight fluted Corinthian columns are arranged with the four widely spaced columns in the center flanked by closely spaced pairs. Its pediment, rising above the cornice, contains allegorical figures, with Minerva, the Roman goddess of wisdom, flanked by Education, Justice and Mining. The north and south facades incorporate smaller porticos with four fluted columns and Corinthian capitals supporting flat roofs. Each also incorporates a balustraded balcony.

Between the first and second floors, flat, square pilasters ending in Corinthian capitals support the cornice that surrounds the building. Windows decorated with ornamental iron are set within the pilasters. Until 1952, in place of an eastern portico, a semicircular bay or apse housed the supreme court and the state library.

Above its roof, a dome rises 220 feet, reflecting the dome that was simultaneously rising on the far-away federal Capitol. It is supported by a two-

Reconstructed stairway inside the capitol.

tiered drum, with the first incorporating a colonnade of Corinthian columns and the second of Corinthian pilasters. Above a columned lantern, covered with a small dome, is a 30-inch gold-covered ball.

Inside, scenes from the state's colorful history, such as the discovery of gold in 1848 and the arrival of the first ship in Monterey Bay, are illustrated in basement murals dating from 1915. Additional historical insight appears in the "Eureka tiles" set into the floor on the first level. Originally installed in 1896 and meticulously reproduced during a 1970 restoration, the 320 tiles contain symbols that also appear in the state seal, including the ever-present Minerva. In mythology, Minerva emerged fully grown, from the head of Jupiter, just as California became a state without first becoming a territory. "Eureka," California's state motto, means "I have found it" in Greek and refers to the discovery of gold. The grizzly bear represents the strength and independence of wildlife, while the sheaves of wheat represent agriculture.

From the first floor, the rotunda, 53 ½ feet in diameter, rises 120 feet within its inner dome. A 90-foot space between the inner and the exterior

A rear view of the California Senate chamber.

dome contains a spiral staircase that climbs to the lantern. Paint analysis during a restoration revealed the rotunda's current gold, blue, pink and beige colors. Other embellishments include reproduced English encaustic tile floors, small bull's-eye windows encircled with lights, painted fleur-de-lis, cast-iron bear heads, niches, griffins, and plaster garlands with cornucopias, further symbolizing California's first-in-the-nation agricultural production.

Standing prominently on the rotunda floor is a statuary group by Larkin Goldsmith Mead. Completed in 1871 and acquired in 1883, it is carved out of a single block of white marble. The sculpture commemorates Columbus's voyage to the New World by portraying Queen Isabella pledging her jewels to help finance the undertaking. At her side is her page, along with Columbus, who holds a sphere in his hand to demonstrate his theory that the earth is round.

Also located on the first floor are historic offices reflecting California's executive branch of government at the time of the 1906 San Francisco earthquake. For example, in the governor's office, the desk overflows with telegrams and newspapers about the disaster. The treasurer's, attorney general's and secretary of state's offices have also been recreated from historical photographs.

The original stairs were replicated, as during an earlier remodeling they had been replaced by elevators. Today, carved bear heads and light fixtures incorporating flying seahorses decorate the newel posts. The mosaic floor, made of six hundred thousand pieces,

The restored California State Assembly chamber.

contains golden poppies, the state flower. It was cleaned and painstakingly replaced by hand during the restoration.

The predominantly red and green colors of the chambers of both the Senate and Assembly were borrowed from the colors found in the British Parliament. Entered via the second-floor corridor through two tall paneled doors,

the Senate features a hand-carved dais, reproduction chairs, and members' desks of carved black walnut with red leather tops. Between 1864 and 1890, the capitol received furnishings for the chambers from a German furniture company, including an order for 120 carved walnut desks patterned after German school desks and costing $13 each.

Another English influence includes two chairs with red velvet cushions standing behind the rostrum, reserved for the king and queen, but always left empty. Above them hangs a portrait of George Washington attributed to Jane Stuart and based on her father, Gilbert Stuart's, famous painting. Given to the Senate in 1854, it is the oldest object in the room. Above the painting hangs a gold state seal and a Latin phrase that means "It is the duty of a senator to protect the liberty of the people." A statue of Minerva overlooks the room.

Gilded Corinthian columns support public galleries that extend across the back and around the side walls. During a 1950 remodeling, the original attached chairs were replaced by theater-type seats, but during a later restoration the originals were found and reinstalled. Above the galleries, plaster pendants hang from pre-cast plaster ceiling coffers. The electric crystal chandeliers and wall sconces are reproductions of the original gas fixtures.

Located at the opposite end of the second floor, the Assembly chamber reflects the British House of Commons in its primarily green tone. The green carpet, of Victorian-era design, is identical in design to the Senate's red carpeting. Original front desks, member desks and chairs date from the 1890s, and except for the portrait of Abraham Lincoln and the Latin admonition meaning "It is the duty of legislators to pass just laws" above the rostrum, everything else in the room is a reproduction. Arched, shuttered windows pierce the green

Hallways in the Annex.

"Eureka tiles" in hallway.

walls between pilasters with gilded capitals. The ceiling contains dropped pendants and coffers with paintings of California wildflowers. The press and constituents who obtain passes ahead of time may observe the proceedings from the floor, behind the rear pillars.

The Senate took twelve years longer than the Assembly to use computers and still votes by roll call. The Assembly adopted electronic voting in 1935 and is now fully computerized. Its sessions and many of its committee hearings are broadcast on cable television stations, and Californians can follow legislation and learn about their representatives on the Internet.

The capitol building has undergone many changes. Electricity replaced gas light between 1892 and 1895. In 1906, a remodeling created additional office space and incorporated technological advances. For the attached East Annex, completed in 1952, the popular rear apse was razed and in its place office space was added for legislators, including the current governor's suite. Constructed of concrete and steel, the East Annex features acoustic tile, fluorescent lighting, aluminum window frames, marble corridor walls, and hallway cases for county exhibits. At that time, the legislative chambers were redecorated in the then-modern style of the 1950s.

Two decades later, after a study of the building showed that it might not withstand an earthquake, the old capitol was entirely reconstructed in order to not only reinforce it but to restore its interior appearance to the period between 1900 and 1910.

Undertaken between 1975 and 1982, the monumental task involved removing the roof and bracing the walls from outside, though the dome remained in place. The insides were then removed one floor at a time. To make the walls stronger, a foot of original brick was removed and replaced by a layer of steel-reinforced concrete three feet thick. New steel trusses were added at the roof level, and the dome was reinforced and covered with copper shingles that duplicate the original. Some roofline statuary, much of which had been earlier removed because of deterioration, was reproduced and replaced.

After the woodwork was removed it was numbered for reinstallation, stripped and refinished. Decorative features were cleaned, restored or recreated as necessary. The estimated cost of the project is believed to have been $68 million. Today, the capitol is considered a working museum, where its elected representatives govern according to California's second constitution, adopted in 1879.

The rotunda has been restored to its early twentieth-century appearance.

MICHIGAN

MICHIGAN STATE CAPITOL

ORIGIN OF NAME: From the Chippewa word *Michigama* meaning "large lake."

CAPITAL: Lansing

CONSTRUCTED: 1872–1878

ARCHITECT: Elijah E. Myers

ADMITTED TO THE UNION: January 26, 1837 (twenty-sixth)

SENATE: 38 members

HOUSE OF REPRESENTATIVES: 110 members

In 1787, the area that is presently the state of Michigan was set aside by the United States Congress as part of the Northwest Territory. In 1805, the Territory of Michigan separated from the Northwest Territory and Detroit became its capital. Upon statehood, the old Michigan territorial courthouse in Detroit became its first capitol. By 1847, fearing a possible British occupation of the area so close to the Canadian frontier and eager to develop the interior of the state, the legislature decided to move the capital to an unsettled location in its wilderness.

At first, the newly created capital was called Michigan. Its name was later changed to Lansing, after the township in Ingham County where it was located. A small frame building served as the capitol until 1871, when planning began for a more permanent structure. Following an architectural competition, Elijah E. Myers was named architect, and Nehemiah Osburn & Company, an experienced firm from Rochester, New York, was appointed contractor. The legislature limited its budget to $1.2 million. Ground was broken in 1872, and on New Year's Day 1879, Michigan dedicated its new capitol. The final cost was $1,427,738.78 — nearly on budget.

Reflecting the expanded Capitol in Washington, D.C., with its horizontal shape, central block and balanced wings, the building is representative of many state capitols constructed during the period between the end of the Civil War and the turn of the twentieth century. Over 420 feet long and 273 feet wide, it consists of a basement and three stories, with a fourth story over the central section. It is 270 feet from the ground to the tip of the finial above the slender, tower-like cast-iron dome, encircled by a colonnade.

The rusticated ground story and upper walls are constructed of local brick and sandstone from neighboring Ohio. The facade incorporates pilasters with Doric capitals on the first floor, Ionic on the next, and Corinthian orders on the third level. The main entrance, through a balustraded double portico within a projecting four-story central pavilion, incorporates columns of the same orders as the corresponding wall order. The pavilion's pediment contains the capitol's only sculpture, symbolizing Michigan's transformation from a wilderness to an agricultural and industrial state. String courses, or continuous horizontal bands around the building's exterior, define each of the floor levels. Windows on the first story are arched, while those on the second and third stories are pedimented.

Myers became an architect not through formal training, with its stylistic

Old Michigan Supreme Court chamber, now a hearing room.

The Michigan State Capitol rotunda; the glass floor transmits light to the areas below.

The Senate chamber.

discipline, but by working his way through the building trades. As a result, he drew his ideas, inspirations and details from a wide range of architectural styles, a technique that sometimes led to professional criticism. But perhaps because of this background, he meticulously designed the interior woodwork, floors, cast-iron stairs, columns and other iron elements, cabinetry and furniture. Instead of producing these features with imported marble and expensive black walnut, Myers integrated local white pine and domestic stone throughout the building. The inexpensive pine, plaster and cast-iron were then faux-painted to look like the more costly marble and walnut.

The pine was more prominently grained by layering brown paint to imitate the striation natural to walnut, then it was covered with colored glazes to give it the appearance of black walnut. The purpose of painting the pine, plaster and cast-iron was not only to make them appear more beautiful and more expensive but also to enable the contractor to stay within the building's statutory budget limit. In addition, every wall and ceiling was hand-painted using bright colors, elaborate patterns and stenciling. The capitol is considered one of the finest examples of Victorian decorative painting.

Only 44 ½ feet in diameter, the rotunda is dedicated to the citizens of Michigan, and it is decorated to inspire them. Cases holding replicas of historical flags surround the first floor. During the Civil War, there were one thousand Michigan soldiers per regiment, each one from a small geographic area. Local women designed and sewed flags that were carried in the middle of a regiment as it marched into battle.

The rotunda also incorporates a unique floor made from 976 pieces of glass, each about 5/8 inch thick. The glass is set into a patterned steel frame and is strong enough to hold 40 tons of weight. Capitol tour guides often suggest that schoolchildren lie on the floor and look up, where they see ring after ring of balconies rising 160 feet into the dome. Portraits of fourteen past governors hang from the walls. One of them, Governor Swainson (1961–1962), is unfinished. This is because he was thirty-seven when elected governor and his career is ongoing (he became a Supreme Court judge). Eighty feet above the portraits, eight allegorical female figures, representing Science, Art, Labor, Education, Law, Commerce, Industry, and Agriculture, overlook the activities of the busy building.

Electric lighting was introduced to the capitol in late 1899 and the summer of 1900. The twenty original "Michigan" gas chandeliers, now electrified, feature the word "Tuebor" (meaning "I will defend"), elk, and other motifs from the state's coat of arms, along with an eagle, representing the United States.

In the House of Representatives, the largest room in the capitol, the members sit at original solid walnut desks. Over the rostrum hangs the Michigan coat of arms. The state seal theme is repeated here and in the Senate in the glass panels of the coffered ceiling, etched with the coat of arms of all fifty states. In the upper chamber, the carpet features the Michigan coat of arms,

A statue of Austin Blair, Civil War governor of Michigan, stands in front of the state capitol.

though the federal seal is displayed over its dais. Throughout the building, doorknobs and hinges are cast with the Michigan coat of arms.

In the old supreme court chamber, designed by Myers, the ceiling, black walnut bench and cabinets are original to the room. Portraits of former justices who served on the Michigan Supreme Court hang on the plaster walls, which are decorated with Moorish swirls. In 1970, the court moved to the nearby Law Building, and the room now serves as a committee room, where senators and representatives work on bills that might become law.

A subdivision of existing office spaces took place between 1970 and 1973, and as the building started to look old and worn, an initiative to replace it with a more modern design was supported by many, including Governor George Romney. Ultimately, Romney moved on to serve in the federal government, and public support for the capitol kept it from demolition. In 1989, a $58-million renovation commenced to restore it to its original appearance, with painters grain-painting and stenciling, and plasterers swirling designs on the walls. The workers and artisans appeared to enjoy the process and the result, just as the original craftsmen undoubtedly had taken pride in their work. Modern technology and conveniences were also added. The rededication took place on November 19, 1992.

By the time of the capitol's rededication, Michigan's Upper and Lower peninsulas, separated by the Straits of Mackinac, were more unified than ever. This was largely due to the

The interior of the Michigan State Capitol dome.

legislature's effort to construct the Mackinac Bridge. The story of Michigan's land acquisitions and the building of a bridge goes back to 1836, when what is now Wisconsin and the present Upper Peninsula lay in the Michigan Territory. At that time, Congress created the Territory of Wisconsin, including that part of the Upper Peninsula area west of a line drawn up through it from the center of Lake Michigan. This wilderness area, given to Wisconsin, was not contested by Michigan when it applied for statehood, but a strip of land across its southern border became a major problem after it was claimed by the state of Ohio.

When Michigan and Ohio could not reach a peaceful settlement, the Ohio militia prepared to invade what was considered by Michigan to be its land.

Congress interceded on June 15, 1836, and granted the nearly 400 square miles of contested land, including the Toledo Harbor, to Ohio. As consolation, Michigan received what now constitutes the Upper Peninsula, taken from the Wisconsin Territory, and it was admitted as a state of the Union.

Although the two peninsulas were united politically, the physical separation of the Straits of Mackinac inhibited economic progress. In the beginning they could only communicate by boat, leaving them completely isolated in winter. With the prosperity following the discovery of vast copper and iron-ore deposits in the so-called Upper Peninsula wasteland, the idea of constructing a bridge took root, even though most people believed that the distance of nearly five miles was too great, the water too deep, the current too swift and the winds during a storm too dangerous.

During the late nineteenth and early twentieth centuries, events such as the completion of the Brooklyn Bridge, improved railroad ferries, an icebreaker ferry, and the development of the automobile spurred the legislature to seek to oversee and promote better connections between the peninsulas. It established a Highway Department and financed an auto ferry service. But the capacity of transportation connecting the peninsulas continued to lag, especially in deer season when waiting periods averaged as long as nineteen hours and lines of cars reportedly stretched for 27 miles. The Depression halted further initiatives.

After the Second World War, with the state prosperous and cars ubiquitous, the legislature finally created the Mackinac Bridge Authority and gave it the go-ahead to build a bridge. Money was raised by selling bonds, to be repaid from tolls paid by those using the bridge. Funds were also appropriated by the legislature to cover part of the bridge's operational expenses. When the bridge was completed in 1957, it was considered an engineering marvel. At 26,444 feet, it was the world's longest suspension bridge, the suspension part of it measuring 8,614 feet, which is 2,000 feet longer than the Golden Gate Bridge across San Francisco Bay. Although it cost $100 million and took nearly four years to build, the bridge is considered to be more than worth the time and expense, because by joining the Upper and Lower peninsulas it ended the Upper Peninsula's isolation.

A cast-iron staircase inside the state capitol building.

CONNECTICUT

CONNECTICUT STATE CAPITOL
ORIGIN OF NAME: The Algonquian word *quinnitkqut* meaning "beside the long tidal river."
CAPITAL: Hartford
CONSTRUCTED: 1873–1878
ARCHITECT: Richard Michel Upjohn
ADMITTED TO THE UNION: January 9, 1788 (fifth)
SENATE: 36 members
HOUSE OF REPRESENTATIVES: 151 members

Before the completion of its capitol in 1878, Connecticut claimed two seats of state government, one in Hartford and one in New Haven, where its legislature met alternately in five state houses. (The first state house on record was constructed in New Haven in 1717.) New Haven's second state house, occupied in 1763, was older than Hartford's old state house (built 1793–1796), located on the site of its first one in the middle of Hartford's business district. The old state house, Connecticut's fourth, is attributed to the architect Charles Bulfinch. A landmark of brick and brownstone built in the Federal style, it was, among other things, the site of George Washington's first secret meeting with the French during the American Revolution and was the seat of state government (1796–1878), and of city government (1878–1915). Washington's full-length portrait, painted by Gilbert Stuart, hangs in the restored Senate chamber.

While Connecticut's legislature met at the old state house, it continued to convene alternately at New Haven's third state house. This small temple-shaped building was designed and built just off the New Haven Green between 1827 and 1830 by Ithiel Town. In 1874, the last session of the General Assembly met there before the building passed into the hands of the City of New Haven and various nonprofit organizations. In 1889 it was torn down.

After a popular referendum, Hartford, the business center of Connecticut, was finally named the only capital and a state capitol commission was formed to build the new capitol. Following an architectural competition, a secular Gothic design by Richard Michel Upjohn was chosen. The estimated cost of construction totaled $875,000. But a year into its construction, the commission decided to alter the design in order to better fireproof the new structure and to make it more reflective of Connecticut's prosperity.

Upjohn, son of well-known church architect Richard Upjohn, initially included a tall clock tower in his design, but at the insistence of the commission

he modified the plans and replaced the central tower with a gold-leaf dome nearly 54 feet in diameter and rising to more than 240 feet. Other modifications included provision of additional space, more columns and carvings. These modifications resulted in a final construction cost of $2,532,524, and after interior decorations and furnishings, it rose to $3,347,550.

Although the building's unusual secular Gothic style is unique in capitol designs, it was a generally popular style during this Victorian period. The marble three-story building incorporates projecting four-story center pavilions, three-story end pavilions, multiple towers and turrets, marble dormer windows with carved trimmings, gables pierced by circular windows, and

The old Connecticut State House surrounded by office towers in downtown Hartford.

The Connecticut State Capitol.

Assembly hall of the Connecticut House of Representatives.

iron cresting. The arcaded center pavilions, five bays wide, feature a carved cornice, Gothic arches containing trefoil windows mirroring the tympana below, pointed towers and a marble balustrade.

The north facade, facing Bushnell Park, features a main entrance with five arches, while the southern facade contains a porte-cochere with vestibule. The eastern end is similar to the north but smaller, with three arches, while the west is the most plain. Each facade reflects American and Connecticut history: the north, Connecticut's founding fathers and colonial history; the east, the Revolutionary War and the founding of the nation; the west, figures representing government service; and the south, the Civil War and forward.

Twenty-six statuary niches with pedestals cover the entrances. Placed on the pedestals is statuary of the state's most admired leaders, such as Joseph Wadsworth, who hid the Royal Charter of 1662 in the Charter Oak tree; and Thomas Hooker, a minister considered to have been the founder of the Connecticut colony.

The east-side niches were filled within the first two years of the building's use. Some pedestals intended for future additions were left vacant, and in 1987 a statue of Ella Grasso was added. Grasso, the eighty-third governor of Connecticut, became the state's first woman to be elected to this position, in 1974.

Interior view of dome showing the Gothic arches formed by the dome's supports.

High above, allegorical figures representing Commerce, Education, Science, Agriculture, Music and Force surround the dome. The 15-foot bronze statue of the Genius of Connecticut originally stood at its top. Replaced by a stone finial, the statue now stands in the interior lobby. Also inside, the Boston decorating firm of William J. McPherson worked nearly two years painting and stenciling the walls and ceilings, manufacturing all the stained glass, and supervising the installation of carpets, fabrics, tiled floors and fixtures. In addition, McPherson worked on the White House, the Treasury Building and the War & Navy Building in Washington, D.C., along with the city hall in Providence, Rhode Island. Moorish and Middle Eastern influences popular during this time, appear throughout but are especially prominent in the two light courts, with ornamental railings and iron columns painted with shiny aluminum paint, while the capitals and bases feature bronze and gold-leaf detailing.

In the middle of the building, near a tall space that is painted in shades of red, gold, green and blue, ten large stone piers support the dome, making an opening that rises to a painted blue sky with gold stars. Two marble staircases flank this space. The interior marble and granite columns, Gothic arches, and marble floors and walls are made from Connecticut, Maine, Vermont and Rhode Island stone. The woodwork finish consists of oak, black walnut and ash.

The Hall of the House of Representatives, located on the second floor, occupies the entire projection of the central portion of the southern facade of the capitol above the porte-cochere and vestibule. There are four entrance doors on the north side and large windows on the other three sides. Flanked by white marble columns, the Gothic upper windows consist of colored glass and leaded sash, while the lower ones integrate stained glass in the transom and plate-glass openings covered with rose curtains.

The gallery occupies the north side of the room and is divided from the chamber by a series of twin columns painted red and separated by bronze

The Charter Oak chair in the Senate chamber was carved from the tree in which the colony of Connecticut's royal charter was hidden from the king's men in 1687. In 1662, King Charles II of England had granted the people of Connecticut a special charter enabling them to govern themselves. Twenty years later, King James II, believing that the people had too much power, sought to rescind it. The people of Connecticut refused, and the king reacted by sending his representatives to Hartford to renegotiate the terms of the charter. At one point, with the charter lying on a table before the opposing parties, the candlelight suddenly went out. By the time they were relit the charter had vanished. Captain Joseph Wadsworth is credited with saving the precious charter by grabbing and hiding it in a giant oak tree. When the tree fell during a storm in 1856, its wood was used to build the chair, carved with oak leaves. So many other objects were purportedly carved from the tree that Hartford resident Mark Twain joked that he had seen "enough Charter Oak to build a plank road from Hartford to Salt Lake City."

guard railings. The speaker's desk, located below and between the double entrance doors, stands on a platform of black walnut. The chairs, with red leather seats, and the desks of the representatives, are arranged upon a circular platform at a slight elevation, one above the other. The woodwork and the furniture, including the original members' desks, are of black walnut. Wainscoting surrounds the room at doorway height. The room is painted predominately in shades of red, yellow and olive green. The state seal is woven into the carpet. The ceiling, above a stucco cornice, includes recessed panels with intersecting ribs supported at the wall ends by carved corbels. Decorative painting and stenciling remain intact after a restoration effort returned the chamber to its 1880s appearance.

The Senate, formerly the state library, was converted to the upper chamber in 1910. Public galleries with mahogany wainscoting were added at the time of the conversion. Other decorative features include red carpeting, stained-glass windows, ceiling rosettes and stenciling. The members' desks form a 25-foot circle, where they are seated by districts, not by party. This unusual nonpartisan arrangement supposedly fosters a more collegial atmosphere. Underneath a clock, the lieutenant governor presides from the Charter Oak chair.

Connecticut's history is honored throughout the capitol. Standing in the east wing is a statue of Nathan Hale. During the Revolutionary War, Hale volunteered to spy on the British forces occupying New York. He was captured by British soldiers while carrying plans for British fortifications and hanged without a trial. The twenty-one-year-old's famous last words, as described on the granite base holding his statue, were, "I only regret that I have but one life to lose for my country."

In the Hall of Flags, where flags carried into battle by Connecticut soldiers are displayed, stands Marquis de Lafayette's camp bed, discovered in Washington's Hartford quarters, and Israel Putnam's gravestone. Putnam commanded Connecticut forces at the Battle of Bunker Hill and is credited with saying, "Don't fire 'til you see the whites of their eyes."

The building originally included space for the Connecticut Supreme Court, state library, a courtroom, state offices, the governor's suite and the legislative chambers. Only the governor and the legislature remain, as all the others were moved to separate buildings. In addition, in 1988 the nearby legislative building was completed at a cost of $61 million. This steel, glass and concrete-block structure is faced with rough and polished granite. Except for the atrium, it is covered by a copper mansard roof. There are offices for the lawmakers and areas where public hearings and legislative committee hearings are held. The cherry-wood doors of the ten hearing rooms are decorated with marquetry, an ancient craft in which wood veneers are cut and pieced together to form a picture. One door includes a map of the state with its eight counties, and others depict the capitol, the state bird, and Litchfield Law School, the first law school established in America, in 1784. This busy building is connected to the capitol through an underground concourse.

This statue of Nathan Hale stands in the Moorish-looking east wing of the state capitol building.

Iowa

Iowa State Capitol

Origin of Name: From *ayuxwa*, a Native American word translated as "beautiful land."

Capital: Des Moines

Constructed: 1871–1886

Architect: Alfred H. Piquenard

Admitted to the Union: December 28, 1846 (twenty-ninth)

Senate: 50 members

House of Representatives: 100 members

The state of Iowa stretches horizontally between the Mississippi and the Missouri rivers. Included in the Louisiana Purchase of 1803, its land became part of the Territory of Louisiana in 1805 and of the Territory of Missouri in 1812. Under the Missouri Compromise of 1820, a part of that territory became the slave state of Missouri, though slavery was prohibited in the area that included the future Iowa.

As European settlers pushed Native Americans westward, fighting broke out between them. After the Black Hawk War (1832), lands guaranteed to Chief Black Hawk if he and his followers would leave Illinois and settle along the Iowa River were taken back and opened for settlement. As Dubuque, Bellevue, Muscatine, Burlington, Fort Madison and Keokuk developed, Congress in 1834 included Iowa in the Territory of Michigan, until two years later when it became a part of the Territory of Wisconsin, with Burlington as its capital.

In 1838, Congress named Iowa a separate territory and appointed the former governor of Ohio, Robert Lucas, governor. Burlington continued as the capital for the new territory, and the first meeting of its legislature took place in an old church. In order to move the capital closer to the center of the territory, a hill on the Iowa River was subsequently chosen as the site for a new capital. The legislature named the site "City of Iowa" or later Iowa City. The stone structure, designed in the Classical style and built as the territorial capitol, later served as Iowa's first permanent capitol. It was designed by John Francis Rague, architect of Illinois' first capitol at Springfield.

Eleven years after Iowa became a state, the legislature decided to relocate even closer to its geographical center by moving to Fort Des Moines, on the Des Moines River. Since there was no railroad west of Iowa City, a stagecoach moved state officials, while furniture, including four large safes, was hauled by ox teams to the new capital. As consolation for losing its status of capital, state officials awarded the state university to Iowa City.

A three-story brick building on a hill in Des Moines housed the legislature for thirty years. Constructed on the same grounds, today's capitol, like many government buildings constructed during the post-Civil War period, contains a dome, rotunda, porticoes and wings. It is, however, the only five-domed capitol in the nation.

Built of brick, it is faced with limestone, granite and sandstone from Iowa, Missouri, Minnesota, Ohio and Illinois. Iowa stone provides the foundation below the rusticated first floor. Rusticated piers support central porticoes on each elevation. Six Corinthian columns, rising two stories in the front

Since 1922 a flag has been suspended from the state capitol's interior dome.

The Iowa State Capitol incorporates five domes.

and back porticoes, support sculpted pediments, while on the wings the porticoes incorporate four Corinthian columns. Rustication is repeated on the quoins, while smooth pilasters and wall surfaces made of Missouri stone surround the windows, which are of varied shapes, many of them arched.

The end sections of the wing incorporate platforms on the corners, from which the four-corner subsidiary domes protrude. Above double-arched windows, covered with pediments, the domes mirror the large dome with bull's-eye windows, though with a smaller lantern and finial. The corner domes are roofed in copper, tarnished to a shade of green.

The central block roof contains a balustrade. Paired Corinthian columns interspersed between long, narrow, arched windows support the central dome with its consoles, smaller paired windows, surrounding balustrade and ornate bull's-eye windows. Revised between 1879 and 1880, the dome is covered in 23-carat gold leaf and rises 275 feet above the ground.

At first the capitol grounds covered only four blocks; however, in 1913 the legislature (in a move that seemed controversial at that time but is now seen as farsighted) bought an additional 84 acres surrounding the building at a cost of about $3 million. A landscaped park replaced the cleared houses, barns and fences, and areas were set aside for future state buildings.

Inside, the three-story building houses a cafeteria and offices on the ground floor, the governor and other elected state officials on the first floor, and on the second floor the House of Representatives and Senate chambers, the state law library, committee rooms and other offices. Originally the rotunda extended above the first floor to the dome, but in the early 1900s a

The mural Westward *is displayed on the upper landing of the grand staircase.*

circular opening was cut into the floor, extending the rotunda into the basement level. With the additional light, the basement expanded from a storage area to provide space for additional offices.

A 1902 renovation included the installation of electric lighting, elevators and a telephone system. A workman installing electrical wiring by candlelight started a fire that destroyed most of the north wing, including the House of Representatives chamber and the ceiling of the supreme court below. But damaged areas were repaired and redecorated following the fire.

The House chamber features stained-glass skylight. Granite columns support the dome, while the columns in the legislative halls are finished in scagliola. They also feature walnut desks and furniture. In the chambers and in the offices of the governor and other state officials, walls and ceilings are decoratively painted and stenciled. Interior woods integrate native Iowa ash, red oak, white oak, chestnut, black walnut, butternut, cherry, mahogany, poplar, catalpa, white and yellow pine. Floors are primarily terrazzo, and twenty-nine varieties of domestic and imported marble are incorporated throughout the building, some of which can no longer be obtained.

After the fire, large pieces of art were purchased for the rotunda. Above the marble grand staircase, a 40-by-14-foot painting entitled *Westward* symbolizes the arrival of the pioneers in Iowa. The artist, Edwin Howland Blashfield, described his work as follows: "A symbolic presentation of the pioneers led by the spirits of Civilization and Enlightenment to the conquest by cultivation of the Great West. The canvas shows a "prairie schooner" drawn by oxen across the prairie. The family rides upon the wagon or walk at

Iowa House of Representatives chamber.

A photograph of the 168th Infantry and a collection of dolls depicting Iowa's first ladies.

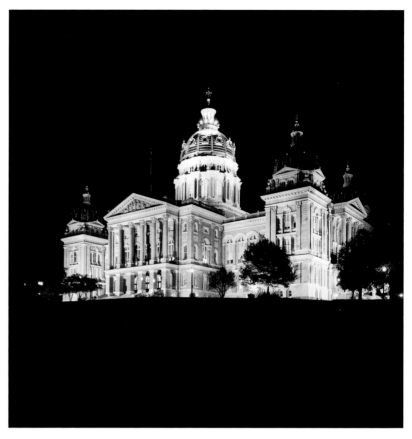

The Iowa State Capitol is visible throughout the downtown area of Des Moines.

its side. Behind them and seen through the growth of stalks come the other pioneers and later men. In the air and before the wagon are four floating female figures; one holds the shield with the arms of the State of Iowa upon it; one holds a book symbolizing Enlightenment; two others carry a basket and scatter the seeds which are symbolical of the change from wilderness to plowed fields and gardens that shall come over the prairie. Behind the wagon and also floating in the air, two female figures hold respectively a model of a stationary steam engine and an electric dynamo to suggest the forces which come with later men."

Located above *Westward* are six arched panels measuring 6 by 14 feet and filled with glass mosaics by Frederick Dielman from the the Murano glass company in Venice, Italy. The sections represent Defense, Charities, the Executive, the Legislature, the Judiciary and Education. They incorporate, among other things, the current capitol and the old capitol in Iowa City into their design.

At the base of the interior dome, which rises 275 feet above the ground floor to a banner depicting the Grand Army of the Republic emblem, eight lunette paintings suspended by piano wire tell the story of the progress of civilization. Twelve statues between them represent History, Science, Law, Fame, Literature, Industry, Peace, Commerce, Victory, Truth, Progress and Agriculture.

At the top of the stairway on the south wall is a painting entitled *Plenty*, depicting a basket of corn. It was part of the Iowa Exhibit at the Pan-Pacific Exposition in San Francisco in 1915, celebrating the opening of the Panama Canal. It and other agricultural references throughout the building reflect Iowa's role in global food production, with an estimated 92 percent of its land devoted to agriculture.

Close by, in the chambers of the Senate and House of Representatives, the Iowa General Assembly adopts policies and laws promoting agricultural production, including its support of renewable fuels such as ethanol, which utilize agricultural products. Ethanol supporters claim that it is not only a market for Iowa's corn products but it lessens the state's dependency upon petroleum products and reduces pollution from the combustion of fossil fuels.

The Iowa legislature increasingly tries to balance agriculture with environmental interests as the state gradually becomes more urban. In 1987, lawmakers passed a groundwater protection law that sought to curtail runoff by restoring wetlands, creating buffers between farms and rivers, and keeping crop residue on the fields after harvests to anchor the soil and prevent erosion. The law also set up an incentive program that pays farmers to use less phosphorus and to stop plowing their fields after each crop, a practice that leaves the soil vulnerable to erosion.

Iowa state library.

ILLINOIS

ILLINOIS STATE CAPITOL

ORIGIN OF NAME: From an Algonquin word *illiniwek,*
meaning "tribe of superior men."

CAPITAL: Springfield

CONSTRUCTED: 1868–1888

ARCHITECTS: John C. Cochrane, Alfred H. Piquenard

ADMITTED TO THE UNION: December 3, 1818 (twenty-first)

SENATE: 59 members

HOUSE OF REPRESENTATIVES: 118 members

Two forces in Illinois history also relate to the story of its state capitols. One pertains to the influence of Kentucky-born Abraham Lincoln, and the other is the competition between the industrial urban colossus of Chicago and the rural communities "Down State."

When Illinois became a state, its northern boundary, fixed by the Northwest Ordinance of 1787 at an east-west line placed at the southern tip of Lake Michigan, was moved 51 miles north in order to give it a Great Lakes shoreline. The principal settlement of the middle Mississippi Valley was the territorial capital, Kaskaskia, and it became the first state capital. Two years later, with the population shifting northward, the seat of government was moved 80 miles northeast to Vandalia. The opening of the Erie Canal in 1825 brought with it the immigration of large numbers of people to Illinois by way of the Great Lakes. Settlement centered at Fort Dearborn, transforming it into the city of Chicago in 1837.

The citizens of Vandalia provided a new building in an attempt to maintain its capital status, but they were no match for aggressive young railroad attorney Abraham Lincoln and his friends who practiced law in Springfield and spearheaded the capital's move from Vandalia to the even more centrally located Springfield. Following their success, John Francis Rague designed a Greek Revival capitol (1839–1853) from pattern books of the time. The stone building housed all three branches of state government and was located across the street from Lincoln's law office.

Because of its close association with Lincoln, the Rague capitol was dismantled and rebuilt in 1966 in order to preserve and reflect its appearance during his time. It is where Lincoln served four terms in the legislature, conducted research in the library, and pleaded more than two hundred cases in the Illinois Supreme Court. It is also where he accepted the Republican nomination for United States senator and, in 1858 in the House of Representatives chamber, began his United States Senate campaign against Stephen Douglas when he addressed the slavery issue and its effect on the country by declaring, "A house divided against itself cannot stand." Although Lincoln lost that election, it introduced him to the national political scene and led to his successful presidential campaign in 1860. Subsequently, Lincoln located his campaign headquarters in the governor's office, where he met supporters, job seekers and the press. Following his assassination in 1865, Lincoln lay in state there before his burial in Springfield on May 3.

In spite of all its history, from the time the old capitol was completed, it was too small for the growing state. As a result, in 1867 the General Assembly authorized the construction of a new capitol in Springfield, much to the chagrin of Chicago promoters. In order to placate the powerful in Chicago, the General Assembly planned to convene its fall 1871 session in that city. But on October 8, the Great Chicago Fire broke out, ruining the city's plans to permanently woo the state government to Chicago. Nevertheless, even today, state government increasingly operates out of Chicago from the distinctive James Thompson State Office Building. At least

The restored House of Representatives chamber in the old capitol.

This statue of Abraham Lincoln stands in front of the Illinois State Capitol.

The rebuilt old Greek Revival state capitol building.

miles of the pressed-paper ornamentation throughout the capitol, made in his specially designed molds and fixed to the wall or ceiling with glue. In addition to Room 212, it can be seen in the House of Representatives, the Senate, and offices of the auditor, the treasurer and the secretary of state.

Construction of the capitol stopped temporarily after Piquenard's death in 1876, and again in 1877, due to lack of funds. It was resumed in 1884 with new appropriations and a fresh perspective from W. W. Boyington, architect of Chicago's water tower. Boyington built the east and north porticoes, supported by Corinthian columns. He also designed the inner dome and added artwork throughout the building. Finally, in 1888, after twenty years of construction, the capitol was completed.

The building measures 379 feet from north to south and 268 feet from east to west. The height from the ground to the top of the dome is 361 feet, and 405 feet to the tip of the flagstaff, reportedly 74 feet taller than the United States Capitol. The dome is supported by a foundation set in solid rock 25 feet below the surface and 17-foot-thick walls constructed of Illinois limestone. Entrance doors are located through rusticated arched piers that mirror the arched windows of the rusticated ground floor. Pilasters separate the rectangular second-floor windows and the arched third-floor windows. Except for where the mansard roof and the pediments cover the roof, a balustrade follows the roofline.

The dome rises from the center of the roof on a rusticated platform with notched corners. The next section contains tall, arched windows below circular ones fronted by porticoes consisting of two pairs and two singular Corinthian columns with another balustrade connecting them. On the next level, shorter pilasters separate windows with another balustrade. Before the curvature of the roof, pairs of rectangular windows provide additional interior light. A protected lookout with a small dome and finial complete the dome.

Inside, Corinthian red marble columns contribute additional support for the dome and form the rotunda. The rotunda highlights artwork, ornate brasswork, and a stained-glass skylight in the design of the state seal. Surrounding it stand eight granite pedestals, featuring life-size bronze Illini including Lincoln; Douglas; Governor John Wood; David E. Shanahan, who was elected speaker of the House five times; Richard J. Barr, who served in the Senate for forty-eight years; Chicago mayor Richard J. Daley, who began his political career as a state representative; Lottie Homan O'Neill, the first woman elected to the Illinois legislature; and Adelbert H. Roberts, the first African-American senator.

High upon the walls of the rotunda, around the base of the dome, are statues featuring eight men prominent in the civil and military history of Illinois, including Ulysses S. Grant and Ninian Edwards, territorial and first governor of Illinois. Above the statues and just below the base of the inner dome, nine plaster relief scenes depict Illinois pioneer life. Murals also illustrate scenes from Illinois history. At the first landing on the grand

one recent governor refused to move to Springfield, perhaps strengthening Chicago's position to make another capital challenge.

Meanwhile, official state business continues in Springfield from the capitol that was built from the prize-winning design attributed to John C. Cochrane of Chicago. It is generally believed, however, that Cochrane's role was limited to convincing the members of the building commission to select the plan that was actually drawn by his then-partner, George O. Garnsey. After the Chicago fire, Cochrane formed a partnership with Alfred H. Piquenard and remained in Chicago, where he carried out commissions to rebuild the city while Piquenard moved to Springfield to supervise construction of the new capitol.

A French immigrant, Piquenard is primarily responsible for the building's exterior appearance, including the design of the dome, the carved stone over the windows, and the columns and pilasters with Corinthian capitals for the third floor, where the legislative chambers are located. He also designed a decorated frieze, along with the mansard-style roofs over the end wings, borrowed from the French Second Empire style. In addition, he was responsible for ornate interior finishes such as the unique carton pierre moldings prominent in the old supreme court chamber, now Legislative Hearing Room 212.

The Illinois capitol is distinguished by its integration of carton pierre, an imitation of decorative plaster made out of paper. Piquenard described it as "a kind of papier mache generally used in Europe." He claimed there were seven

The recently restored House of Representatives chamber.

staircase is a large mural, measuring 40 feet by 20 feet, showing George Rogers Clark making a treaty with Native Americans in 1778 after the capture of Fort Gage, thus ending British occupation.

Originally, both chambers contained central stained-glass skylights, but the round House skylight has been replaced by a solid circle with eight spokes representing the letters of Illinois, while the Senate's has a solid square design. Also in the House, four 980-prism crystal chandeliers from Austria hang from the ornate ceiling. Each weighs about 1,000 pounds and

is suspended by a half-inch steel cable. The cable is controlled from the attic and requires twenty-four turns to raise or lower each chandelier a foot. For cleaning, all 980 prisms, each measuring 8 inches long and weighing half a pound, are removed and washed in a commercial dishwasher, hand-dipped in ammonia, and then dried with an electric fan.

Over the years the capitol has been remodeled a number of times, with some changes quite controversial. During the late 1960s, lawmakers decided to update its mechanical and electrical systems and to add legislative offices.

Committee hearing room featuring carton pierre (a type of papier mache) decoration.

The statue Illinois Welcoming the World, *from the Columbian Exposition in Chicago.*

Since funding was not available for a separate building, they decided to convert the capitol to serve as both a capitol and a legislative office building.

In addition, by 1973, concern for the building's integrity led to the formation of the Architectural Advisory Committee for the Illinois State Capitol Complex. They sought to remove the capitol's remodeling from the influence of personal preferences and make it more accurate to its period and style. The space problem was later alleviated by construction of the nearby legislative building and a 2002 restoration of the capitol.

Not far from the capitol, because of the General Assembly's zoning legislation, another preservation effort protected the historic character of the four-block district around Abraham Lincoln's home. Illinois zoning laws grant municipalities the right to divide into districts and impose restrictions on the use of property in those districts for the overall benefit of the community.

Communities may also enact regulations protecting historical areas such as the Historical District around Lincoln's home in Springfield. The district was established to ensure that the surrounding area relates sympathetically to Lincoln's home. An inspiration to visitors, the house was purchased by Lincoln in 1844, enlarged in 1856, and was the only home he ever owned. In enacting the National Historical Preservation Act of 1966, Congress declared that "the historical and cultural foundations of the Nation should be preserved as a living part of community life and development in order to give a sense of orientation to the American people."

The barrel-vaulted stained-glass ceiling above the grand staircase illuminates this mural.

INDIANA

INDIANA STATE HOUSE

ORIGIN OF NAME: Given by Congress when it carved the territory from the Northwest Territory, "the Land of Indians."

CAPITAL: Indianapolis

CONSTRUCTED: 1878–1888

ARCHITECTS: Edwin May, Adolf Scherrer

ADMITTED TO THE UNION: December 11, 1816 (nineteenth)

SENATE: 50 members

HOUSE OF REPRESENTATIVES: 100 members

In 1937, Indiana's General Assembly adopted the state's motto, "The Crossroads of America." More than a century earlier, when Indiana became a state, it was not a crossroads but a wilderness situated between Lake Michigan and the Ohio River. Settlers occupied the southern part of the state along the Ohio River, while the central and northern portion belonged to Native Americans. In 1818, the federal government purchased land in central Indiana in order to encourage white settlement there. Known as the New Purchase, this land was officially opened in 1820.

The first Indiana State House was erected in 1813 in Corydon. It served as the seat of the territorial government before it became the first state house. On January 10, 1825, Indianapolis was created, near the geographic center of the state, specifically to serve as the permanent capital. A decade later, a Greek Revival state house was completed on the grounds of the present state house. This controversial building, surmounted by an Italian Renaissance dome, was no longer considered safe after the ceiling of the House of Representatives collapsed in 1867. Although it was to some extent repaired, the legislature created a board of state house commissioners to oversee the construction of a new state house at a cost not to exceed $2 million.

The commission chose Indianapolis architect Edwin May, and along with his draftsman, Viennese-trained Adolph Scherrer, he designed the Renaissance Revival state house. May did not see his design completed because he died two years into the project. Scherrer succeeded him as supervising architect for the next eight years.

Indiana is known for its limestone quarries, and native stone covers its state house. It is designed with a central dome flanked by four-story wings running north and south, intersecting at their ends with projecting wings running east and west. The wings feature Corinthian pilasters separating the windows. Corinthian-columned porticoes, extending from the top of the second floor to the top of the fourth, front the entrance pavilions centered at each wing. The main entrance pavilion faces north toward downtown Indianapolis. A plain stone beltcourse defines the first-floor window line, while a sculpted one separates the second and third floors from the area above.

Emerging from the roof is a two-tier copper-covered dome, the first tier measuring 73 feet in diameter and the second 15 feet. The French Second Empire-influenced design incorporates four corner towers, with a pyramidal dome topped with a cupola. On the roofline of the south facade is an

Rear view of the Indiana Supreme Court.

Full-ceiling skylights illuminate the court and its marble columns.

eagle mounted above statues of a Native American family, a pioneer family, a blacksmith and a hunter.

Initially, the state house accommodated all the governmental offices, but as Indiana's population increased and its state government expanded, many offices were moved to buildings located west of the state house. Today, only the General Assembly, the governor and the supreme court work in the state house.

Edwin May's interior design differed from the usual capitol floor plan in that the legislative chambers were placed on either side of the rotunda, rather than at opposite ends of the building. The end wings were reserved for the supreme court and the state library, though the library was moved across the street from the state house in 1934.

Upon entering the building through the hand-carved wooden doors, 68-foot-wide corridors lead into the rotunda. This central area is surrounded by piers of Vermont marble supporting the dome. Statuary representing Law, Oratory, Agriculture, Commerce, Liberty, Justice, History and Art stands on ledges of the second level. The sculptor, Alexander Doyle of Ohio, lived in Bedford, Indiana, while carving the figures from Carrara marble. A Bedford judge's wife posed for the figure of Justice, and her likeness stands out among the other classical figures.

The skylights of the grand courts of the north and south wings fill the interior with natural light, highlighting the marble floors and stairs. The marble columns and pilasters were originally to be made of limestone and cast-iron in order to stay within the statutory budget, but were changed to marble shafts with limestone and granite caps and bases. Original gas light fixtures have been wired for electricity.

After the Second World War, but before the influence of the historic preservation movement, a major renovation was undertaken. Although the remodeling created additional legislative office space, it diminished the size of the House and Senate by constructing floors for small offices between the outside walls and today's chambers. In the process, the original granite columns, wooden balconies and ornamental plaster ceilings were ripped out and destroyed. Murals were added to both chambers.

In 1966, the House was remodeled, with Indiana walnut paneling replacing earlier blond oak paneling. The brass chandelier, manufactured for the room, contains one hundred bulbs, one for each representative. It can be lowered electronically in order to clean and change bulbs. *The Spirit of Indiana* mural by eighty-year-old Indiana native Eugene F. Savage remains, but a Senate mural was removed during the 1974 remodeling to a Colonial Revival style.

One room in the state house that has remained in its original condition is that of the supreme court. The woodwork is hand-carved Indiana white oak, as are the walls, though they are partly covered by acoustic tiles. The imported French brass chandelier weighs about 1,500 pounds, and its gas jets are now electrified. Lining the walls are portraits of past justices, including one of the first chief justice of the Indiana Supreme Court, James Scott.

Scott became a judge of the General Court of the Indiana Territory from 1813 until the constitutional convention of 1816, when he became a member of the judiciary committee and assisted in the drafting the Judiciary Article of the Indiana Constitution. On December 28, 1816, Scott became a supreme court justice, serving until 1831. He is famous for his written opinion in the case *State v. Laselle*, in which the court held that the Indiana constitution prohibited slavery.

The House of Representatives chamber.

The state house rotunda.

Indiana's state senators work in offices overlooking the Senate chamber.

Indiana's previous state house was completed in 1835. Following an architectural competition, the plans submitted by the New York firm of Town & Davis were selected by the General Assembly. The most influential architectural firm of the period, it promoted the Greek and later Gothic Revival styles and is noted for designing the old North Carolina Capitol (1832–1840) and Town's then recently completed capitol in New Haven, Connecticut (1827–1831).

This first major public building erected in Indianapolis cost approximately $60,000 and was a brick, wood and stucco Greek Revival building. Although Town was experienced in adapting the temple form to a state house, this was the first time he experimented with the temple and dome combination, as well as with the use of Doric piers along the sides, which were placed to hide necessary windows.

It proved to be a controversial design, differing from both the Parthenon (on which it was based) and the highly regarded Connecticut Capitol.

Pilasters replaced the Parthenon's colonnade, which surrounded the temple, and while the Parthenon's porticoes incorporated double columns, here there were only end columns. Its most notorious feature was its dome, rising from a large drum crowned by a lantern. Based on an idea an idea from the Italian Renaissance, critics considered the combination of a dome and a Greek temple to be "a distasteful and unnatural marriage."

Not only was the design objectionable, but apparently the capitol's construction was defective, because it soon started to disintegrate. Bankruptcy of the state government in 1843 and then the Civil War prevented the state from providing adequate upkeep. In December 1867, just before the convening of the legislature, the ceiling of the House chamber collapsed. One newspaper reporter noted that if the House had been in session, "there would have been a lot of busy Hoosier undertakers." The damage was repaired, but its ongoing problems and small size led to the construction of the present state house.

The Indiana State House.

TEXAS

TEXAS STATE CAPITOL

ORIGIN OF NAME: From the Caddo word *tejas*, meaning "friend" or "ally."

CAPITAL: Austin

CONSTRUCTED: 1882–1888

ARCHITECT: Elijah E. Myers

ADMITTED TO THE UNION: December 29, 1845 (twenty-eighth)

SENATE: 31 members

HOUSE OF REPRESENTATIVES: 150 members

Austin became the capital of the three-year-old Republic of Texas in 1839. Its first state capitol (1853–1881) was constructed on Capitol Square. Planning for the current Renaissance Revival capitol began the year before the previous building burned. The capitol building commission announced a national design competition for a new capitol with specific requirements: the budget was to be $1.5 million, the building was to be centered on Capitol Square, facing south, constructed of stone, and it was to incorporate the highest standards for fire protection, heating, water facilities, lighting and ventilation.

Eleven designs were entered in the competition under pseudonyms such as Architect Texan, Pay as You Go, San Jacinto, Tuebor, Woglosnop, and Lone Star. On May 6, 1881, Tuebor, or Elijah E. Myers, was chosen. Pseudonyms are often required in architectural competitions so that the best design is chosen without the influence of the architects' names. At the time of the Texas competition, Myers was by far the most well-known architect, having completed the Michigan State Capitol in 1878. Tuebor, from the Michigan coat of arms, was also his pseudonym in that competition.

Subsequently, Myers revised a proposed square tower to a dome, as requested by the commission, and helped stake out the site for the building in 1882, but he failed to revise the architectural drawings or meet periodically in Austin. Instead, Myers spent his time working on other projects at home in Michigan, and his relationship with Texas officials deteriorated until, by the end of 1886, his duties as architect were essentially over. It is disputed as to whether he was actually fired, but by that time the building was far enough along that the commission decided not to replace him. As a result, the design of the capitol remains essentially Myers'.

Although fiscally impoverished following the Civil War, Texas remained land rich, and since Texas did not belong to the federal government prior to statehood, it managed to retain its public lands at that time. To raise the necessary funds, the state set aside three million acres of those lands either to sell in order to pay for the capitol's construction or be used as the means of payment itself.

Then the commissioners advertised for a contractor: "Sealed proposals for supplying all materials and completing every class of work required in the construction of a new state capitol, in Austin, Texas, will be received up to twelve o'clock (noon) on the 15th day of November, 1881. Payment for the entire amount to be made in lands and the award to the lowest and best bidder." The state valued the largely unpopulated and undeveloped land at 50 cents an acre, but since contractors were to be compensated in acreage rather than money, the winning bid specified the smallest number of acres rather than the lowest cost.

A syndicate led by Farwell Brothers & Company from Chicago prevailed. It received as payment three million acres of land (about the size of Connecticut) taken from ten counties located in the Texas panhandle, adjacent to New Mexico and Native American land in the north. In exchange it agreed to furnish all materials and labor to construct the capitol. The syndicate considered selling the land or colonizing it with

The south lobby.

The Texas State Capitol.

settlers and farmers, but because of low land prices it decided to develop it as the XIT Ranch, a well-known business venture. Meanwhile, it used its own funds and those borrowed from Great Britain to build the capitol. By 1915, the heirs of XIT had sold off the semi-arid land.

Originally, the capitol's exterior veneer was to be made up of local gray limestone, but the supply was insufficient and it contained too much iron, resulting in discoloration, so that granite, a harder and more expensive stone, was proposed as a substitute. It took two years to finally agree on a red granite donated by its owners, from Marble Falls, in exchange for the state agreeing to build a 50-mile railroad between the site and Austin. Then the state gave the stone to the contractor, along with at least five hundred convicts to quarry it. When, in 1885, the granite cutter's union objected to the use of convict labor and boycotted, the contractor responded by importing sixty experienced stonecutters from Scotland.

The rough red granite faces the walls of the Classical capitol. Smooth granite is confined to the shafts of the columns and pilasters, with plain capitals, that line the walls. The lower floor incorporates larger granite blocks, while smaller blocks finish the upper floors and in the solid parapets concealing the copper roof.

The north and south elevations of the three-story building consist of five parts. The center section contains the main entrances, with the north entrance set within a three-story columned portico, while the south entrance is through a recessed columned porch within a large stone arch, extending up through three stories and into a fourth, or attic. Mosaic seals of the nations that governed Texas were added to the north and south pediments in 1976.

The rotunda.

The east and west elevations were originally planned to feature porticoes similar to the one on the north, but they were eliminated after the granite substitution and because of their expense. The middle wing sections, location of the legislative chambers and below the slightly protruding skylights on the roof, are recessed from the central block. The flanking end pavilions also form the east and west elevations, and are covered by convex mansards.

The Renaissance-inspired, ribbed dome is supported by a Corinthian colonnaded drum and is painted to match the color of the granite. The lantern, fitted with a nighttime beacon, contains a second version of the goddess of liberty, with her raised left hand holding a gilded five-pointed star. The first zinc statue was removed in 1983 and recast in lighter-weight aluminum.

Soon after the capitol's completion, the legislature appropriated $35,000 to improve and fence the 26 acres of capitol grounds. The ornamental cast and wrought-iron fence originally incorporated 8,282 five-pointed stars. Seventeen monuments adorn the grounds. The first, installed in 1891, commemorates the heroes of the Alamo.

Works of art in the south foyer tell the story of Texas by commemorating events and people relating to the state's separation from Mexico. The 1930s terrazzo floor memorializes twelve battles fought on Texas soil: the Alamo, Anahuac, Bexar, Coleto, Galveston, Goliad, Gonzales, Palmito, Palo Alto, Sabine Pass, San Jacinto and Velasco. Flanking the arched doorway leading to the rotunda are marble statues of Stephen F. Austin, considered the "Father of Texas" because of his early colonization efforts, and Sam Houston, commander in chief of the army during the Texas Revolution, president of the Republic of Texas, United States senator, and governor of Texas.

The House of Representatives chamber.

One of two large paintings depicts the surrender of Santa Anna on April 21, 1836, after the Battle of San Jacinto. During this final battle in the fight for independence, the Texas army surprised the Mexican army and captured Santa Anna. This painting has been on display at this location since February 1891. The other painting portrays Davy Crockett, former United States congressman and state legislator from Tennessee, who migrated to Texas in 1835 and died at the Alamo.

The south foyer also introduces decorative features found throughout the building, such as the cast-iron columns with Corinthian capitals, ornamented ceilings, plasterwork, wainscoting and elaborately detailed doorframes with pediments, most of which are of carved oak, similar to doors incorporated in the Michigan State Capitol. Woodwork throughout consists of oak, pine, cherry, cedar and walnut. Brass door locks, doorknobs and hinges are decorated with the Lone Star of Texas.

The old supreme court chamber.

The terrazzo floor design in the rotunda replaced Myers' glass-block tile floor, also similar to the floor in Michigan's capitol. Installed to celebrate the 1936 Texas Centennial, it includes the state's seal surrounded by the seals of the countries whose flags flew over Texas. They are Spain (1519–1685 and 1690–1821), France (1685–1690), Mexico (1821–1836), the Republic of Texas (1836–1845), the Confederacy (1861–1865), and the United States (1845–1861 and 1865–present).

The rotunda features four stories with rings of balconies supported on large console brackets of cast-iron. Portraits of the former presidents of the republic and governors of the state circle the walls in reverse chronological order. The star, in the apex, dates from 1958 and measures 8 feet wide.

Off the rotunda, cast-iron staircases lead to the floor above, the location of the legislative chambers. The Senate chamber, restored to its circa 1910 appearance, features its original walnut podium. A hand-carved Lone Star encircled by live oak and olive branches decorates the front of the podium. Behind the podium hangs a dark-green-fringed drapery, a replica of the original, and a mid-nineteenth-century portrait of Stephen F. Austin.

The senators' original walnut desks have been modified by the addition of microphones, telephones connected to their offices, and Internet access. Senators speak from their desks and may speak as long as they wish. Voting remains traditional.

The long windows along the walls of the two-story chamber are covered in replica pine shutters stained to match the furnishings and woodwork throughout the room. The coffered ceiling of galvanized metal contains hanging pendants and glass-paneled skylights. Barriers were added between the skylights and the roof to regulate the chamber's heat and sunlight. Two large brass chandeliers, installed in 1890 with pipes for gas, spell out "Texas." The capitol was prepared for gas, but the pipes were never used because it became one of the first electric buildings in Texas.

Flanking the room's entrance, two large paintings by Texas artist Henry Arthur McArdle commemorate significant state historical events. *Dawn at the Alamo* depicts the thirteenth and final day on March 16, 1836, when every one of the 189 men fighting for Texas died, and *The Battle of San Jacinto*, which depicts the battle in which 600 Mexican soldiers were reportedly killed during the eighteen-minute confrontation.

Located on the other side of the rotunda is the red-carpeted House of Representatives, also restored to its circa 1910 appearance. Introductory legislation is read in its entirety from the front podium. Behind it hangs a portrait of Sam Houston and, when in session, the only flag carried by the Texas Army during the Battle of San Jacinto (otherwise a replica is displayed). The flag depicts a woman with a drawn sword and a sash with the words "Liberty or Death."

The original desks are oak, with chairs dating from 1941. Although the representatives can vote electronically from their desks, they can only speak from a stand in the aisle for a ten-minute time period. Long lines of representatives often form behind the recognized lawmaker, waiting for their turn to speak. The chamber contains spectators' galleries on three sides. As in the Senate, decorative Corinthian pilasters support a full entablature below the ceiling.

Damage from a 1983 fire, along with overcrowding (it was designed for 350 occupants but by 1980s there were 1,300 working there) and overall deterioration led to a decision to return the building to its 1888–1915 appearance and to update vital systems while constructing an extension to its north side. The extension was added underground in order to protect the architectural integrity of the historic building as well as its view of Austin. The project's final cost was estimated to be $189 million, plus $5 million contributed through fundraising.

The two-story, open-air, upside-down rotunda is an example of the effort made to design the extension to complement the capitol's architecture. The bronze star on the floor reflects the star hanging from the ceiling of the dome. Both have letters between their points spelling out "Texas." Committee rooms surround the well. Six rows of skylights, patterned after the skylights in the legislative chambers, provide natural light to members' offices and other facilities two floors underground.

During the 1991–1994 exterior renovation, the metal dome was stripped, restored and recoated with a protective paint. Many of the deteriorated sheet-metal leaves on the columns surrounding the dome were reproduced and replaced. In addition, the roof, windows and doors were repaired, and the granite was cleaned and the mortar repaired. A complete interior restoration was undertaken between August 1992 and 1994.

The Senate chamber.

GEORGIA

GEORGIA STATE CAPITOL
ORIGIN OF NAME: Named for King George II of England.
CAPITAL: Atlanta
CONSTRUCTED: 1884–1889
ARCHITECTS: Frank P. Burnham, Willoughby J. Edbrooke
ADMITTED TO THE UNION: January 2, 1788 (fourth)
SENATE: 56 members
HOUSE OF REPRESENTATIVES: 180 members

In 1732, King George II granted James Edward Oglethorpe the right to establish Georgia, the thirteenth British colony. Oglethorpe sought to help debtors, who under the harsh laws of the time were sometimes confined indefinitely in jail, by giving them a fresh start in the New World. The king's motives included providing a buffer for Carolina against Spanish Florida. In 1733, Oglethorpe and 114 settlers landed in what became Savannah, the capital of colonial Georgia. When Georgia failed to prosper, it reverted to the Crown in 1752.

After the Revolutionary War, the Georgia General Assembly met alternately in Savannah and Augusta. As development continued westward, the capital moved to Augusta in 1786, to Louisville in 1796, and to Milledgeville in 1807. Following the Civil War, Atlanta became the transportation and financial center of Georgia, and its city council lobbied to make it the capital by promising to donate land for use by the state for its seat of government. A statewide vote in 1877 approved the move from Milledgeville, and Atlanta became Georgia's permanent capital. However, because of the unsettled conditions so soon after the Civil War, funds for a building were not available until 1883, when the General Assembly appropriated $1 million, or one half its budget, for its construction.

A board of five commissioners, along with consultant George B. Post, a New York architect and engineer, supervised the building project. The board launched a nationwide competition to choose the architect and selected Chicagoans Willoughby J. Edbrooke and Franklin P. Burnham. When the Classical Renaissance capitol was completed in a style somewhat similar to the federal Capitol in Washington, D.C., many believed it expressed Georgia's new nationalism.

Located in a slightly elevated five-acre square, the capitol faces west toward downtown. Its grounds, enclosed by stone walls, contain a variety of monuments and markers relating to Georgia history. These include

plaques by the Atlanta chapter of the United Daughters of the Confederacy describing the "Siege of Atlanta" and the "Evacuation of Atlanta"; statues of Georgian politicians such as President Jimmy Carter and Senator Richard Russell Jr.; along with a replica of the Statue of Liberty and a monument dedicated to the Spanish War veterans.

The legislative act enabling the capitol's construction specified that "all materials used in the construction of said building shall be those found and procured within the state of Georgia; provided that same can be procured in said state as cheaply as other materials of like quality in other states." The building commission sought to comply as much as was practical, but

The Senate chamber.

Christmastime in the rotunda of the Georgia State Capitol.

discovered that it was cheaper to import Indiana limestone for the exterior than to obtain Georgia marble from then-undeveloped quarries.

The building's west facade features an entrance pavilion with a shallow portico supported by six rusticated piers, and a stone pediment held up by six Corinthian columns. Behind the columns, arched two-story windows indicate the interior location of the House of Representatives. The Great Seal of Georgia, carved on the pediment, is flanked by two figures representing Agriculture and Commerce. The rear facade is similar to that of the west, though it lacks columns.

Above a half-basement story of rough blocks and arched windows is a base of smooth block masonry, with rectangular windows separated above and below by a string course. The upper floors consist of smooth wall surfaces pierced by pedimented windows below smaller rectangular ones. Along the wings, Corinthian pilasters frame the windows.

A solid parapet conceals the roof and skylights. Above the center of the roof, lifted by a tall stone drum, is the Renaissance dome. The drum features detached Corinthian columns between pedimented windows. Above the columns, brackets continue the upward line into the ribs of the dome, which is crowned by a lantern that echoes the dome's form.

Originally sheathed in tin, the surface of the dome was covered with 43 ounces of gold donated to the state by Lumpkin County. Georgia claims to be the site of the first gold rush in the United States, in 1828.

The hand-carved state seal of Georgia.

Gold for the capitol was delivered from Dahlonega by a wagon train on August 7, 1958, and applied to the dome the next year, again in 1979, and again in 1998. Surmounting the dome is a 15-foot Miss Freedom, holding a torch and a sword representing freedom and commemorating the state's war casualties.

The capitol originally consisted of three main stories and a basement with stables for use by state officials and legislators while the General Assembly was in session. The basement was later converted into offices and the floors were renumbered. The basement became the first floor and the main entrance, with the rotunda, is now considered the second floor.

The rotunda's height from the floor to the ceiling of the inner dome is 237 feet. Paired pilasters with Corinthian capitals flank the piers supporting the dome. Except for the plaster motifs inside the dome, there is little interior wall ornamentation, because when Georgia budgeted the $1-million limit to build the capitol there was no remaining money for murals and other artwork. In 1955, the General Assembly established a Georgia Hall of Fame in the rotunda. The four oldest portraits, depicting George Washington, Benjamin Franklin, Thomas Jefferson and the Marquis de Lafayette, had been bought for $5,000 in 1868 and moved from the old capitol in Milledgeville.

Other portraits include those of James Edward Oglethorpe, Robert Toombs, Benjamin Harvey Hill, and Alexander H. Stephens. Busts in the Georgia Hall of Fame include three signatories of the Declaration of Independence: George Walton; Button Gwinnett; and Lyman Hall, M.D.; as well as two of Georgia's signatories of the United States Constitution, Abraham Baldwin and William Few.

Portraits of past governors line the upper-floor hallways. There is also one of Dr. Martin Luther King Jr., dedicated February 17, 1974, the first African-American to be represented in the capitol. King played a significant role in the civil rights movement and in 1964 became the first Georgian awarded the Nobel Peace Prize.

Galleried light courts connect the flanking office wings with the rotunda. They feature marble staircases, Doric and Corinthian columns, marble balustrades and Georgia oak doors and surrounds. In contrast to the exterior limestone, the interior stone, incorporated into the finish of the wainscoting, walls, floors and steps, consists of white and pink marble quarried in Georgia.

Located on the third floor, the legislative chambers are balanced front and rear instead of located in the wings. The similarly designed chambers contain high ceilings, with Classical pilasters and shuttered windows along the walls, pedimented doorways and brightly figured carpets replicating original patterns. In the House of Representatives, Georgia cherrywood predominates, including original desks, a restored ceiling and old-style light fixtures reproduced from photographs. The red carpet was also

The Georgia State Capitol.

reproduced from photographs. The smaller Senate, on the other hand, features oak with blue carpet.

The capitol was equipped with elevators, central steam heat, sanitary facilities and electric lights from the beginning, so there have been few structural changes, though the building's interior design has been altered over the years. In 1993, the General Assembly approved the restoration of the House of Representatives, Senate, Appropriations Room and public spaces to their 1889 appearance, while at the same time incorporating state-of-the-

art telecommunications systems. All legislators' desks were refurbished and equipped with new data, power, audio, microphone and voting capabilities.

The restoration process included a paint analysis to determine the original colors used on the wall and ceilings. The original stencil patterns, many of which remained intact underneath layers of paint, were redrawn and reapplied. Forty-eight colors were used in painting the walls and ceiling of the House, while twenty-six different colors were incorporated in the Senate.

Before restoration, in 1992, the legislature enacted the Georgia Lottery

A statue of Thomas E. Watson, U. S. senator, on the plaza in front of the capitol.

for Education Act. Georgia lottery monies are directed not only toward education but for specific programs — college scholarships, pre-kindergarten classes, and technology for classrooms.

The Lottery for Education Act set up the program Helping Outstanding Pupils Educationally (HOPE). In the beginning HOPE provided up to two years of free tuition at a public college for any high-school student with a B average and family income of less than $60,000 a year, provided they maintained a B average. HOPE also provided free tuition for diploma-granting programs at Georgia's technical institutes, and freshman and sophomores at in-state private colleges received a second-tier Tuition Equalization Grant of $500. Early on, monies purchased hardware and software for adult literacy programs, workplace literacy programs and construction of schools. Over the years HOPE increased its coverage by, among other things, increasing the

family income cap until it was removed altogether (making HOPE a merit-based benefit), adding juniors and seniors to the pool, adding fee and book allowances, including home-schooled students, and increasing the amount available for students attending in-state private colleges.

According to the Georgia Lottery Corporation, as a result of the lottery's first decade, there has been a rise in test scores, and the merit-based program has kept Georgia's top students in the state, leading to a better-educated workforce and a better state economy. In addition, its program to send over half a million to pre-kindergarten programs makes Georgia the largest state to offer fully funded universal pre-kindergarten for every four-year-old. Not only does this program help working families, but tests indicate that those with pre-kindergarten perform better academically.

Portraits of famous Georgians line the capitol hallways.

NEW JERSEY

NEW JERSEY STATE HOUSE

ORIGIN OF NAME: For the Isle of Jersey, where colony leader Sir George Carteret had been governor.

CAPITAL: Trenton

CONSTRUCTED: 1885–1889

ARCHITECTS: Jonathan Doan, John Notman, Samuel Sloan, Lewis Broome

ADMITTED TO THE UNION: December 18, 1787 (third)

SENATE: 40 members

ASSEMBLY: 80 members

Since 1935 visitors driving into Trenton from the west have been greeted by a 327-foot-wide sign with 9-foot-tall letters mounted on the Delaware River Bridge announcing the city's slogan: "Trenton Makes, the World Takes." When the motto was adopted, Trenton made, among other things, rubber, steel rope, mattresses, linoleum and pottery. Today it mostly makes laws from a frequently modified state house.

Because of the many changes, the state house contains a mixture of architectural motifs. It is generally considered a Classical Revival building because of the many Classical reinterpretations adapted by its architects. The building's conception can be traced to November 25, 1790, when an act of the legislature named Trenton the state capital and the General Assembly passed a law to construct a building for itself. Completed in 1792 by the master builder Jonathan Doan, the first state house was built in the Colonial style and consisted of two stories, with arched windows on the ground floor and square windows on the second, a pedimented central doorway and an open cupola attached to the center of the roof.

John Notman expanded the state house between 1845 and 1848 by adding a third story, a porticoed front, Italianate features and a Classical 80-foot dome. Samuel Sloan extended the south wing in 1871 and added an Italianate windowed block over Notman's addition. On March 21, 1885, the state house partially burned, but Lewis Broome repaired the damaged sections and designed the present building in the French Classicism or Second Empire style. Today's dome and rotunda are also attributed to Broome.

Later phases of construction included the 1891 Assembly wing and the Senate wing of 1903. In 1906, a four-story structure replaced half of the 1792 building, and additions were added during 1911 and 1912. The most recent add-on, a two-story granite-faced south addition, provides office and mechanical space along with a new entrance. Completed in the 1990s, it was added in conjunction with an overall building renovation to address safety issues and accessibility requirements. It involved the collaboration of more than 130 experts and consultants.

The foundation and trim of the state house consist of New Jersey stone, while its walls are constructed of brick and faced with Indiana limestone. Limestone detailing continues at the windows, doors and corners. Situated close to the public sidewalk, the building's shallow entrance pavilion contains a two-tiered portico with a balcony supported by polished granite columns with Corinthian capitals. The New Jersey coat of arms is incorporated into an arch reaching into a pediment above the portico. The entrance and arched windows grace the ground floor, while the second floor contains rectangular windows with curved stone hood molds supported by brackets, and at the top, flat hood molds supported by brackets. Above, the gold dome incorporates a peristyle and is topped with a lantern and a gold mini-dome that rises from a section of the state house behind the Broome front.

The interior consists of a mixture of Victorian and remodeled space. The rotunda is 39 feet across and rises 145 feet to the top of the stained-glass dome. Prominently displayed is a bronze of Abraham Lincoln by Daniel

The state house dome seen from across the Delaware River in Pennsylvania.

The Senate chamber in the New Jersey State House.

Chester French. It was cast from a plaster study for the Lincoln Memorial in Washington, D.C., and commemorates Lincoln's visit to the state house in 1861, on his way from New York City to his first presidential inauguration.

Beyond the rotunda and off a hallway, buried within the building's thick walls, are the remains of the original state house. Today it is a very small part of the governor's wing. The legislative chambers are located on the same floor.

The Assembly features wainscoting with polished white Italian marble that rises to the windows and forms the sills. Other details include sconces, an original stained-glass ceiling and windows, and restored original desks. Gold leafing enhances the pilasters that line the walls between windows and other plasterwork. A gallery with a mahogany rail surrounds the chamber.

A large brass chandelier, attributed to Thomas Edison's workshop in Menlo Park, hangs from the center of the ceiling. The 1,240-pound chandelier contains parts dating to the 1850s.

Along with the chandelier, the focus of the chamber is the speaker's podium, which stands before an arch supported by Corinthian columns and topped with painted plaster figures of Liberty and Prosperity. Above the marble wainscoting, the walls are covered with plaster panels. The door leading into the speaker's room is paneled oak.

No photographs or pieces of the chamber's carpeting could be located during its restoration. A new carpet design wove in such state symbols as the eastern goldfinch, red oak leaf, honeybee and purple violet.

Dating from a decade later than the Assembly, the smaller Senate chamber integrates scagliola plasterwork rather than marble. Other features include slender columns supporting the galleries, reproduction mahogany

A recent addition to New Jersey's state house.

desks, and a gold- and silver-leaf decorated ceiling divided into sections. Each section refers to someone who played a role in New Jersey history.

Just below the ceiling, fifteen murals painted by William Brantley Van Ingen and refurbished during the 1990s occupy arched spaces in the vaulting. Along with the Van Ingen located over the president's desk, entitled *Liberty and Prosperity,* they present a historic panorama of New Jersey. The others are entitled *Washington, Electricity, Education, The Stone Industry, Agriculture, The Battle of Monmouth, Machinery, Lexington, Commerce, The Battle of Trenton, The Battle of Princeton, The Silk Industry, The Pottery Industry, Building,* and *The Glass Industry.*

New Jersey's past includes an industrially rich history. But ever since Trenton was selected as New Jersey's seat of government, reportedly because of its convenient location on the stagecoach route between New York City and Philadelphia, the state has sought to distinguish itself from those cities, particularly New York.

A dispute over access to the Hudson River lasted well over a century, but with the early nineteenth-century invention of the steamboat and its impact on commerce along the river, the states were forced to resolve the matter, leading to the Compact of 1834. Approved by the state legislatures and Congress, the compact drew the boundary between the states down the middle of the Hudson River. But in order to achieve this outcome, New Jersey legislators conceded that all the islands in the Hudson, including Ellis and what is now Liberty, were part of New York. The treaty gave New York the above-water land, while New Jersey received the water or submerged area surrounding the islands on its side of the river.

The New Jersey Assembly chamber.

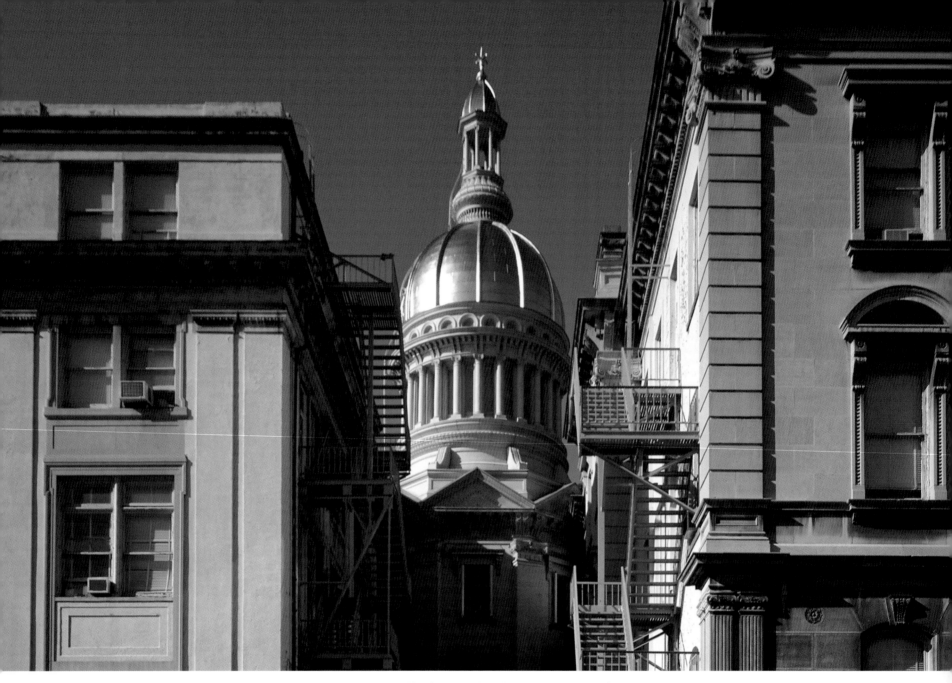

New Jersey's golden dome rises above disparate architectural styles.

At that time, Ellis Island was a low-lying 3.3 acres, but after 1892 it became the location the nation's main immigration center. By 1954, over twelve million immigrants had entered the United States through the Ellis Island center. The ever-increasing waves of immigrants necessitated expansion of the island with landfill, mostly from the excavation of New York City's subway construction, and it grew to 27.5 acres.

In 1986, New Jersey governor Thomas Kean and New York governor Mario Cuomo negotiated an agreement to share sales-tax revenues from the Ellis Island museum and gift shop and to use the money to support a program for the homeless. The New Jersey legislature ratified the agreement, but New York's did not. This led, in 1993, to New Jersey filing suit against New York in the United States Supreme Court, arbiter of territorial conflicts between states, to decide whether New York or New Jersey had sovereignty over the filled land.

New Jersey claimed that nearly 90 percent of the island belonged to it, basing its claim on the 1834 agreement that was signed when the island mass was only three acres. New York contended that when that area was filled in, it became part of New York. The U.S. Supreme Court found that New Jersey could claim the land to the low-water mark. This meant the lands surrounding the original island remained the sovereign property of New Jersey when the landfill was added. The original three acres remain under New York's jurisdiction.

The interior dome dates from 1885.

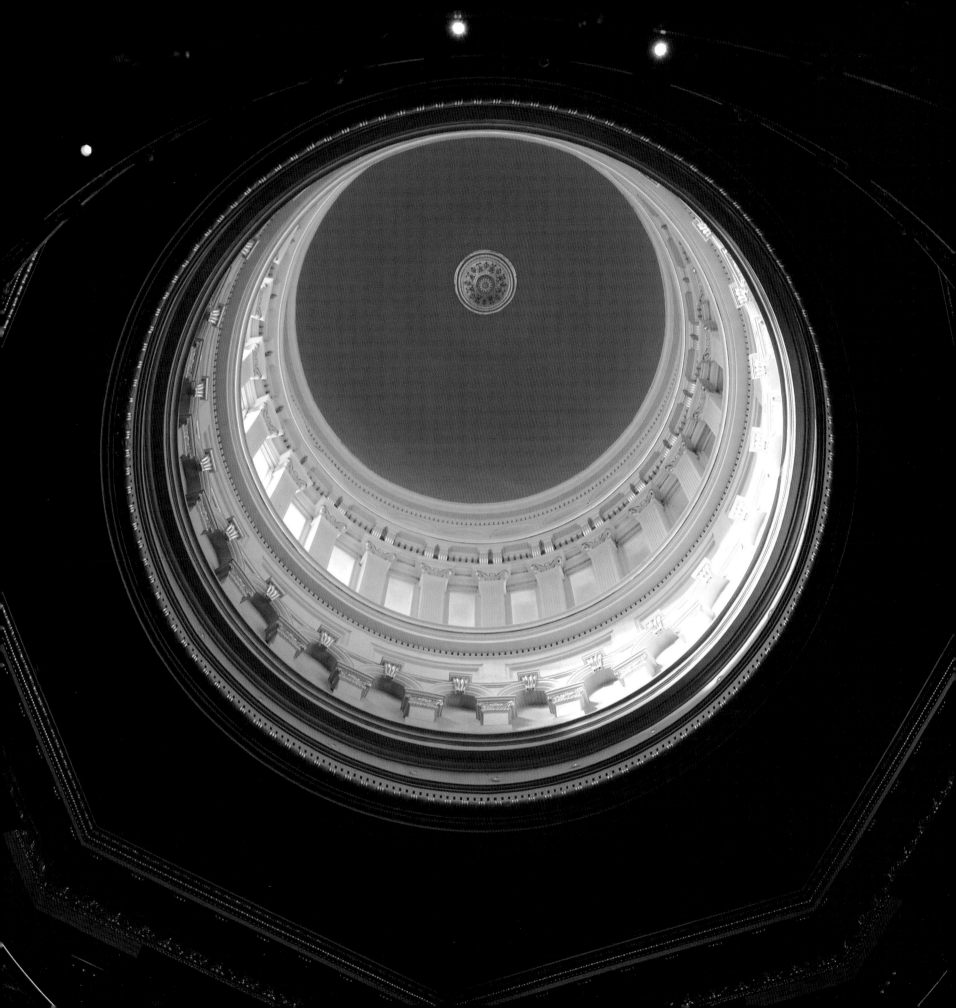

NEW YORK

New York State Capitol

Origin of Name: For the Duke of York, after the British captured the
area from the Dutch in 1664.

Capital: Albany

Constructed: 1867–1897

Architects: Thomas W. Fuller, Henry H. Richardson,
Leopold Eidlitz, Isaac Perry

Admitted to the Union: July 26, 1788 (eleventh)

Senate: 61 members

Assembly: 150 members

In 1865, New York lawmakers passed an act authorizing construction of the capitol. This post-Civil War period fostered public building on an unprecedented scale, characterized not only by a new level of extravagance but often by an uninhibited mingling of architectural elements from various historical sources. New York's capitol exemplified this trend. It was designed by three groups of architects who drew elements from disparate European architectural styles, especially the Renaissance and Romanesque.

In 1868, Thomas Fuller, architect of the Parliament buildings in Ottawa, Canada, was appointed architect for New York's capitol. But after eight years, the first building commission was replaced because of mismanagement and its association with New York City's controversial and scandalous William M. "Boss" Tweed. The new commission decided to change architects, even though construction was beginning on the third story of the building. Fuller was dismissed and replaced by Leopold Eidlitz and Henry H. Richardson. One of the most influential American architects of the period and originator of the popular Romanesque Revival style, Richardson was well regarded because of his work on Trinity Church in Boston. His joint appointment with Eidlitz resulted in the notorious "Battle of the Styles" controversy.

It began when Eidlitz and Richardson took down some of Fuller's stonework above the second floor and made the third story transitional. Above the third story and all around the building, Eidlitz incorporated a beltcourse that divided the work of Fuller and that of the newly appointed architects. The fourth story integrated Romanesque features, with among other things, tile roof, rough-faced stone, gables containing arched windows supported by columns, and a dentil cornice running under the roof eaves, all superimposed on Fuller's Italian Renaissance style. The building's roof is in the French Renaissance style.

Not only is there some architectural confusion in the capitol, but it was constructed during a period of transition in construction materials, which also influenced its design. It was one of the last large buildings constructed in the United States to use masonry load-bearing walls (over 16 feet thick), with brick arches in the basement supporting the massive granite building. Toward the end of its thirty years of construction, at a time when skyscrapers were starting to rise, steel I-beams were incorporated into the upper stories.

Another design issue involved the provision of adequate lighting and ventilation. The quality of light produced by gas and early electrical systems was poor, and mechanical ventilation systems did not exist. Light courts, constructed in open and unoccupied space surrounded by walls and windows, were frequently incorporated to provide natural light and fresh air to large buildings such as this one. But the importance of the light courts diminished as electricity replaced them.

A solid stone rectangle, the capitol measures 400 feet long and 300 feet wide. At each corner is a tower accentuated by tall gabled dormers. The main, or east, elevation is fifteen bays wide. The arched main entranceway, located in a slightly protruding pavilion, is reached by climbing seventy-seven steps. Unlike the grassy park-like settings surrounding many state capitols, the New York Capitol anchors the mostly concrete Governor Nelson A. Rockefeller Empire State Plaza (1965–1979), named for the former governor, who promoted its creation at a time when state government needed more office space.

The $1-billion plaza occupies 98 acres and consists of a quarter-mile-long concourse filled with modern art and sculpture and eleven government, business and cultural buildings. These include the New York State Museum, the Convention Center, legislative office buildings, the Justice Building, and the Performing Arts Center (a flying-saucer-like structure known as "The Egg"). There are also memorials, along with shops, banks and restaurants, in the lower public space. At the time of construction, the plaza was controversial because it displaced churches, schools and many homes in forty city blocks.

Inside the capitol, Eidlitz and Richardson divided the space between them. Eidlitz planned the Assembly chamber and the Assembly and Senate staircases, while Richardson concentrated on the Senate chamber, the Executive chamber and the Great Western Staircase, also known as "The Million Dollar Staircase." This division resulted in a mixed interior design and further accentuated the separate competitive domains of the Senate and Assembly.

The New York State Capitol.

Done in the Gothic style and completed in 1879, the Assembly chamber incorporated a stone-vaulted, arched ceiling with the keystone of the central vault 56 feet above the floor, supported by four giant pillars of polished red granite. But apparently the ground shifted and the stone roof gutters began to leak, with water seeping inside the walls and dangerously cracking the ceiling. The first evidence consisted of a small amount of dust on members' desks, then one day a lawmaker arrived to reportedly discover a bowling-ball-sized piece of the ceiling on his desk. Since the ceiling was not considered reparable, a flat wooden ceiling, 20 feet lower, replaced the original in the 1880s, sealing off the great vaults from public view.

On the other side of the building, the richly decorated and more intimate Senate chamber remains intact. Few, if any, cost-saving devices, such as local stone or wood, were integrated into its decor. The general prosperity and confidence of post-Civil War New York is reflected in this room. Mexican onyx panels across the middle north and south walls are among its special features. Yellow Sienna marble and red granite from Scotland are also incorporated into the decor. The ceiling consists of hand-carved, deep-paneled oak. Red Spanish leather and carved Caribbean mahogany paneling cover the walls below the galleries, while 23-carat gold leaf coats the walls above the arcade.

Two fireplaces at the rear of the chamber are called the "Whispering Fireplaces." No longer used for heating, they are large enough for a person to stand in and senators use them to conduct private conversations. Also notable is a large case clock designed by Richardson.

But in 1883, after Eidlitz's death and after Richardson's connection with the capitol had ended, the reform administration of Governor Grover Cleveland hired Isaac Perry, from Binghamton and Elmira, to complete the building. He is credited with the ceremonial approach to the main entrance and the final design of the Great Western Staircase.

Perry executed the staircase of sandstone imported from Scotland. He especially favored hand-carving, so it far surpasses what Richardson had planned for it. The elliptical arches, other carvings, and especially the portraits distinguish the staircase, including those of famous Americans such as George Washington, Thomas Jefferson, Alexander Hamilton, and Benjamin Franklin, along with literary figures such as Albany resident James Fennimore Cooper.

The Civil War was recent history, and there are numerous war heroes represented, such as president Abraham Lincoln and Generals Ulysses S. Grant, William Tecumseh Sherman and Philip Sheridan. Also recognizable are John Brown, Harriet Beecher Stowe, and the Abolitionist leader Frederick Douglass. Among the hundreds of carvings are numerous unrecognizable images. Many of these are probably craftsmen's friends or even strangers who paid to be immortalized. Perry's own daughter and granddaughter are among them.

The finest contemporary artists and craftsmen were hired to detail the features and finishes of the capitol during its long construction period. Thousands of laborers arrived in Albany to work on it, including more than five hundred stonecutters and carvers employed at various times to work on the Great Western Staircase during the last fourteen years of construction.

The final cost of the staircase was closer to $1,500,000. It measures 119 feet to the skylight. During an ongoing restoration and renovation, workers reconstructed the staircase's skylight, which was covered with

New York's Assembly chamber.

New York's Senate chamber.

fabric and painted during the Second World War. The covering was to prevent potential enemy bombers from using its light to locate the nearby Watervliet Arsenal.

After thirty years of construction, Governor Theodore Roosevelt finally declared the capitol complete. It wasn't. The Senate chamber, for example, features unfinished carving over the stone fireplaces and the capitals of the columns.

Roosevelt is just one of many important politicians to occupy the New York governor's office. His portrait hangs along the long wall leading to the governor's office, joining portraits of John Jay, George Clinton, DeWitt Clinton, Martin Van Buren, Grover Cleveland, Samuel J. Tilden, Al Smith, Franklin D. Roosevelt, Charles Evans Hughes, William Averell Harriman, Thomas E. Dewey, Nelson A. Rockefeller, and others.

Governors often clash with lawmakers, and the legislative halls are the theater of memorable political maneuvering and oratory. This was especially evident during the early twentieth century, with progressives such as Alfred Smith, Robert F. Wagner, and Jimmy Walker championing the working class and workers' safety. After a fire at New York City's Triangle Shirtwaist

The lower ceiling on the assembly chamber covers the great vaults.

factory in 1911 killed 146 women who were trapped in the factory, reform efforts such as regulation of sweatshops and factory safety were promoted.

Earlier, during the 1880, 1881 and 1882 sessions, Theodore Roosevelt served in the legislature. He is considered one of the twentieth-century's greatest conservationists, and in recognition of his contribution to the state of New York, an unnamed peak in the Adirondacks was named for him on the centennial of his term as governor. The tribute reflects his love of the Adirondacks, which he supported when he became President of the United States.

Prior to 1885, lumbermen bought Adirondack timberland from the state at a low price, and many proceeded to damage it by overharvesting pine, spruce and other softwoods. Later, they often abandoned the land rather than pay taxes. Because of the extensive logging and the growing concern for conservation, the New York legislature created a forest preserve out of what was left of the public domain in the Adirondacks. This law was the source of

the phrase "Forever Wild," stating: "The lands now or hereafter constituting the forest preserve shall be forever kept as wild forest lands. They shall not be sold, nor shall they be leased or taken by any person or corporation public or private."

In 1892, the legislature created Adirondack Park, defined by a line drawn around some 2.8 million acres, with the state owning about 550,000 acres. The border was drawn in blue on the official state map, and ever since then the boundary has been known as the "Blue Line." Effective January 1, 1895, a constitutional provision guaranteed that the forest preserve would "be forever kept as wild forest lands."

The park is one of the nation's oldest preserves and has expanded to encompass almost six million acres, making it the largest state park in the contiguous United States — about the size of the state of Vermont or the size of Yellowstone, Yosemite, Grand Canyon, Glacier, and the Great Smoky Mountains national parks combined.

The Great Western Staircase with carvings of Zachary Taylor and Thomas Jefferson.

Montana

Montana State Capitol

Origin of Name: From the Spanish word for mountains.

Capital: Helena

Constructed: 1899–1902

Architect: Charles Emlen Bell

Admitted to the Union: November 8, 1889 (forty-first)

Senate: 50 members

House of Representatives: 100 members

Before the arrival of settlers, the vast and largely uninhabited region of Montana was administered as part of seven different United States territories: Louisiana, Missouri, Oregon, Washington, Nebraska, Dakota, and finally Idaho. In 1863, when the Idaho Territory was created, it included present-day Idaho, Montana and most of Wyoming. The next year, Congress created the Territory of Montana and named Virginia City as the capital.

For many Montanans, the construction of a permanent capitol building symbolized the state's growth into a full-fledged member of the Union. This achievement took thirteen years, largely because of a controversy over the location of the permanent state capital, with an especially acrimonious debate between Helena and Anaconda, and problems with financing.

Soon after Helena became the capital, the legislature named a state capitol commission to oversee the capitol's design and construction. Although the commission successfully sponsored a nationwide competition to select a design, after two years the only signs of its work were a $40,000 debt and the beginnings of an excavation for a proposed $1-million building that the legislature decided the state could not afford.

The legislature formed a new commission, instructed it to hire only Montana builders and architects, and authorized a $350,000 bond issue, securing the bonds with the 182,000 acres of land granted by the federal government at statehood. Discouragingly, the bonds' low interest rates made them unattractive investments and none of them sold. When it appeared that the construction of a capitol would be further delayed, a wealthy Helena miner agreed to purchase the entire issue, and work on the Neoclassical capitol finally began.

Its construction proceeded in two phases. The original building incorporated Montana sandstone. Matching east and west wings built of local granite were completed in 1912. The rectangular capitol consists of five connected blocks, including flanking wings, their connecting sections, and the central section topped by a square platform capped with a dome.

A central portico located over the front entrance is approached by a 35-foot-wide granite stairway with ornamented light standards. The portico incorporates 25-foot fluted Ionic columns that support an entablature with "Montana" carved into its frieze. Above are brackets dividing three panels. On the central panel, the M is set against a bas-relief background of two crossed torches and a garland wreath. Carved into the left and right panels are "1889" and "1899," the year Montana achieved statehood and the year construction of the capitol began. Above the main entrance is a large semicircular window with radiating glass dividers, flanked by two circular windows. Four windows covered with swan-necked pediments also border the portico.

The rear entrance, also located in the central block, features a semicircular art-glass window between two Ionic pilasters. In addition to the Ionic

The Senate chamber.

Statues of Mike and Maureen Mansfield face the mural Driving the Golden Spike *above the grand stairway.*

columns on the front portico and rear entrance, a number of two-story Ionic pilasters adorn the 1902 wings, and two-story Ionic colonnades form inset pavilions on the three full sides of each of the 1912 wings.

The ground-floor exterior is composed of rusticated smooth ashlar. The smooth walls of the second and third levels are topped by a parapet that rises above the cornice. A one-story square platform with a balustraded parapet rises from the central block and is topped by a second platform containing pediments on all four sides. All facades incorporate three vertical windows separated by Corinthian pilasters and topped with semicircular windows. The copper-covered dome rises from the platform along with four copper

half domes at the corners. The addition of copper was more appropriate than gold because of the surrounding copper-rich mining area. In accordance with the architect's original plans, construction began on a low round dome, but a last-minute change substituted the taller dome. It culminates with a bronze statue of Liberty.

In contrast to the capitol's intact Neoclassical exterior, its interior has undergone a number of changes. The east wing was remodeled in 1955, and the two lower levels of the rotunda (including much of the French Renaissance decor) and the west wing were remodeled in 1964–1966. Also at that time, the vaulted art-glass ceiling over the marble stairway leading up from the rotunda was removed and the space was filled with a committee hearing room.

An eight-year project completed in 2001 included cleaning and repair of the exterior, installation of new entry doors, upgrades to office space, mechanical, plumbing and electrical systems. In addition, public areas such as the rotunda were restored to their original French Renaissance appearance.

F. Pedretti & Sons of Cincinnati, Ohio, completed the original frescoes, stained-glass and murals, which were not of the allegorical subjects often associated with Classical buildings, but were instead popular Montana themes suggested by elected officials. Other retouched features include scagliola columns topped with gold-leaf composite capitals, gilded niches and projecting balconies, a marble staircase with newel posts topped with light standards, a floor of glass tiles, and a band of sixteen circular art-glass windows in the dome. The interior dome paintings depict such frontier figures as a Native American chief, a cowboy, a prospector and a trapper.

The hallways leading from the rotunda contain Tennessee marble pilasters and wainscoting. At the top of the Grand Staircase and at the end of the stained-glass-decorated barrel- vaulted ceiling hangs the painting *Driving the Golden Spike*, completed in 1903 by artist Amedee Joullin

A statue of Jeannette Rankin, congresswoman, peace activist and advocate of women's rights.

and paid for by the Northern Pacific Railroad. It shows former president Ulysses S. Grant preparing to drive the last spike to complete the the transcontinental Northern Pacific Railroad on September 8, 1883, at Gold Creek, Montana. This event connected a northern transcontinental route that was to be economically significant to the state.

On the third level, the former Montana Supreme Court chamber (old Senate) features scagliola columns and pilasters supporting an ornamental cornice from which panels curve toward the art-glass skylight. The panels contain Pedretti murals with Montana-related themes: *Gates of the Mountains, Emigrant Train Being Attacked by the Indians, Signing of the Enabling Act, Lewis' First Glimpse of the Rockies, Signing of the Proclamation of Statehood, The Chase of the Buffalo*, and *Farewell to the Buffalo*.

The Senate chamber (former House of Representatives), also on the third floor, was altered during an earlier remodeling and wallpapered below the cornice level, but like the court chamber, it incorporates a cornice leading up to the skylight and Pedretti murals that also depict Montana themes, including *The Louisiana Purchase, Lewis and Clark at Three Forks, Old Fort Benton, Prospectors at Nelson Gulch, Old Fort Owen*, and *Custer's Last Battle*. Other decorative elements include pilasters with composite capitals, a brass chandelier, desks with the original chairs, galleries on three sides and a partial fourth gallery, along with the original mahogany rostrum.

The House chamber is tucked away in the building's 1912 west wing. Six paintings by Edgar Samuel Paxon decorate the House lobby: *After the Whiteman's Book, The Border Land, Lewis at Black Eagle Falls, Pierre de La Verendrye, Surrender of Chief Joseph*, and *Lewis and Clark at Three Forks*.

The intact House chamber incorporates Vermont marble Ionic columns, a visitors' balcony with brass railing, a barrel ceiling skylight, and oak desks with original oak-and-leather chairs. Behind the speaker's oak podium, a Charles Russell painting depicting Lewis and Clark meeting the Flathead Indians at Ross's Hole in 1805 dominates the room.

Ralph Earl DeCamp, another Montana artist, was chosen to decorate the 1912 wings. The scenic landscape murals for the original law library in the east wing include *The Gallatin, Gates of the Mountains, Last Chance, St. Ignatius, Lake McDermott, Above Timberline, The Rosebud River, Holter Dam*, and *The Flathead*.

Since its construction, the capitol's interior decor has served to remind visitors, and especially lawmakers, of Montana's history and scenic beauty, and has served as the center of Montana's political life. One of the remaining vestiges of the frontier west in Montana survives in Montana's approach

Interior view of windows above the main entrance to the Montana State Capitol.

to open-range laws. The open-range tradition stems from the nineteenth-century western custom of allowing livestock to graze on unoccupied federal land.

The practice became law when Montana's territorial legislature passed an open-range statute allowing cattle to roam freely on unenclosed private lands. The consequence was that if farmers wanted to protect their land and crops, it was up to them to enclose their fields to keep out someone else's livestock. In contrast, other states require the livestock owner to restrain his or her animals from running at large or be held responsible for any damages caused by livestock trespassing on private land, whether fenced or unfenced.

Over time, with growing population, increasing urbanization and high-speed automobiles, open-range issues began to shift from farmer and rancher to motorist and rancher, especially claims for death or injury resulting from vehicle accidents caused by livestock wandering onto highways. During the latter part of the twentieth century, though accidental trespass by livestock at large continued to be protected by the open-range laws, some limitations evolved, such as liability for negligent livestock herding or the destruction

of property. The open-range doctrine became further restrictive through judicial interpretation.

For example, after a woman was seriously injured when she hit a bull on a public highway, a Montana court found that both the driver and the livestock owner were responsible. This decision set a precedent for consideration of the facts of each case before assessing liability. Ranchers, insurance agents, county commissioners and other Montanans objected that the apportionment of liability was too inconsistent and unclear. Twenty-three of the state's fifty-six counties, nearly half of its total geographic area, remain a frontier with less than two people per square mile, and where grazing is a necessary way of life. In response, lawmakers sought to write a flexible open-range law that could adapt to growing urban centers with responsible drivers as well as traditional rural communities. In March 2001, the Montana legislature passed a law making only irresponsible livestock owners liable by providing that a livestock owner is not liable for livestock-vehicle collisions unless "grossly negligent or engaging in intentional misconduct." Hence, gross negligence might apply only if a livestock owner knew cattle were continually on the roadway, causing accidents, and did nothing to prevent it.

The House of Representatives chamber.

Kansas

Kansas State Capitol

Origin of Name: From a Sioux word meaning "people of the south wind."

Capital: Topeka

Constructed: 1866–1903

Architect: John C. Haskell

Admitted to the Union: January 29, 1861 (thirty-fourth)

Senate: 40 members

House of Representatives: 125 members

The state capitol of Kansas stands on 20 acres of land donated to the state for the site of its seat of government by Topeka developers in 1862. Unable to build during the Civil War, the legislature, conducting business in rented facilities, authorized the construction of the capitol in 1866. Work soon began on the east wing, and by 1870 both the Senate and the House of Representatives convened in what is now the Senate chamber, with a temporary wall dividing them. The wing was not entirely completed until 1873, when the portico and trim were added.

Further construction of the capitol proceeded in stages as money became available, with work on the west wing beginning in 1879. In 1881, members of the House of Representatives assembled in their unfinished chamber (completed in 1883). A covered wooden walkway, nicknamed "Cave of the Winds," connected the wings. During the 1881 session, lawmakers authorized the completion of the north and south wings, along with the central domed section to tie the wings together. Work started on the last part in 1884. In order to support the dome, its foundation was set on bedrock, approximately 25 feet below the surface.

The cruciform-shaped building, with each wing a slightly different length, was basically completed by June 1903. Built in the Classical style, the native limestone capitol incorporates Corinthian composite details. Stone steps lead to the south portico or main entrance, where stone columns support the entablature with its stone cornice. The entrances to the other wings are similarly designed. On the north and south porticoes, pediments consist of rough stone and were intended to incorporate relief sculptures, though never authorized.

Above the rusticated base, pilasters with Corinthian capitals line the smooth walls of the north and south wings and separate the rectangular windows, which decrease in size from the second floor to the fourth. The architecturally similar east and west wings, where the legislative chambers remain, contain four Corinthian pilasters covered with pediments, and arched windows. The east wing also incorporates small circular windows. All windows have cut-limestone sills and lintels.

At the roofline, a partial balustraded parapet, pediments and an extra floor on the north and south conceal the roof from where a three-story drum lifts the dome high above Topeka. Its first floor incorporates paired plain columns in front of arched, rectangular and square windows. Paired pilasters surround and separate the arched windows of the second story. The narrow highest story contains single pilasters between square windows. Circular

Entrance to the House of Representatives chamber.

The Kansas State Capitol.

windows and supporting ribs protrude slightly from the copper roof of the dome, which is topped by a cupola and the bronze statue *Ad Astra*.

> "Since undertaking the project of murals for the Kansas state capitol I have received many suggestions relating to subject matter and the mode of approach. In such a situation the court of last appeal must be the artist himself. The theme I have chosen is historical in more than one sense. In great measure it is the historical struggle of man with nature. This struggle has been a determining factor in my art expression. It is my family's tradition and the tradition of a great majority of Kansas people. And though I fully realize the importance of Kansans in the fields of politics and the various phases of education and human welfare, these phases are removed from my vital experience, and that experience is necessary for me to make a forceful art expression. Back of the historical allegory is the great back-drop of the phenomena of nature and to those who live and depend upon the soil for life and sustenance in these phenomena is God."
>
> John Steuart Curry

Lawmakers originally planned to place a statue of Ceres, the Roman goddess of agriculture, on top of the dome. But when many Kansans objected, contending that Ceres was not worthy to adorn the capitol because of her reputed immoral behavior with other gods, lawmakers refused to appropriate the necessary funds. One Kansas legislator even suggested: "If we want to honor grain, why don't we put a giant box of Wheaties on top of the Capitol?" Ignoring his suggestion and raising money from private sources, the statue of a Kansa Native American was finally placed on the dome in October of 2002.

The statue, *Ad Astra*, stands about 22 feet tall and weighs 4,420 pounds. Its name is an abbreviation taken from the Kansas motto, *"Ad Astra per Aspera,"* or "To the Stars through Difficulty." *Ad Astra* not only honors the Kansa, a tribe of hunter-gatherers that once lived in the Topeka area, but the pioneers, by pointing his bow to the North Star that guided them on their journey westward.

Inside, the limestone capitol incorporates many different marbles, including stone from Tennessee, Georgia, Mexico, Belgium, Italy, Africa and France. Fresco murals along the marble walls on the first floor of the rotunda illustrate the state's history. Dating from 1953, they are *The Coming of the Spaniards, The Chisholm Trail, The Coming of the Railroad, The Santa Fe Trail,*

Tragic Prelude *by John Steuart Curry.*

Lewis and Clark in Kansas, Building a Sod House, The Battle of Mine Creek, and *The Battle of Arickaree.*

Upstairs in the second-floor corridors located just off the rotunda are murals painted by John Steuart Curry, a native of Kansas. In the east corridor, two panels entitled *Tragic Prelude* refer to newspaperman William Allen White's description of the pre-Civil War anti-slavery movement in the Kansas Territory, "A tragic prelude to the tragic years to come." Beginning with the conquistadors, the artist shows Francisco Vasquez de Coronado and Father Padilla, a Franciscan missionary. Padilla ministered to Native Americans, who loved him. When he thought his mission was completed and wanted to move on, they stoned him to death rather than let him depart. To the left is a plainsman standing by his slain buffalo, and herds of buffalo pursued by Native Americans.

Directly across from the governor's office, Curry painted an oversized figure of free-state advocate John Brown as a fanatic. In his outstretched left hand he holds the word of God and in his right hand a "Beecher Bible" (a rifle). In 1859, Brown was hanged for treason after leading a raid on the federal arsenal at Harpers Ferry, now in West Virginia. Swirling behind

The rotunda.

him, tornado and prairie fires represent the violence and storms of war that first gathered on the plains of Kansas before sweeping the country. Flanking him and facing each other are the contending free-soil and pro-slavery forces, symbolizing brother against brother. The two dead soldiers at Brown's feet represent the more than one and a half million men who were either killed or wounded during the Civil War. In the background are pioneers with their wagons moving toward the West.

In the west corridor, Curry portrays a later period of Kansas. On the north wall is his interpretation of the Kansas oil fields, *The Riches of the Land.* On the west wall, the ten-foot figures of a young farmer, his wife and children stand before a farmhouse under an evening sky. The south mural shows the Kansas landscape with a Hereford bull, steers and hogs, fields of grain, a grain elevator, and a grove of Osage orange trees before a setting sun.

Originally, Curry planned to tell his story in three parts. The first two were the settlement of Kansas, including the conquistadors, the plainsmen, and John Brown, and the life of the homesteader and pastoral prosperity, including modern Kansas with its farms and industry. After he completed the first two parts, he asked that eight marble panels in the rotunda be moved to the third floor so that he could paint in their place the life of the homesteader. But the Kansas Council of Women, overseeing the capitol decor, opposed the removal of the marble because they felt that the murals "do not portray the true Kansas. Rather than revealing a law-abiding, progressive state, the artist has emphasized the freaks in its history — the tornadoes, and John Brown, who did not follow legal procedure."

Others, preferring waving wheat fields, sunflowers, and scenes of its industry, criticized Curry's portrayal of Kansas as too rough. They thought the Hereford bull was too red and his neck was too thick. The tail of the pig was painted incorrectly, as was the woman, too big with too short a skirt. Critics of *The Riches of the Land* complained that the nighttime prairie scene could be mistaken for an ocean, with a coyote looking like a seal and oil derricks appearing as ship masts.

Kansas newspaper editors, longtime supporters of Curry and artistic freedom, tried to persuade the council to let him complete his work, but the marble remained and the work went unfinished. Curry then complained that "the work in the east and west stands as disjoined and un-united fragments. Because this project is uncompleted and does not represent my true idea, I am not signing these works."

Finally, in 1976, the Kansas legislature decided to commission murals for the vacant space. Since Curry had completed sketches from which he planned his work, the legislature directed the new artist to refer to them in preparing the new murals. A committee selected Lumen Martin Winter, another Kansas native. His works, entitled *Colonel John C. Fremont*, *The Sacking of Lawrence*, *Threshing*, *Well Digging*, *Education*, *The Governor's Mansion*, *Sowing*, and *Commerce*, were dedicated in 1978.

Also contributing to the decor of the second-floor rotunda are four limestone statues of famous Kansans, installed four years later. They portray Dwight David Eisenhower, commander-in-chief of the Allied Armies in Europe during the Second World War and President; William Allen White, editor and publisher of the *Emporia Gazette* and Pulitzer Prize winner; Arthur Capper, twentieth Kansas governor and United States senator, who established the Capper Foundation for children with disabilities; and Amelia Earhart, the first woman granted a pilot's licence and first woman to fly solo across the Atlantic Ocean.

The inner dome's height is 75 feet below that of the outer dome, and part of its embellishment aroused a controversy predating the Curry mural fracas. The bitterly divided political parties dominating the state in 1898 fought over the propriety of its artwork. Originally, the Populist Party authorized the painting of sixteen Grecian women holding garlands of flowers and vases. The upper half of the figures was nude and the lower half obscured by flowers, almost mermaid-like. Measuring between 8 and 10 feet, they sat within a 16-foot-high panel encircling the dome. The opposing Republican Party found the figures too risqué, nicknaming them the "Nude Telephone Girls," and once in power replaced them with four allegorical murals — *Knowledge*, *Power*, *Peace* and *Plenty*. When the *Peace* panel was cleaned 1978, the restorer added his own self-portrait..

The Senate and the House of Representatives continue to be located on the third floor in the oldest wings. The Senate's decor dates from 1885, after the House moved into its own chamber. The lower wall, just above the

baseboards, is covered in an unusual gray-blue marble from Belgium. Above it and running horizontally around the room is Mexican onyx. White marble above the onyx is Italian Carrara. Tennessee beige marble surrounds the door. Round stained-glass windows imported from France line the walls.

Another prominent feature of the Senate includes a group of twenty-eight bronze columns and pilasters, all hand-cast with hand-hammered designs of morning glories and roses, by artisans who were brought from Italy to finish the intricate work. It took one man an entire day to complete a cluster of three leaves. The bases of the columns consist of black cast-iron with grillwork that at one time provided ventilation for the room.

The senators' desks and chairs are handmade from native cherry. Two lamps representing Eternal Peace sit on the president's hand-carved rostrum. Public galleries are situated in the front and back of the room.

Opposite the rotunda is the House of Representatives, restored in 1998 to its original appearance. During the restoration, circa 1882 allegorical ceiling murals representing Law, History, the First Dawn of Liberty and Justice were discovered and subsequently restored. Above the windows, the names of ten men prominent in the Abolitionist or Free-State Movement during territorial Kansas were also discovered and repainted. They include T. W. Barber, killed by pro-slavery men in 1855 and namesake of Barber County; Andrew Reeder, the first territorial governor; Charles Robinson, the first state governor; and John Brown.

The coved and paneled ceiling is made of decorative plaster. The public gallery is located in the back of the chamber, while the front gallery is reserved for invited guests of members. Accents of 23-carat gold leaf top the pink scagliola columns, and Belgian black marble forms their base. Tennessee marble is incorporated throughout the room and trimmed with Italian Carrara. The speaker's podium is comprised of walnut surmounted with hand-carved walnut urns.

The current interior restoration is scheduled to be completed by 2007 along with an overlapping eight-year exterior restoration project. Especially important is the work being done to slow the deterioration of the limestone exterior caused by weather, air pollution, de-icing compounds and other chemicals, which is most prominent in the earliest constructed areas, where a poorer-quality sandstone was initially used. Today, at least in outward appearance, the capitol looks much as it did at the time of its completion over a century ago.

The Kansas Pastoral *by John Steuart Curry viewed through an archway.*

Interior view of the Kansas State Capitol dome.

MISSISSIPPI

Mississippi State Capitol

Origin of Name: From a Native American word
meaning "Father of Waters."

Capital: Jackson

Constructed: 1901–1903

Architect: Theodore C. Link

Admitted to the Union: December 10, 1817 (twentieth)

Senate: 52 members

House of Representatives: 122 members

The state of Mississippi dedicated its capitol on June 3, 1903. The dedication date was specifically selected by officials because it coincided with the birthday of Mississippian Jefferson Davis. Thousands of visitors arrived in Jackson for the ceremony, many by the Illinois Central Railroad, which added sixteen special trains in order to accommodate them. The event's patriotic fervor intensified further because the annual reunion of the Confederate veterans was also being held in Jackson on that day. One newspaper reported that the city took on the appearance of a Confederate encampment, with tents pitched everywhere and the gray uniforms of the Confederate Army visible throughout the crowds.

The dedication celebration's *pièce de résistance* occurred when switches turned on the Beaux Arts capitol's nearly five thousand electric lights. The capitol was Jackson's first all-electric building, but to assuage those who doubted electricity's future, every third light fixture was also equipped with a gas jet.

The Illinois Central Railroad played another role in the history of the Mississippi Capitol. When the old capitol (1839–1903) became too small and financing a new one seemed impossible, an alert state treasurer discovered and collected back taxes owed to the state by the railroad. Those receipts financed the capitol's total cost of $1,093,641. Later, from 1979 to 1982, a largely federally financed renovation restored public areas, including the House and Senate chambers, the rotunda, corridors, and the Governor's Reception Room. Mezzanines were also installed to increase its office space.

The symmetrical building is composed of three connected blocks measuring 420 feet wide and 180 feet high to the top of the dome. The exterior walls consist of concrete and Indiana limestone. The rusticated base course of Georgia granite was completed in less than one year with the help of laborers from the state penitentiary.

Windows decrease in size and the amount of their decoration from the second floor to the fourth. The entablature above the third floor is decorated with dentils and modillions. The legislative wings include a slightly projecting pavilion decorated with columns and pilasters and end in semicircular Corinthian colonnades topped with saucer domes. Flags fly over the domes of the chambers to announce when the legislators are in session.

A pavilion with an entrance portico of six Corinthian columns supporting a pediment projects from the center of the south facade. The bas-relief sculp-

Fish-scale consoles support the gallery in the House of Representatives chamber.

The rotunda of the Mississippi State Capitol.

Stained-glass windows on a landing of the grand staircase.

ture within the pediment, with Miss Mississippi in the center, allegorically represents Agriculture, Industry and the Arts. Above the portico, metal-and-glass globe-like finials decorate the short corner towers of the central block, below the dome. A peristyle of Corinthian columns surmounted by a balustrade encircles the base of the dome. High atop the dome's lantern rests a gold-plated eagle, 8 feet tall with a wingspan of 15 feet.

Inside, Italian white marble adorns the walls, with Belgian black marble molding and coffered ceilings. On the second floor, bronze tongue-and-dart molding outlines marble pilasters with bronze capitals. The old supreme court chamber and the old state library, at opposite ends of the corridor, incorporate pedimented entrances supported by Tuscan columns of white marble.

The second-floor rotunda also consists of white Italian marble, with black Belgian and New York marble trimming, along with scagliola columns. Four large piers with marble niches and scagliola columns, topped by composite capitals, support the dome. A relief sculpture of blindfolded Justice with magnolias, the state flower, in her hair, decorates the top of the four arches. In the dome, painted medallions depict scenes from Mississippi history — two involving Native Americans and the other two depicting a Spanish explorer and a Confederate general. A cast-iron balustrade surrounds the opening in the floor.

The architect was interested in light and incorporated 750 of the building's 4,750 exposed electric lightbulbs in the rotunda. In addition, light filters through the stained glass of the rotunda dome, the skylights and domes in the chambers, and the glass-block floor of the fourth floor below stained-glass skylights down to the third floor.

Off the rotunda, the marble grand staircase leads to the third floor. At the first landing, three stained-glass windows depict a Native American, Mother Mississippi, and a pioneer settler. Marble lions' heads decorate the landing's newel posts. Toward the fourth-floor mezzanine, the ceiling is decorated with ornamental painted plaster garlands and flowers.

The hallways leading to the legislative chambers, located at the ends of the third story, incorporate marble, bronze and scagliola. Fluted columns and pilasters of marble decorated with brass anthemia, egg-and-dart molding and Ionic capitals flank the arched entrances to the chambers. Visitors enter the chambers from the front, enabling them to observe the faces of the Mississippi lawmakers.

The Senate chamber.

The Senate chamber, of a higher status politically than the House of Representatives, reflects its position in its bold decorative features. Corinthian columns of violet and purple scagliola support a domed, stained-glass and coffered ceiling. Written in the center of the dome is the declaration: "The people's government, made for the people, made by the people, and answerable to the people." Exposed lightbulbs in guilloche molding encircle the base of the dome. The senators' chairs are new, though the desks date from the 1930s. The design of the carpet replaces original tile floor in the same pattern. The Senate retains the roll call or voice vote.

At the other end of the building, the House of Representatives also features scagliola along with wainscoting of Belgian black marble. Corbels support the visitors' galleries. Mississippi's coat of arms, with added cotton bolls, decorates the midpoint of the four arches. The arches support the saucer-domed ceiling, which is highlighted, once again, by exposed lightbulbs and stained-glass coffers. The members' oak desks date from 1903. The original oak rostrum and clerk's desk contain fruit carvings, flutings, and egg-and-dart moldings. Behind the speaker's chair, consoles flank an original brass wall sconce bearing the state coat of arms. It is here that the lawmakers vote electronically on the important matters of the day.

It was during a special session of the Mississippi legislature on October 10, 1969, that the state's first Medicaid program was adopted. A minimum program, it brought into the state approximately $30 million of federal money to match a lesser amount of state funds in order to provide certain health-care

Mississippi's House of Representatives.

benefits and long-term care to low-income and needy people.

The federal government contributes 50 percent of a state's administrative expenses, though state expenditures for medical benefits are matched by federal payments. The size of the match is determined by the state's per capita personal income compared to the national average for the three preceding years. Medicaid matching rates range from a floor of 50 percent for wealthier states to as high as 77 percent. The rates are recalculated each year. An aging population and skyrocketing costs for leading-edge medical treatment have made Medicaid the fastest-growing category of state spending in Mississippi.

The Mississippi State Capitol building.

RHODE ISLAND

RHODE ISLAND STATE HOUSE

ORIGIN OF NAME: For the Greek island of Rhodes or *Roodt Eylandt*, meaning "red island" in Dutch.

CAPITAL: Providence

CONSTRUCTED: 1895–1904

ARCHITECT: McKim, Mead & White

ADMITTED TO THE UNION: May 29, 1790 (thirteenth)

SENATE: 50 members

HOUSE OF REPRESENTATIVES: 100 members

Every day, outside the entrance to the Senate chamber of the Rhode Island State House, a fireproof steel vault is opened to reveal King Charles II's original 1663 parchment charter granting Rhode Island colonists freedom to govern themselves and freedom of religion. The charter remained in force until 1843, when it was finally replaced by a state constitution.

During the colonial period, Rhode Island instituted an itinerant legislature that met throughout its counties at Providence, Newport, Warwick, Portsmouth, Pawtucket, East Greenwich, Bristol, South Kingstown and Narragansett. In 1840, the legislators reduced the rotation of their sessions to four sites: Bristol, East Greenwich, Newport and Providence, with the site of South Kingstown reinstituted three years later. By 1854, lawmakers decided to establish Newport and Providence as co-capitals.

As the economy shifted from shipping to industrialization, the business of the state became more centered in Providence than Newport. The constitution was thereby amended, establishing that all future legislative sessions be held in Providence. By the late nineteenth century, Rhode Island, the smallest state in size, was the richest state per capita. Coincidentally, many of the nation's wealthy and powerful citizens summered at Newport, giving the state national influence far beyond its diminutive size. The 1760 Providence State House was soon deemed to be inadequate.

During the January 1890 session, the legislature authorized the construction of a new state house and appointed a board of state house commissioners to build one that would better reflect Rhode Island's status. The eight commissioners representing the state's five counties were considered some of its most influential and cosmopolitan politicians and businessmen. They announced an architectural competition to create a design for a capitol.

In the interest of fairness and professionalism, the American Institute of Architects encouraged anonymous submissions to national competitions for public buildings. Not only was Rhode Island's competition not anonymous, it was unusually structured with two tiers. Only Rhode Island architects were invited to compete in the preliminary tier, in order to ensure that certain local architects were represented. After winners were chosen from that group, national architects, or rather three architectural firms from New York and Boston, were selected to compete with the local firms in a second and final tier. While deliberating, the commissioners visited such renowned architectural structures as Grant's Tomb in New York City, Hartford's new capitol, Boston's public library (designed by the firm of McKim, Mead & White of New York and one of their best-known buildings in the American Classicism style), and the planned addition to the Massachusetts State House.

In 1892, the commissioners announced their choice, McKim, Mead & White, one of the most prestigious and internationally recognized architectural firms during this period and architects of many homes and buildings in nearby Newport. The commissioners praised their state house design for its "artistic effect and practical arrangement, its monumental character and

Rhode Island's Royal Charter dating from 1663.

Massive piers support the dome of the Rhode Island State House.

classic type, as most closely associated with the best civic examples." They also cited its compactness, the clarity of its plan, and the manner in which the interior features were expressed externally.

After Rhode Island voters approved a bond issue of just over $1.5 million to fund construction, the plans were approved, including a stipulation that the building be of brick and iron-beam construction, faced and ornamented with white Georgia marble. The decision to construct the state house of white marble in a city of red brick was probably influenced by the overall white-themed World's Columbian Exposition in Chicago in 1893, for which McKim, Mead & White were simultaneously designing the Agriculture Building in their increasingly influential American Classicism style.

On October 15, 1896, U.S. President Grover Cleveland attended the state house cornerstone ceremony. The interior finish work and landscaping were completed in 1904, with the final cost rising to approximately $3 million, an excessive sum for that time, especially for a small, albeit wealthy, state.

In order to be visible the state house was carefully sited on Smith Hill, where today it continues to dominate the city of Providence. Its self-supporting dome, at nearly 250 feet high and 50 feet in diameter, is the second largest of the four self-supporting marble domes in the world (after St. Peter's Basilica and larger than the dome of the Minnesota State Capitol and the Taj Mahal). Topping the dome is a classically draped statue, *Independent Man*, cast locally in bronze by the Gorham Manufacturing Company.

On a colonnaded drum, the dome is surrounded by four smaller cupolas, or tourelles, each with its own dome and supported by a Corinthian colonnade. On either side of the dome are seven bay wings with saucer domes surmounted by flagstaffs over the legislative chambers. A small shallow

The dome is illustrated with allegorical figures of Education, Literature, Commerce and Justice.

balcony is located on both sides of each wing. The ground-level windows are arched, mirroring the nearby arched entryway, while the next story incorporates rectangular-shaped openings, and the windows on the top floor are square.

To the north, a center projecting pavilion with an arcade protects a covered carriageway. The portico, without a pediment, is inscribed as follows:

PROVIDENCE PLANTATIONS
FOUNDED BY ROGER WILLIAMS, 1636

PROVIDENCE, PORTSMOUTH,
NEWPORT INCORPORATED
BY PARLIAMENT, 1643

RHODE ISLAND —
PROVIDENCE PLANTATIONS
OBTAINED ROYAL CHARTER, 1663

IN GENERAL ASSEMBLY DECLARED
A SOVEREIGN STATE, MAY 4, 1776

A similar arcade is featured on the opposite side, with a two-story loggia at the second-floor level overlooking the city. Bronze statues of Rhode Island native sons Commodore Oliver Hazard Perry and General Nathaniel Greene face downtown Providence.

From the entrances, visitors move through vestibules to the rotunda, where the Classical white of the exterior continues on the lower levels. Color and texture are introduced above through coffering and paintings, culminating in the 1947 mural circling the interior of the dome. The 50-foot mural depicts Roger Williams buying land from Native Americans in 1636 as he sought religious freedom after his banishment from Massachusetts.

The legislative chambers retain their original colors, with the Senate predominantly green and the House red. The Senate chamber is almost a cube, 56 feet wide, 44 feet long, and 45 feet high. On the archway above the dark green velvet-draped rostrum are the seals of the original thirteen states, with Rhode Island's in the center. The House is larger, with a coffered ceiling and a skylight. Tapestries simulate gardens on the sides of the

The Governor's Reception Room.

chamber, giving the impression of open space in a room without windows and natural light.

The state library is decorated in terracotta colors, conducive to study and reflection. The coved ceiling is decorated with gold-leaf paint, carvings of the seals of famous university printing houses, and exposed lightbulbs (a tribute to the the relative newness of electricity at the beginning of the twentieth century). Especially apparent in the library is the addition of computer technology, a difficult installation task in a solid-stone structure.

Used for official events and entertaining important visitors, the Governor's Reception Room features a gilded, coved ceiling, with a central panel of clouds in a blue sky, gold-topped and variegated marble pilasters, matching carved white marble fireplaces, a crystal chandelier, and oversized oak doors. The architects chose the room's furnishings in the style of Louis XIV. It is also a repository of Rhode Island artifacts, including the well-known portrait of George Washington painted by Gilbert Stuart.

As in other states, it is the Rhode Island legislature's responsibility to keep and maintain its state government facilities, including the state house and its paintings, furnishings and fixtures. In 1800, the Rhode Island General Assembly ordered two portraits of George Washington "drawn at full length, by some eminent artist, with suitable frames, be procured at the expense of the State, and that one of them be placed in the Senate chamber in each of the State Houses of Newport and Providence." It further voted to pay $1,200 for the portraits and $400.05 apiece for the frames, plus the cost of transporting them from Philadelphia. The legislature also agreed to pay $115.13 to hang the Washington portrait in the Newport Courthouse, and $120.03 to place the other in the Providence Courthouse.

The Rhode Island State House, facing north.

The "eminent artist" referred to by the lawmakers was native Rhode Islander Gilbert Stuart, who painted three portraits of George Washington from live sittings and many replicas. The Rhode Island portraits are believed, along with the Gilbert Stuart replica in the old Connecticut state house in Hartford, to be copies of the Lansdowne portrait that Stuart had painted from a sitting with Washington in 1796. It was commissioned by Senator William Bingham of Pennsylvania and his wife, Anne, as a gift for William Petty, Lord Shelburne, the first Marquis of Lansdowne, a British supporter of the American cause in Parliament during the American Revolution. The original now hangs in the National Portrait Gallery of the Smithsonian Institution.

In the Governor's Reception Room, specifically designed with the portrait in mind, a full-length, standing Washington is painted in civilian clothes. His left hand rests on his dress sword and his right hand on a document on the table beside him. Lower portions of two columns and a red curtain form the background. He wears a black suit and a white shirt, frilled at the neck and cuffs, and powdered hair. The oil-on-canvas portrait measures 95 by 60 inches, and its frame is decorated with cross-ribbons, a shield, an eagle, clusters of flags, and weapons.

The General Assembly also enacted a law in the 1870s entitling every Rhode Island governor to one portrait. As a result, portraits of former governors line the state house corridors.

The state library.

PENNSYLVANIA

PENNSYLVANIA STATE CAPITOL

ORIGIN OF NAME: Latin for "Penn's woods." Named by King Charles II
in honor of Admiral William Penn, the father of the colony's founder.

CAPITAL: Harrisburg

CONSTRUCTED: 1902–1906

ARCHITECT: Joseph M. Huston

ADMITTED TO THE UNION: December 12, 1787 (second)

SENATE: 50 members

HOUSE OF REPRESENTATIVES: 203 members

Pennsylvania played a central role in the formation of the United States. The State Assembly first met upstairs in the old state house now known as Independence Hall, in Philadelphia, with the Second Continental Congress meeting in a 30-by-40-foot room on the first floor. In this space debates raged over the Revolutionary War with Great Britain; the Declaration of Independence was adopted on July 4, 1776; George Washington was named commander of the Continental Army; the Articles of Confederation were written; and, in the summer of 1787, the United States Constitution was drafted. It also housed the art studio of Charles Willson Peale and his son, Rembrandt.

The construction of Independence Hall began in 1731. Between 1750 and 1753, a tall bell tower was added with an open hall and staircase. The Georgian state house consists of a central building flanked by smaller wings joined to the central block by loggias open to the north.

But when the 1790 constitution set up a bicameral legislature, and Independence Hall had room for only one chamber (the location of which lawmakers from outside Philadelphia argued was too far from the center of the state and who also refused to enter the city when it was particularly hard hit during the yellow-fever epidemic of the 1790s), the legislature briefly moved to the county courthouse in Lancaster before settling in what is now Harrisburg. There, the first legislative session convened during December 1812, temporarily residing in the Dauphin County Courthouse. In 1816, the lawmakers authorized a capitol to be constructed on land along the Susquehanna River using the proceeds from the sale of Independence Hall to Philadelphia.

The Greek Revival capitol, with a colonnaded portico and a low dome, was completed in 1822. Destroyed by fire during a snowstorm on February 2, 1897, its replacement, to be constructed on its ruins, was never completed.

Instead, a building commission appointed Philadelphian Joseph M. Huston as architect for a capitol budgeted at $4 million and to be more representative of Pennsylvania's growing industrial strength and power. Huston designed a Renaissance Revival building in the style of St. Peter's Basilica and other European buildings he had admired on his grand tour of Europe after his graduation from Princeton.

When the building was completed and dedicated by President Theodore Roosevelt, it was one of the largest and most expensive capitols in the United States. With over six hundred rooms on six floors covering two acres, it cost over $13 million to construct, decorate and furnish. Today the capitol and

Independence Hall, Philadelphia.

Interior dome of the Pennsylvania State Capitol.

The House of Representatives celebrated the 100th anniversary of the Teddy Bear in 2002.

its modern east wing, dedicated in 1987, anchor a complex of commonwealth buildings that include the 1894 restored Executive, Library and Museum Building, now known as the Legislative Office Building.

The 520-foot-long and 254-foot-wide capitol is constructed in three primary blocks that house the rotunda and the legislative chambers. Faced with Vermont granite, the exterior is ornamented with paired Corinthian columns and pilasters, pediments, marble balustrades, varying fenestration, a parapet and subsidiary domes rising out of both wings.

Sixteen piers ornamented with pairs of Corinthian columns, support the dome. Above, a cornice and a course of egg-and-dart molding separate the granite from the green-glazed tiles of the roof. The roof incorporates bull's-eye windows, which add light to the rotunda's interior. The cupola repeats the pattern of the dome and is crowned by a gilt ball holding a bronze-and-gilded statue, facing west.

Huston sought to build a "palace of art," and commissioned artists to fill it with their works. A white Carrara marble staircase, inspired by the staircase of the old Paris Opera House, and a 272-foot-high interior dome dominate the ornate and brightly lit rotunda or Grand Hall. It is here that the capitol's artwork is integrated into its architecture, including medallions representing Art, Law, Religion and Science, along with larger murals illustrating the state's primary industries at the time of the capitol's construction — coal, oil and steel. Images of William Penn's ships coming to the New World fill the lunettes. These works are attributed to Edwin Austin Abbey.

Allegorical figures, "Angels of Light," designed and paid for by the

The Pennsylvania State Capitol.

architect after the newel posts were cut from the budget, stand at the bottom of the staircase. They hold crystal globes containing nearly two thousand beads strung on silver-coated copper wire. Electrical wiring to each globe is threaded through the pedestal base, the garment folds, and into the uplifted arm, coming out of the palm of the hand.

The opulent decor of the Grand Hall continues in the legislative chambers. Pennsylvania's House of Representatives membership, at 203, is the second largest of all the states, after New Hampshire, though its population is ten times that of New Hampshire. Within its great chamber, the largest mural in the capitol, Abbey's *The Apotheosis of Pennsylvania*, hangs directly behind the speaker of the House's podium. Measuring 35 feet square, it depicts the Genius of Pennsylvania with fifty distinguished sons at her feet, including intellectual, spiritual and military leaders and explorers. William Penn stands at the center of the work, with Benjamin Franklin at his side.

Murals flanking *The Apotheosis* include Abbey's *Penn's Treaty with the Indians*, featuring William Penn, who was granted all the land in Pennsylvania in 1681 by England's King Charles II. Penn reportedly decided not to sell or settle any of the land without first buying the claims from Native Americans who lived there. The tree under which the sale takes place dominates the painting. On the other side, Abbey's *Reading of the Declaration of Independence* shows the first public reading of the document in Philadelphia on July 8, 1776.

Abbey's circular ceiling mural, *Passage of the Hours*, represents the passage of day and night, with twenty-four maidens against a dark blue background designating each hour of the clock rotating over and over from day to night. The artist completed the painting on a large wheel in his London studio.

Also notable are fourteen round stained-glass windows created by William B. Van Ingen, 4 feet in diameter, weighing 200 pounds each, and framed in gold leaf. They represent such themes as Education, Justice and Abundance. Chandeliers weighing between 2 and 4.5 tons also brighten the room.

Throughout the chamber the new is assimilated into the old. Since 1961, electronic voting-board tallies have covered the third and fourth windows. Laptop computers rest on the members' original mahogany desks. The Speaker of the House sits in a chair specially designed by Huston. Columns made from Pennsylvania steel are topped with plaster Classical capitals. The coffered flowers in the ceiling hide a modern sprinkler system.

Abbey died before he completed his work, but a twenty-eight-year-old muralist from Philadelphia, Violet Oakley, succeeded him. She worked for over a quarter of a century to produce forty-three murals in the capitol, reportedly the largest public commission assigned to a woman up to that time. Oakley's paintings in the Senate chamber took her more than eight years to complete. Divided into sections, *The Creation and Preservation of the Union* overlooks the room from behind the speaker's podium. One of two side panels shows George Washington presiding over the constitutional convention in Philadelphia in May 1787, while the other depicts Abraham Lincoln at Gettysburg in November 1863. Above, as a painted frieze, Oakley painted her vision of a united world. Works depicting the end of warfare and the end of slavery flank Unity.

As throughout the capitol, the crystals in the Senate's bronze light standards are cut in such a manner that the lights appear as an X. Other features include the green Connamara marble lining the walls, which complements the original mahogany desks and Tiffany stained-glass.

The capitol reportedly contains more murals than any other public building in the United States. It also boasts 16,000 square feet of hand-crafted Moravian mosaic tile covering its floor. Created by Bucks County craftsman Henry Chapman Mercer at his Doylestown tile factory, the mosaic tiles are set chronologically according to the historical events they portray, beginning with Native American activities circa 1600 and ending in the early 1900s with the automobile and the telephone.

In the tradition of Pennsylvania's early German potters, Mercer hand-made the tiles using local clay. The floor consists of field tiles — the square background tiles that are various shades of red, orange and darker colors, and the mosaics — the hand-cut tiles that make up the pictures. Over the years, heavy traffic caused damage to many of the tiles, requiring constant upkeep, but it was never an option to replace them with an easier-to-maintain surface.

Identical hand-laid Mercer tiles also pave the floors of the modern east wing. The wing added 400,000 square feet of space to the capitol and houses almost one hundred legislative offices, rooms for public hearings, a public cafeteria, and a welcome center. Its exterior granite is from the same Vermont quarry as that of the capitol.

The means for building the opulent capitol came from Pennsylvania's industries, especially coal and steel. Coal replaced wood as the source of fuel in the early 1800s, and since that time Pennsylvania has supplied 20 percent of the "soft" coal and nearly 100 percent of the "hard" coal used in the United States, even though the state contains only 7 percent of the coal reserves in the country. Coal's higher temperatures and greater burning efficiency led to the production of steel. The first blast furnace appeared in Pittsburgh in 1851, and it soon became known as "the Steel City," with entrepreneurs such as Andrew Carnegie and Henry Clay Frick building over 350 steel mills. During the twentieth century, Pennsylvania produced over half of the nation's iron and steel, a role it continues in the twenty-first century.

Detail of Mercer floor tile.

The Senate chamber.

MINNESOTA

MINNESOTA STATE CAPITOL

ORIGIN OF NAME: From the Dakota word *minisota*, meaning "water that reflects the sky."

CAPITAL: St. Paul

CONSTRUCTED: 1896–1905

ARCHITECT: Cass Gilbert

ADMITTED TO THE UNION: May 11, 1858 (thirty-second)

SENATE: 67 members

HOUSE OF REPRESENTATIVES: 134 members

Minnesota undertook its state capitol project after its first capitol, dating from 1853, was destroyed by fire. It outgrew the second one just ten years after it was completed in 1883. Although Minnesota was less than fifty years old, the construction of its American Renaissance capitol integrated works of art glorifying the state with marble from around the world. This conveyed to the world a more urbanized and sophisticated state rather than one comprised mostly of farmers living at the edge of the frontier.

The capitol's style was undoubtedly influenced by Rhode Island's state capitol, as the architect, Cass Gilbert, had worked as a draftsman for McKim, Mead & White, the architectural firm that designed the Providence building. After working for McKim, Mead & White, Gilbert established an office in St. Paul and designed large homes and churches in the nearby Summit Avenue neighborhood. Gilbert eagerly sought the capitol commission, and following the capitol's completion he went on to design the sixty-story Woolworth Building in New York City (at that time, in 1912, the world's tallest building); the United States Supreme Court Building in Washington D.C.; the state capitols in Arkansas and West Virginia; and many other museums, libraries and public buildings.

A perfectionist, Gilbert involved himself in the smallest detail in his projects, even the doorknobs and furnishings. When he sought to commission works of art to decorate the capitol, he found the board of state capitol commissioners, made up of members mostly from rural communities, reluctant to spend the amount of money necessary. In order to convince the commissioners, Gilbert took them to see buildings with mural paintings in Philadelphia, New York, Boston and Washington, D.C. The paintings in the Library of Congress were especially convincing, and today murals decorate the rotunda, hallways and public rooms of the capitol.

Later, Gilbert related: "When the Minnesota Capitol was constructed... one of the Commissioners stated that people of modest means could not afford to embellish their homes with works of art and that it was a reasonable function of the state in the direction of culture and education, and in the development of civilization, to provide in the State Capitol, which is owned and used by all of the people, suitable mural decorations of idealistic and historic character, and the expenditure necessary for doing it was justified. As a result of this advice, the comprehensive program was carried on and it has resulted in the growth of state pride. The building is visited annually by many thousands, school children and citizens, who learn there of the history of the state and of the ideals upon which it is founded."

From the outside, visitors can determine the capitol's internal arrangement. It is rectangular, 433 feet by 120 feet, with a central portico and

The Minnesota State Capitol dome.

The rotunda of the Minnesota State Capitol.

The House of Representatives chamber.

balanced wings containing the Senate chamber in west wing and the Minnesota Supreme Court in the east. A central wing on the north, or rear, measures 106 feet by 108 feet and contains the House of Representatives. The three distinct blocks are decorated with pilasters and connected by linking sections. At the ends of the building, columned pavilions contain two-story loggias with columns. Loggias are also suggested in the wings beneath shallow glass domes.

The capitol consists of white Georgia marble veneer over a steel frame. Initially, when Gilbert suggested the marble, with its veins of black and silver-gray, Minnesotans objected to incorporating out-of-state stone, wanting to use only their own state materials. Civil War veterans, with vivid memories of the divisive war, opposed using marble from the South. Gilbert finally suggested an acceptable compromise — gray St. Cloud, Minnesota, granite and sandstone for the foundation, steps, terraces and ground-floor walls, and Georgia marble for the walls above. In addition, the stone was delivered in raw blocks so that local stonecutters could dress it. This arrangement resulted in the rusticated basement and first floor, set apart from the floors above them.

Facing south, the central pavilion contains three arched doorways below a double-columned, arched loggia. The columns support an entablature decorated with statues representing the underlying virtues of good citizenship: Wisdom, Courage, Bounty, Truth, Integrity and Prudence. Instead of a pediment, a square pedestal tops the portico. Upon it, at the base of the dome, stands a gilded quadriga, *The Progress of the State.*

This steel-and-copper, gold-leaf-covered sculptural group consists of a chariot drawn by four leaping horses, with figures of a young man and two young women. It was created by Daniel Chester French and Edward C. Potter, who designed the horses to represent the forces of nature: Earth, Wind, Fire and Water. The charioteer symbolizes Prosperity by holding a horn of plenty filled with Minnesota's bounty and a banner with the word "Minnesota." The women represent Farming and Industry.

Behind the quadriga and rising from the center of the roof is one of the largest self-supporting marble domes in the world, 89 feet in diameter and internally supported by a cone of steel and brick. The dome is surrounded by pairs of Corinthian columns, each supporting a hand-carved marble statue of an eagle. Pedimented windows in between the columns allow light to naturally brighten the interior. The roof features stone ribs and a double row of bull's-eye windows. A columned circular lantern is topped by a copper orb 223 feet above the ground and covered in gold leaf.

A variety of both domestic and European marbles, as well as polished Minnesota Kasota limestone and granite, are incorporated into the capitol interior. The vaulted ceilings and wall panels of the corridors are decorated with hand-painted garlands representing fruits, grains and vegetables grown in the state, in ivory, gold, blue-green and rose colors.

The Governor's Reception Room.

Minnesota is known as the "North Star State," a translation of the French inscription on the state seal, *L'Etoile du Nord.* A large eight-pointed glass star in a brass framework is embedded in the limestone-and-marble floor directly under the dome. The brass-and-glass design is repeated in the colored marble of the surrounding floor.

The second floor of the 142-foot-high rotunda includes a circular balustrade of French marble, with balusters of Skyros marble from Greece. Monolithic Corinthian columns of Minnesota granite incorporate gilded Corinthian capitals with the state flower, the lady's slipper. From this floor, the circular rotunda becomes octagonal, with the walls forming piers that support the dome. In each of the piers is a niche containing a bronze statue of a Minnesotan who served in the Civil War.

Above, the interior of the dome is a great blue-and-gold vault with an Austrian crystal chandelier, six feet in diameter and holding ninety-five lights, suspended from its center. Four murals entitled *The Civilization of the Northwest* decorate the pendentives. They tell the story of a young man leaving home led by a woman symbolizing Wisdom. In the second, he drives out Cowardice, Ignorance and Sin in his new land by clearing the land. The third shows him using the resources of the earth, and in the fourth, he watches the winds scatter Minnesota products all over the world, with the state capitol in the background. Other ceiling adornments include paintings representing the signs of the zodiac in twelve lunettes.

Grand marble stairwells, with no two balusters alike in color or pattern, rise from the east and west of the rotunda and are lighted by barrel-vaulted skylights. Eighteen Italian marble columns, with Corinthian capitals, surround each of the stairwells. Featured in the skylight lunettes are Minnesota historical scenes.

These stairs lead to the second or "grand" floor of the capitol containing the chambers of the Senate, the House of Representatives, and the Minnesota Supreme Court. The Senate and House were restored to their 1905 appearance between 1988 and 1990, and contain their original mahogany furniture.

The square Senate chamber is covered with a domed skylight. The cornice is supported by French marble columns in shades of cream and violet. Pendentives between the arches opening to the spectators' galleries in the east and west arches are decorated with figures of Freedom, Courage, Justice and Equality. The inscription of the surrounding frieze, chosen by Gilbert, is attributed to Daniel Webster: *Let us develop the resources of our land, call forth its powers, build up its institutions, promote all its great interests, and see whether we also, in our day and generation, may not perform something worthy to be remembered.*

Filling the lunettes of the north and south walls are murals by Edwin Blashfield. To the north is *The Discoverers and Civilizers Led to the Source of the Mississippi*, and on the south wall, also by Blashfield, is *Minnesota, the Granary of the World*. In the latter, in the Medieval tradition of including the artist's patrons, added to a bottom corner of the painting are portraits of Cass Gilbert and Channing Seabury, head of the capital commission, in contemporary clothing.

A light fixture in the Senate chamber.

The semicircular House chamber incorporates a half dome ceiling, with five arches opening into spectator galleries and lighted by a gilded skylight surrounded by a broad frieze incorporating the letter M. Names on the ceiling such as La Salle, Hennepin and Duluth honor early French explorers in the Northwest. White Vermont marble Ionic columns flank the original speaker's desk, and a portrait of Abraham Lincoln hangs behind it. Between Ionic pilasters, the walls are covered in red wallpaper. During the late 1930s, a gallery above the speaker's rostrum was walled off in order to provide additional office space. Covering the wall now fronting the chamber is a sculpture grouping entitled *Minnesota — Spirit of Government*.

In this work, the dominant central figure represents Government, with a scepter in one hand symbolizing Authority and an open book in the other showing the dates of the establishment of the territory and the state, 1849 and 1858 respectively. On one side are a French explorer and a pioneer, while on the other are Native Americans. "The Trail of the Pioneer Bore the Footprints of Liberty" is written below.

The supreme court chamber in the east wing mirrors the Senate chamber in shape and is also lighted with a dome skylight. The justices' bench, opposite the door, is backed by four Ionic columns of white Vermont marble. Four lunette paintings on the upper portions of the walls include *The Moral and Divine Law*, showing Moses receiving the Ten Commandments on Mount Sinai. The others are entitled *The Recording of Precedents*, *The Relation of the Individual to the State*, and *The Adjustment of Conflicting Interests*.

The Governor's Reception Room, the most elaborate room in the capitol, features dark white oak woodwork from Minnesota, intricately decorated with painted plaster and covered with gold leaf. The ceiling and cornice are also in gold leaf. Gilbert designed the original hand-carved mahogany table where the Electoral College meets. Gold grillwork on the walls features a metal M. The fireplace consists of unpolished marble, *fleur de peche*, from France. Reproduction lightbulbs with tungsten filaments provide a dim light, aided by Austrian crystal chandeliers also designed by the architect.

Six large paintings illustrating scenes from Minnesota's history cover the walls. One depicts Father Hennepin at the Falls of St. Anthony, which he named in 1680 in honor of this patron saint. Another depicts the signing of the Treaty of Traverse des Sioux in 1851. In this treaty with the Native Americans of Dakota, the United States obtained the land that now forms much of southern Minnesota. Other paintings honor Minnesota regiments that fought in the Civil War, including one entitled *The Battle of Nashville*, showing the 5th, 9th and 10th Minnesota Infantry Regiments capturing the Confederate last line of defense on December 16, 1864.

Above the four doors in the reception room are spaces intended to hold the portraits of the state's four greatest governors. Perhaps because the choice is left to the governor in office, they remain empty. Additional portraits of past governors line the corridors.

The Minnesota State Capitol.

SOUTH CAROLINA

SOUTH CAROLINA STATE HOUSE

ORIGIN OF NAME: After King Charles I of England.

CAPITAL: Columbia

CONSTRUCTED: 1855–1907

ARCHITECTS: John R. Niernsee, James C. Neilson, Frank M. Niernsee, Frank P. Milburn, Charles C. Wilson

ADMITTED TO THE UNION: May 23, 1788 (eighth)

SENATE: 46 members

HOUSE OF REPRESENTATIVES: 124 members

South Carolina's first small frame state house, located in Charleston, burned to the ground in 1786. Because of increasing westward expansion, the General Assembly decided to move the capital to a more central location, and it founded Columbia, one of the first planned cities in the United States. Subsequently, the legislature became so concerned that the second state house, also made of wood, might burn that it authorized construction of a stone state house in 1851. When cracks appeared in its walls, lawmakers decided to tear the unfinished building down and start over. They appointed John R. Niernsee as architect for a third state house in 1854.

Although construction of the state house took over fifty years to complete, Niernsee's proposed Classical Revival design largely endured. The building's native blue granite was excavated by a slave-dominated labor force and hauled to the construction site first by wagon and then by a specially constructed three-mile railroad. Niernsee oversaw construction to nearly 66 feet above the foundation before work was disrupted by the Civil War and General William Tecumseh Sherman's burning of Columbia in February of 1865.

Sherman reportedly ordered a number of public buildings, including the old wooden state house, torched, though he mostly spared the unfinished one. Many suggested it was because Sherman admired its beauty, while others claimed he wanted to save the explosives it would have taken to destroy the solid stone walls. Bronze stars on the south and west facades still mark the slight damage caused by Union shells. Stockpiled building materials were destroyed by Union soldiers, as well as Niernsee's drawings and written specifications, somewhat altering the state house's completion as originally planned.

The walls remained unfinished at the time of South Carolina's readmission to the Union in 1868, during Reconstruction, and even after federal troops

left the state in 1877. Niernsee was not authorized to continue his work until 1885. He died later that year. Covered by a temporary roof, the state house's construction stalled further as the state and the South's economy suffered. When Niernsee's former associate J. Crawford Nielson replaced him, Nielson completed the chambers and galleries for the Senate and House of Representatives. In 1888, Niernsee's son Frank took over as architect. Before his death, the younger Niernsee added the cornice, balustrade and roof, along with library features such as cast-iron stairs, galleries and balconies.

In 1900, Frank Pierce Milburn became the fourth state house architect. He installed a new roof and substituted the dome for the tower John Niernsee envisioned, reportedly modeled after Tennessee's. Niernsee had

A staircase from the ground floor to the lobby.

The South Carolina State House.

intended to add piers from the basement through each level to support a tower, but with his plans lost, the piers were omitted as the second and third floors were constructed. Lacking the vertical support necessary for a traditional dome design, Milburn worked with the American Bridge Company of Pittsburgh to implement a steel-truss support system. Finally, from 1902 to 1907, a new architect, Charles Coker Wilson, completed the exterior by adding the north and south porticoes.

On the exterior, granite stairways consisting of fifty-two steps ascend to the pedimented porticoes that provide access to the second floor. They are supported by Corinthian columns (twelve on the north and ten on the south) and pilasters. The fluted columns, hand-carved from a single piece of stone, stand 43 feet high. Entrance to the building from the front portico is through a large double doorway surrounded by fluted Corinthian pilasters that reach to the portico ceiling. Adjacent to the pilasters on the lower level are panels with carved Roman fasces, and above these are hand-carved eagles. Over the entrance is a smaller, arched doorway with a marble balustrade. This doorway is flanked by bas-relief medallions featuring likenesses of Robert Hayne and George McDuffie, early nineteenth-century governors of South Carolina and United States senators. The doors of the main and south portico entrances are oak with glass panels.

The first story consists of rusticated stone and semicircular arched windows. The second- and third-floor walls are smooth-surfaced, with rusticated quoins. Bracketed pediments top rectangular windows on the second floor, and the smaller third-floor windows incorporate bracketed sills.

A view of the lobby from the balcony.

Rising from the center of the hipped balustraded roof is an Italianate dome. On its lower section, the dome incorporates eight pairs of semicircular arched windows separated by pilasters and topped by hood molds with keystones. On top of this section is a copper-faced roof with bull's-eye windows. The wooden cupola above is also sheathed in copper and surmounted by a flagpole flying the flags of the United States and South Carolina.

Inside are two lobbies: a lower lobby located on the ground floor, and the main lobby, which is on the second or main entrance floor. Thirty-two granite Doric columns support the white vaulted ceiling of the lower lobby. Walls in some areas are six feet thick. The floor is marble and uncarpeted.

Two staircases ascend from the lower lobby to the main lobby. The stairs feature black wrought-iron railings with a mahogany banister. Wide painted metal cornices decorate the lobby's upper walls below the pressed-metal ceiling. This ceiling and the false dome were installed at the same time as the outside dome but do not connect. A six-foot-wide balcony, supported by decorative cast-iron brackets, extends around most of the lobby and is reached by twin cast-iron staircases located against the rear wall. This balcony provides access to the galleries of the legislative chambers on the third floor. An arched mosaic rose-glass window depicting the state seal adorns the balcony's rear wall.

The carpets incorporate borders with South Carolina's state tree, the palmetto. A reproduction of the *Ordinance of Secession* hangs from a wall, memorializing South Carolina's status as the first state to secede from the Union in 1860. Also prominent is a statue of South Carolinian

The restored House of Representatives.

John C. Calhoun, a model for a marble statue that stands in the national Capitol's Statuary Hall. Calhoun was a political voice for states' rights and supported the theory of nullification as a method of invalidating unpopular federal laws, thus becoming associated with pro-slavery or segregationist philosophy. He served as vice-president under John Quincy Adams and Andrew Jackson, two terms as United States senator, and twice as a cabinet member.

At the rear of the lobby's south wall, three marble-framed arched doors with leaded stained-glass fanlights surrounded by Tennessee marble provide entry into the vestibule of the state library or joint legislative conference room. This is the only room in the state house that remains in its original condition. Black wrought-iron spiral staircases rise to a balcony that is supported by black iron columns and ornamented by a grillwork railing and a mahogany banister. Other features include a pressed-metal ceiling and the only original chandelier in the state house.

At the east end of the main lobby, a door opens into a marble-floored foyer that leads into the Senate chamber. Corinthian columns and ornamental brackets support a balcony with a polished brass railing. The focal point of the chamber is the hand-carved mahogany rostrum dating from 1915, with its oil portrait of Calhoun. Smaller paintings of other South Carolinians line the walls: Isaiah DeQuincy Newman, first African-American senator after Reconstruction; Mary Gordon Ellis, first female senator;

Henry Timrod, poet laureate of South Carolina and author of the song "Carolina"; and J. Strom Thurmond, governor of South Carolina and the longest-serving United States senator.

Directly across the lobby from the Senate chamber is the 6,405-square-foot hall of the House of Representatives. A balcony with an 1887 brass railing, decorated with a palmetto design, extends around the chamber below the plaster coffered ceiling. The speaker's hand-carved desk, made of British Honduras mahogany, dates from 1937. During legislative sessions, the flags of the United States and South Carolina are mounted above the speaker's desk. There are also portraits of South Carolinian Andrew Jackson; Confederate General Thomas "Stonewall" Jackson; Thomas Jefferson; Benjamin Mays, president of Morehouse College and mentor to Martin Luther King Jr.; and Woodrow Wilson.

The paintings, furnishings and occupants of the state house were moved out in 1995, and the building was renovated to its nineteenth-century appearance. An earthquake-proof foundation was constructed, repairs were made to the slate roof, and the copper dome was replaced. Inside, the renovation work included asbestos removal, mechanical and electrical system updates (including new heating and air-conditioning systems), accessibility upgrades in compliance with the Americans with Disabilities Act, and replacement of members' desks to allow for new technology.

Lawmakers seeking a respite from their increasingly difficult work may wander outside to walk through the 18 surrounding acres filled with flowers, trees, pathways, and more than twenty monuments. The oldest monument is the cast-iron Palmetto Monument, dedicated to the men of the Palmetto Regiment, which served in the Mexican War. Other monuments include a gun from the battleship *Maine*, a statue of Strom Thurmond, and a Confederate women's monument. A life-sized bronze statue of George Washington stands at the north entrance. It is one of six replicas cast in 1853 from the Houdon statue at the Virginia Capitol. Washington visited the old state house in 1791 as part of a tour of the southern states. During the occupation of Columbia by Sherman's army, Union soldiers reportedly broke off the lower part of Washington's walking stick, and in order to make a point about the soldiers' disrespectful attitude, it was not repaired.

Before the main entrance stands the Confederate Monument memorializing those who died during the Civil War. The Carrara marble monument

The George Washington statue in front of the state house.

consists of a standing Confederate soldier on a pedestal. It was ordered in 1872 from the Muldoon Monument Company of Louisville, Kentucky, at a cost of $10,000, arrived in Columbia in 1875, and was erected on the grounds in 1879. Originally located closer to the east side of the building, its visibility became enhanced after the legislature passed a controversial law removing the Confederate flag from the flagpole on top of the state house and instead flying it next to the monument.

This last Confederate battle flag to fly from a capitol dome flew there for thirty-eight years, starting in 1962. That year the South Carolina General Assembly approved a resolution to place the Confederate battle flag atop the state house as a part of the state's centennial celebration of the "War of Northern Aggression." It soon raised controversy and intense passion. Flag supporters said it represented the state's heritage and honored the memory of those who fought and died for South Carolina. Opponents contended it was a symbol of slavery and oppression, and opposed the Civil Rights Movement.

In January 2000, nearly 6,000 people gathered on the state house grounds to urge lawmakers to continue flying the flag. A little more than a week later, nearly 456,000 rallied at the same spot to demand that the flag be removed. More rallies followed, as did a march from Charleston to Columbia. Ultimately, a plan to take away the flag and raise a similar one on the state house grounds passed the legislature. According to the law, the South Carolina infantry battle flags of the Confederate States of America were also removed from the rostrum in the chambers of the House of Representatives and the Senate.

The African-American history monument to the east of the house was dedicated on March 29, 2001. South Carolina is the only state to have an African-American memorial on its capitol grounds. The $1.2-million monument portraying the history of African Americans and their contributions to South Carolina was financed by private donations. It includes an engraved ship depicting 336 slaves chained together on the trip to the United States, many to Charleston. A 23-foot obelisk is flanked by 25-foot curved granite walls that hold bronze panels of bas-relief depicting twelve scenes from African-American history, including slaves on the auction block, as well as black astronauts, tennis player Althea Gibson, and jazz trumpeter Dizzy Gillespie.

The African-American Memorial on the east side of the state house.

COLORADO

COLORADO STATE CAPITOL

ORIGIN OF NAME: A Spanish word meaning "red."

CAPITAL: Denver

CONSTRUCTED: 1886–1908

ARCHITECT: Elijah E. Meyers

ADMITTED TO THE UNION: August 1, 1876 (thirty-eighth)

SENATE: 35 members

HOUSE OF REPRESENTATIVES: 65 members

In 1861, following the 1858 discovery of gold near Denver, the United States Congress created the Territory of Colorado from a ragtag group of gold-rush camps. The first territorial legislature convened in Colorado City, now a part of Colorado Springs. The next year, lawmakers met again in Colorado City, but only for nine days before they adjourned to Denver. There, the legislature changed the capital to Golden, until December 9, 1867, when the legislature voted Denver to be the permanent capital. Lawmakers met in rented quarters.

In 1868, Henry Cordes Brown gave ten acres of land, located on a ridge overlooking the Rocky Mountains to the Territory of Colorado on the condition that it become the future capitol building site. An itinerant carpenter from Ohio, Brown initially bought 160 acres for $1.25 an acre under the Homestead Act. Not only did he became wealthy from the Denver real-estate holdings that grew out of his initial investment, but he became known for building the Brown Palace Hotel on the triangular plot of ground that was his cow pasture after another hotel reportedly declined to serve him because he wore cowboy boots. His motives for assisting the state were not entirely unselfish, because he undoubtedly believed that if he donated the land (costing him a pittance) and the capitol were built there, his remaining land would increase in value.

After a number of years, when nothing was constructed on the donated parcel, Brown sued for the return of the appreciated land. Following seven years in the courts, with hearings by the Colorado Supreme Court in 1881 and the United States Supreme Court in 1882 and 1886, it was finally determined that the ten acres belonged to the state of Colorado, not Brown.

Perhaps the lawsuit brought to the attention of state officials the necessity of providing a permanent capitol for conducting government business. Soon after Colorado became the "Centennial State," so named because it was admitted to the Union the year of the nation's centennial, the board of capitol managers appointed Elijah E. Myers architect for the Classical Renaissance project.

Primarily constructed of native Colorado materials, its exterior consists of gray granite from quarries near Gunnison. The stone was transported across the Continental Divide by a narrow-gauge railroad. The five-foot-thick foundation is made up of sandstone quarried in Fort Collins.

A flight of steps leads to porticoes containing three arches centered on each elevation of the three-story building. Above, Corinthian columns two

The golden dome of Colorado's state capitol building.

Corinthian columns in the west lobby of the capitol.

stories high support a pediment. Carved within the western-facing tympanum are bas-relief figures representing a homesteader, a miner and a cowboy, patterned after drawings by Myers. Along the walls, pilasters with plain capitals separate symmetrically spaced rectangular windows. Without rustication, the walls from the ground to the roof are smooth.

Above, a parapet surrounds the hipped roof, from which a gold dome rises 272 feet above the ground. It is supported by a drum incorporating free-standing columns and two stories of narrow, arched windows. Its walls, balconies and columns are made of cast-iron designed to look like Gunnison granite. The cast-iron was substituted because masonry was considered too heavy at that height.

Although the capitol is famous for its gold dome, Myers initially chose to cover it in copper. But gold, unlike copper, is native to Colorado, so in 1908 the Colorado Mining Association donated 200 ounces of 24-carat gold leaf to cover the dome, at a cost of $14,680. As a continual reminder of the state's mining heritage, the dome is periodically re-covered with gold leaf. In 1950, the gold cover cost $25,000; in 1980 it was $190,000; and in 1990 weather damaged the gold, necessitating another recovering the next year, at $223,200.

The sixteen windows of the dome contain stained-glass portraits of people who played a role in the growth and development of Colorado. The Colorado Hall of Fame was added in 1900. First selected was Chief Ouray of the Utes, who worked for peace between Native Americans and settlers and was instrumental in deeding large land areas to the U.S. government. Others chosen included William Gilpin, first governor of Colorado Territory; J. W. Denver, Denver's namesake, governor of Kansas Territory, part of which became Colorado when gold

The north wing seen from the rotunda.

was discovered; Kit Carson, Colorado pioneer who helped open the West; Frances Wisbart Jacobs (the only woman), who founded many charities in Colorado, one of which was the Community Chest; along with other governors, legislators, educators, industrialists, and early transportation leaders.

Inside, corridors leading from the four entrances meet at the rotunda. Filling the rotunda is a grand staircase consisting of 77 marble steps and 176 brass balusters. Eight murals, completed in the 1940s, decorate the walls of the small space. They emphasize the importance of water to the development of Colorado and the West.

Polished marble from the town of Marble, located near Aspen, and a rare rose onyx marble discovered southwest of Pueblo, near Beulah, are incorporated into the stairways, interior columns, floors and wainscoting. It took craftsmen over six years to complete the marble installation. The onyx marble is extraordinarily precious because almost all of it was integrated into the capitol, and to the bewilderment of geologists, it has never been found anywhere else in the world.

The largest room in the capitol, the House of Representatives, is located in the central block, while the Senate occupies the east wing. Both remain in nearly original condition, though brighter lighting systems designed for television cameras were installed. The chandeliers weigh nearly 1,500 pounds and contain forty-eight lights, one for each state before Alaska and Hawaii were admitted to the Union. With 160 rooms including the basement, all legislators have their offices in the capitol building.

The stained-glass likeness of railroad entrepreneur David Moffat overlooks the Senate chamber, while scenic paintings decorate the House. In 1987, representatives passed a resolution establishing an arts committee to

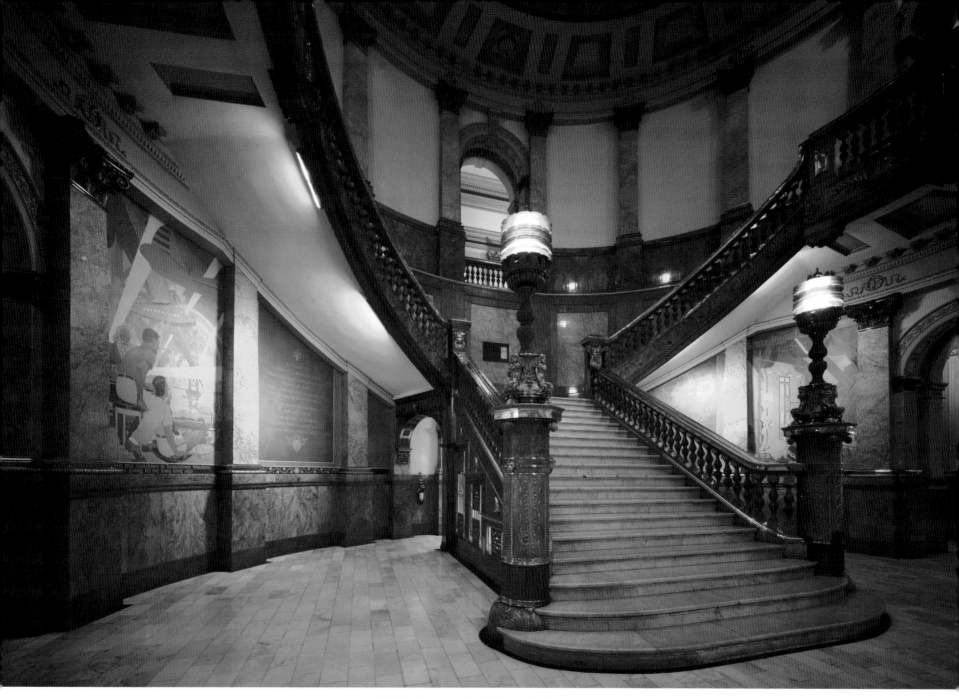

The first-floor rotunda with its grand staircase.

raise funds from private sources to purchase "a beautiful scene of Colorado" to hang behind the speaker's podium. Not only was the painting depicting Long's Peak acquired for this purpose, but four other works, also representing Colorado were purchased using private donations.

Elevator doors also depict scenes from the state's history: bison indicate the remote country before man appeared; tepees symbolize the long reign of Native Americans; covered wagons, the arrival of the first pioneers; pick and shovel, crossed before a miner's pan, indicate the discovery of gold, silver and other metals responsible for much of Colorado's rapid growth; a train represents the arrival of modern transportation; agriculture and livestock,

the two industries that are major sources of Colorado income; and the cog wheel, suggesting the important role industry plays in the state's present and future.

In 1955, the Corinthian-style building was redecorated in bold and authentic Corinthian colors. Building officials contend that the capitol is the only building in the United States of this authentic vivid Corinthian decoration. An ongoing renovation started in the 1990s.

Mining, so often symbolically referred to in the capitol, promoted Colorado's settlement and growth. The state still contains valuable minerals, but those hoping to recover them, along with those "mining white gold," or

The Closing Era became the first gift of art to Colorado's capitol in 1898.

skiing, often find themselves in conflict with the preservation of Colorado's environmental assets, especially its water. Historically, the state's water laws expose complex and contentious social and cultural forces not only within the state but outside its borders.

These forces arise from the fact that Colorado is situated at the center of the Rocky Mountains, with the Rio Grande connecting it to the Southwest, the Colorado River to the range and plateau of the West, and the Platte and the Arkansas rivers to the Great Plains. These water resources played a significant role in the development of the West and continue to do so in this increasingly arid region of the United States, with its rapidly growing population. In an effort to protect its water and its sovereignty, Colorado battles with both its neighbors and the federal government over who controls the water in the rivers running out of the state. Despite its resources, it controls less than one half of its own water and receives almost no water from other states.

In the beginning as the miners migrated to the region they developed the "first in time, first in right" rule to appropriate and make use of water,

a right superior to the rights of later consumers. They rejected the idea that they could not reduce the availability of water to other users downstream. Though surface water cannot be owned, the right to use it is a property right and subject to private ownership. And the rights of all property owners are further subject to regulation by state and federal governments. Today, state legislation protects the public. Federal regulations set further boundaries on the individual's freedoms of use.

In 2003, economic growth, demographic changes and drought in the West forced the upstream states to demand enforcement of a 1920s compact. The resulting agreement, brokered by the federal government, required California, the country's thirstiest state, to gradually reduce its dependence on the Colorado River, allowing the six other Colorado River Basin states (Colorado, Wyoming, New Mexico, Utah, Nevada and Arizona) to receive their share. Because of finite supplies, it was determined that the water reserved for irrigating crops must be increasingly diverted to urban areas. The situation continues to develop, further eclipsing Colorado's water laws and the system of Western water law that has evolved over the last century.

The Colorado State Capitol.

KENTUCKY

KENTUCKY STATE CAPITOL

ORIGIN OF NAME: From the Iroquoian word *Ken-tah-ten*, meaning "land of tomorrow."

CAPITAL: Frankfort

CONSTRUCTED: 1905–1909

ARCHITECT: Frank Mills Andrews

ADMITTED TO THE UNION: June 1, 1792 (fifteenth)

SENATE: 38 members

HOUSE OF REPRESENTATIVES: 100 members

In 1792, the state of Kentucky was carved out of Virginia and became the first state organized from a territory west of the Appalachian Mountains. As a compromise, Frankfort, a small town located between political and business rivals Louisville and Lexington, became the state capital. After the state's first two small capitols burned, Gideon Shryock designed a temple-shaped structure that was built on the square between 1827 and 1830.

Restored to its original appearance, the old state capitol incorporates an Ionic-columned front portico. Inside, a self-supporting circular stone stairway leads from the lobby to the second-floor legislative chambers. Today, the landmark functions as a cultural and educational center.

Years after the old state capitol was constructed, a conflicted Kentucky remained loyal to the Union during the Civil War. After Confederate troops captured Frankfort, the state government briefly moved to the Jefferson County Courthouse in Louisville before returning to the old capitol. In 1904, Kentucky sought and received a million-dollar settlement from the United States government for damages incurred during the Civil War and for services provided during the Spanish-American War. The General Assembly, still meeting in the old capitol, decided to appropriate the settlement, along with an almost equal amount, to construct today's capitol. Since the site on the square was deemed too small, the old capitol was saved from demolition and the new capitol was constructed on the other side of town, overlooking the Kentucky River.

Architect Frank Mills Andrews, an enthusiastic Francophile, designed the capitol in the Beaux Arts style, combining French decorative features and elements of Classical architecture. Built on a rusticated Vermont granite base, the symmetrical three-story building is faced with Indiana limestone. Running through the second and third floors and encircling the building,

building are seventy monolithic Ionic columns. The columns, 27 feet 10 inches tall and weighing about 18 tons each, support a wide entablature.

Over the north entrance, the central portico contains a carved pediment with a female figure symbolizing Kentucky surrounded by figures representing Progress, History, Plenty, Law, Art and Labor. At one end, two Native American figures crouch apprehensively as they watch settlers encroach upon their land.

The old capitol portico.

The Kentucky State Capitol.

From the flat roof of the central section rises the steel-and-concrete dome. Andrews modeled the dome after the one on the Hotel des Invalides in Paris, where Napoleon's tomb lies. This time, Andrews incorporated twenty-four Ionic columns to surround the dome, covered by 1,621 terracotta blocks. They are made up of thirty-five shapes so as to curve on both a horizontal and vertical plane. The average block measures 2 by 2½ feet, is 6 inches thick, and weighs approximately 200 pounds.

The terrace, 212 feet below the lantern topping the dome, surrounds the capitol. At the rear stands the unique Floral Clock, dedicated on May 4, 1961. Measuring 34 feet across, it slopes at an angle of 26 degrees so that it can be easily seen. The minute hand weighs 530 pounds and the hour hand 420 pounds. It can take as many as twenty thousand plants, grown in a state-owned greenhouse located near the capitol, to cover the clock. Sometimes numbers are replaced with letters spelling out the name "Kentucky," or perhaps "Peace on Earth" during the Christmas season.

Inside, the over 300-foot-long nave, or Great Hall, with its stairways, balustrades and banisters, imitates the interior of the old Paris Opera. The walls and staircases incorporate white Georgian marble, while a light-colored Tennessee marble and a dark-green Italian marble cover the floors. Light filters into the space through curved art-glass skylights and high arched windows cut out of the barrel-vaulted ceiling. Thirty-six monolithic Ionic columns of Vermont granite, 26 feet tall and weighing 10 tons apiece, support the dentil cornice.

The granite for the columns arrived in Frankfort on river barges and was transported to the building site on railroad tracks constructed specifically for that purpose. Since at that time the only power-driven machine avail-

The Senate chamber.

able was a steam-powered concrete mixer, men and pulleys lifted the heavy columns into place.

At both ends of the nave, murals adorn the lunettes with painted scenes of early Kentucky history. One depicts explorer Daniel Boone and his men when they first saw the Bluegrass Region in 1769. The other shows the negotiations for the Treaty of Sycamore Shoals, which led to the purchase of the Cherokee land that became Kentucky.

Below the Great Hall, in the 57-foot-diameter rotunda, statues of prominent Kentuckians make up the Bluegrass Hall of Fame. The members include the 14-foot-high figures of Abraham Lincoln and Jefferson Davis. These Kentucky natives, born within a year and 100 miles of each other, served as presidents for the Union and the Confederacy during the Civil War and symbolize the divided loyalties that existed in Kentucky during that time. The statue of Senator Henry Clay is a copy of the one in Statuary Hall at the Capitol in Washington, D.C. Alben W. Barkley, vice-president under Harry S. Truman, and Dr. Ephraim McDowell, a pioneer in surgery and also represented in the Statuary Hall in Washington, D.C., complete the members.

French influence continues in the Governor's Reception Room. Designed to be the official reception room where the governor entertains dignitaries, it is based on Marie Antoinette's drawing room in the Grand Trianon Palace at Versailles and furnished after the period of Louis XIV. Murals, hand-painted in oil to resemble tapestries, depict scenes of gardens and ruins in Versailles. The Galerie des Glaces (Hall of Mirrors), also in the palace, influenced the careful placement of the cut-crystal chandeliers such that they create an image of infinity from the mirrors over the fireplaces, which are copies of fireplaces found in Versailles.

Statues of Kentuckians Henry Clay, Jefferson Davis and Abraham Lincoln in the rotunda.

Other features in the reception room include scagliola pilasters and egg-and-dart trim. The Kentucky state seal is above the fireplace and incorporated into the hardware of the entrance doors. Fine furnishings include original hand-carved French Baroque furniture covered in silk brocade, an Italian marble table, and a rug hand-woven by a group of Austrian nuns.

Art-glass skylights cover the ceilings in the House of Representatives and Senate chambers. Pink scagliola pilasters line the walls in the House, and buff-colored columns are incorporated into the smaller Senate. Both chambers contain pedimented and columned backdrops for the front podium. All the woodwork is hand-carved Honduras mahogany, and both chambers feature original roll-top mahogany desks and upholstered leather chairs. Spectators may watch the proceedings from the recessed balconies. Modern chandeliers replaced the originals in the 1970s, in order to provide stronger light for television.

The last, and most expensive, room to be completed in the capitol houses the Kentucky Supreme Court, the highest court in the state. The Electoral College also meets here to cast votes for the president of the United States. Paneled in solid Honduras mahogany, the chamber features egg-and-dart molding, a coffered ceiling covered in metal hammered to imitate bronze, and brass chandeliers and sconces imported from England. A special beam holds the chandeliers because of their one-ton weight.

In a state where an appeals court blocked an ordinance to ban smoking in public places, smoking is allowed and ashtrays are provided throughout the capitol. Tobacco remains Kentucky's leading cash crop, and the state

The Kentucky House of Representatives.

is second in the nation, after North Carolina, in tobacco production. Coal is also a significant industry. But it is the horse industry that plays a special role in Kentucky.

The fertile soil in the 8,000-square-mile area surrounding Frankfort, called the Bluegrass Region, was formed from limestone. Containing the mineral phosphate, it is considered some of the best soil for crops, pasture, and raising Thoroughbred horses. The horses assimilate some of the mineral from the grass and water, and that apparently helps to build the sturdy bones that make racing champions.

The breeding, selling, raising and racing of horses, along with such related industries as paramutuel betting, tourism, veterinary medicine, photography, auction companies, equipment manufacturers and boarding stables, are a multi-billion-dollar addition to Kentucky's economy. Syndication also began early in the state's history when Henry Clay reportedly bought a prize horse in Virginia and later sold shares to four other Kentuckians in order to spread his risk of loss.

Today, unless a syndicated contract is carefully drafted to ensure that it complies with Kentucky law, federal securities law prevails. When federal law does not supersede, the Kentucky General Assembly traditionally provides sweeping support for the horse industry through its laws and regulations. A racing statute establishes a racing commission and a regulatory agency with rules and administrative procedures. Funded by the state, the agency provides, among other things, the means to detect illegal performance-enhancing drugs in horses and to license racetrack employees.

The Great Hall.

SOUTH DAKOTA

SOUTH DAKOTA STATE CAPITOL

ORIGIN OF NAME: From the Sioux word for "friends" or "allies."

CAPITAL: Pierre

CONSTRUCTED: 1907–1910

ARCHITECT: Charles Emlen Bell

ADMITTED TO THE UNION: November 2, 1889 (fortieth)

SENATE: 35 members

HOUSE OF REPRESENTATIVES: 70 members

After the Dakota Territory was created in 1861, consisting of present-day North Dakota and South Dakota as well as parts of Wyoming and Montana, Yankton became the capital. Seven years later, following the establishment of the territories of Idaho, Montana and Wyoming, the Dakota Territory was reduced to the approximate area of today's North Dakota and South Dakota. By 1874, there was a gold rush into the Black Hills, an area located in the southwest of the territory that was part of the Great Sioux Reservation. When the federal government's policy of ejecting miners as trespassers on Native American land proved increasingly futile, the Sioux and some Cheyenne fought for the control and protection of their land. After the Battle of Little Bighorn (1876), where the Sioux killed Lieutenant Colonel George Armstrong Custer and over 250 United States soldiers, the tribes were subdued, and an uneasy peace followed as the Black Hills were subsequently opened to miners and others.

In the meantime, railroad construction through the area brought even more settlers to the Dakotas. In 1883 the capital was relocated from Yankton to Bismarck, in the northern part of the territory. Those living south of the 46th parallel were so unhappy that they petitioned Congress to divide the territory. This led to two separate states and initiated a fight among towns in South Dakota over which would become its seat of government.

In 1904, in the last of three statewide elections to select a capital site, Pierre finally prevailed. The 1905 legislature sought to eliminate further attacks on Pierre's selection by proposing construction of a permanent capitol there using proceeds from the sale of public lands under the auspices of the South Dakota State Capitol Committee.

The first official act of the committee was to travel to Helena to inspect Montana's state capitol. The commission liked the Montana Capitol so much it decided to simulate it in Pierre. In order to cut costs, architect Charles Emlen Bell agreed to reuse his Montana blueprints for the South Dakota capitol, while adapting them to comply with its requirements.

The result is a Neoclassical capitol in the American Renaissance style. The raised foundation, steps and window trim consist of native granite and the first level of painted rusticated sandstone, while smooth Indiana limestone covers the upper-level walls. Originally, the building measured 124 feet wide, 292 feet long, and 161 feet high from the ground to the lantern. An annex in keeping with the style of the original building was added to the rear in 1932.

A central portico located over the arched main entrance incorporates Corinthian columns that support an entablature with "South Dakota" engraved upon its frieze. Slightly protruding end sections are decorated with pilasters, quoins and pediments similar to the central section. Featured above the ground-floor end entrances are Ionic columns, arched windows and a plain pediment. The walls of the second and third levels are broken by rectangular windows and topped by a parapet. A one-story square platform with

The Governor's Reception Room.

The second-floor rotunda of the South Dakota State Capitol.

The House of Representatives chamber.

a balustraded parapet projects above the central portico and is topped by a pediment. The dome and its lantern rise from the platform and incorporate niche-like protruding pendentives and Corinthian columns.

The original cast-iron dome had a three-inch-thick concrete shell covered with copper, but the copper roofing leaked and water seeped through it to the concrete. Following years of freezing and thawing, large chunks of concrete broke off and fell to the floor below. In the 1960s, the copper roof was re-moved, steel replaced the concrete, and a new roof replaced the old one. Also added was a new copper lantern topped with an orb finial.

The main entrance leads into the second-floor rotunda. It is 96 feet from the glass prisms set in the center of the marble terrazzo floor to the inside of the stained-glass dome. Sixty-six Italian workmen hand-laid the mosaic floor, a work of art. In order to sign it, each workman placed a blue stone somewhere in the floor, but over the years, only fifty-five blue signature stones have been found.

In the 1930s, $30,000 furnished by state and $60,000 in WPA money from the federal government financed the repair of cracks in the walls and terrazzo tile floors caused by settling. Original concrete pilings 40 feet below the surface of ground were replaced by 24 additional feet of poured concrete under the foundation. This stabilized the building, and it has not moved since. This time, tile workmen left stones in the floor in the shape of hearts as their signatures, though one broke his heart in half before cementing it into the floor after reportedly receiving a "Dear John" letter.

While scagliola columns with gilded capitals are incorporated throughout the rotunda, the grand stairway and the wainscoting in the corridors surrounding the rotunda on the second and third floors consist of veined marble. Above, the pendentives in each corner of the inner dome contain circular murals portraying Greek gods and goddesses such as Venus, Ceres, Minerva and Zeus, which are also meant to symbolize such South Dakotan assets as Family, Agriculture, Mining and Livestock. Below the murals are the painted seals of France, Spain, South Dakota and the United States, all of whom have governed what is now South Dakota. Their flags, and flags such as those of the United Sioux Tribes, the 50th Anniversary of Mount Rushmore flag and a Native American Warrior Eagle Staff flag, fly from niches on the second level. Below the flags, another series of niches contain centennial sculptures representing Wisdom, Vision, Courage and Integrity.

Under a leaded stained-glass barrel-vault ceiling, the grand staircase leads to the third or legislative floor. The staircase integrates marble balustrades, where the artisan left his signature by inverting the third baluster from the top. A mural entitled *The Advent of Commerce*, showing a Native American and an explorer making a trade, occupies the end wall space of the barrel vault.

The Senate chamber.

Located on the east side of this floor, the House of Representatives features decorative plaster, oak wainscoting and original oak roll-top desks containing electronic voting systems. Also included are the original hand-carved oak rostrum, 1910 replica carpeting, restored stenciling, a gilded eagle and a leaded stained-glass ceiling ornamented with coved panels. Modesty curtains cover the railings of the recessed visitor galleries. The chandeliers date from 1910 but are not original to the room. They were removed from the old federal courthouse and installed in the House.

Over the speaker's bench is the mural *The Peace that Passes Understanding*, measuring 12 by 20 feet. It depicts the first recorded act of religious worship in South Dakota, in 1823. Although it was not originally illuminated, one of the representatives could not see it clearly, so he personally paid for the indirect lighting. On one side of the House is a private lobby for members and their staff, while on the other is a lobby for lobbyists.

To the west, the restored Senate contains scagliola columns with gilded capitals, Vermont marble wainscoting, cherry-wood roll-top desks, the original mahogany podium, reproduction light fixtures, decorative ceiling stenciling and Tiffany-style stained glass. The coved ceiling panels are ornamented with stencil decorations, except for the large panel over the president's desk containing a mural entitled *The Louisiana Purchase*. South Dakota was carved from the Louisiana Purchase. The painting depicts a Native American woman, representing Louisiana, with another woman, America, placing the United States flag over Louisiana after having dropped the garment of France. France, by her side, holds a copy of the treaty by which the purchase was ratified. During the 1970s, a senator introduced a bill to remove or cover the mural because he objected to the United States

The South Dakota State Capitol.

flag touching the ground and covering the woman. He maintained that the flag should only drape the coffins of war dead. The mural survives in its original form and is a reminder of the period when it was painted.

In 1978, the Governor's Reception Room was the first room in the capitol restored to its original 1910 condition. Today, it features original mahogany furniture and woodwork, decorations such as the painted deep soffit ceiling, along with pilasters and moldings with gilded relief ornamentation. The reproduction carpet has the same pattern as the carpet covering the Senate floor.

At the west end of the room is a nine-foot-square mural entitled *The Spirit of the West*, painted by Edwin Blashfield. In the work, Blashfield represents South Dakota as a woman, with a figure of Hope floating above her and

pointing forward. Native Americans are shown clinging to the clothes of South Dakota while being shoved to the ground by men representing the United States Army as white settlement advances into the Dakotas by prairie schooner, seen in the background.

Because it is considered politically incorrect, the work is now hidden behind a cover, though the cover can easily be removed.

The working South Dakota Supreme Court chamber was also restored in 1978. Following the discovery of the border decorations and designs under many coats of paint, they were restored, and today the room features hand-drawn wall stencils, brass light fixtures, velvet draperies, original furniture and carved mahogany woodwork. Over the bench the mural *The Mercy of the Law* shows an angel as goddess of justice.

The Advent of Commerce fills the end of the stained-glass barrel-vaulted ceiling.

UTAH

Utah State Capitol

Origin of Name: From the Ute tribe, meaning "people of the mountains."

Capital: Salt Lake City

Constructed: 1912–1915

Architect: Richard Kletting

Admitted to the Union: January 4, 1896 (forty-fifth)

Senate: 29 members

House of Representatives: 75 members

The area encompassing what is now Utah was under the control of Mexico when it was chosen in 1847 by members of the Church of Jesus Christ of Latter-Day Saints (LDS), more commonly known as Mormons, as a refuge from persecution. Here, the Mormons founded a theocratic society separate from the rest of the United States, with small self-sufficient agricultural communities. Their isolation was short-lived, however, because in 1848 Utah became part of the United States under the Treaty of Guadalupe Hidalgo at the end of the Mexican War. The completion of the transcontinental railroad in 1869 brought social diversification, with immigrants passing through Utah on their way to the gold-rush camps in California and to work in Utah's silver, copper and coal mines.

Fillmore was selected as Utah's territorial capital in 1851 by a commission appointed by Brigham Young, who served simultaneously as the governor of the Utah Territory and the head of LDS. Fillmore was centrally located, and Young planned to settle Mormons throughout the territory. In 1852, construction started on a red sandstone building using a $20,000 appropriation by the federal government. Just one wing was completed, and lawmakers only met there in 1855 before Young persuaded the legislature to move the territorial capital from Fillmore to the more rapidly growing Salt Lake City the following year.

Within Salt Lake City the home of the territorial government changed many times, to its county courthouse, the city hall, and the present Romanesque City and County Building. One of the reasons a capitol was not immediately constructed in Salt Lake City was that Congress considered the funds appropriated for the first one to have been a waste of money and declined to appropriate more for another building. In addition, the people of Utah elected Mormon officials and lawmakers, while the territorial officials, appointed from Washington, D.C., were generally non-Mormon, resulting in tension and conflict.

In 1888, anxious to reclaim the use of the City and County Building, local officials donated land on a hill overlooking Salt Lake City to the state for construction of its capitol. In 1909, the Utah state legislature created a seven-man commission to select its design. On March 1, 1911, the state received a welcome windfall — payment of an inheritance tax totaling $798,546 to settle the estate of the onetime president of the Union Pacific Railroad, Edward H. Harriman. Lawmakers quickly responded by approving a similar amount, and Utah's capitol was finally a reality.

Throughout the capitol building, the decor reflects the continued intertwining of government and religion in Utah. This is immediately apparent upon entering the building, where a larger-than-life statue of Brigham Young can be viewed directly across the rotunda. Other references to religion in the state government building include artwork recalling Utah's religious past and a recurring beehive motif.

The beehive symbolizes the social order that the Mormon pioneers hoped to establish when they fled westward. It offers protection, shelter and sustenance to those who work for the benefit of the group. Upon arriving in what is now Utah and most of Nevada, the Mormons called their new home Deseret, from a word in the *Book of Mormon* that means "land of the honey-

The beehive symbol is seen throughout the building.

The Utah State Capitol.

bee." The beehive became the emblem for the provisional state of Deseret in 1848 and was kept, along with the word "Industry," on the seal and flag when Utah became a state. In 1959, the beehive and the motto "Industry" became official Utah symbols.

Bronze beehives also flank the flagpoles before the steps leading to the capitol's main entrance. The three double-entrance doors are part of the central portico, which includes an unadorned pediment and eight Corinthian columns. In addition, fifty-two columns and the exterior walls, above a rusticated base, consist of unpolished gray granite quarried from nearby Little Cottonwood Canyon. Stone was also taken from there to construct the Salt Lake City Latter-Day Saints Temple in downtown Salt Lake City. A copper dome, reflecting Utah's role as the second leading producer of copper in the United States, rises above the balustraded roof. The dome features a colonnade of twenty-four Corinthian columns supporting another balustrade below a second surround of windows. It is crowned by a cupola topped with a light.

Although the capitol commission sought to enlist Utah labor and materials in the building's construction whenever possible, the cost of Georgia marble proved such a savings that it was substituted in the interior's main floor. Twenty-four monolithic Ionic columns, each weighing 25,000 pounds, line the marble halls. At two columns per railroad flat car, it took forty-six carloads to ship the marble from Georgia to Utah.

Coffered arches support the interior dome, rising 165 feet to its ceiling. There, painted seagulls commemorate the legend of the birds saving the Mormons from starving by eating the crickets that were threatening their crops. While the gulls appear about their natural size from the floor, they actually measure about six feet wide.

Statues of Brigham Young (front) and Philo T. Farnsworth.

Suspended from the dome is a giant brass chandelier decorated with an eagle. The fixture weighs 6,000 pounds, and its steel chain is 95 feet long.

As construction neared completion, few funds remained despite plans calling for "extensive pieces of art work." The only artworks initially commissioned were paintings in the House chamber, the Senate, the State Reception Room, the lunettes, and an oversized portrait of the capitol commissioners. Later, 1930s depression era murals, painted on canvas and attached to the walls, were added to encircle the base of the dome. They depict historical scenes: the Dominguez-Escalante Expedition of 1776, which undertook the first documentation of the area; John C. Fremont, who mapped the West for the federal government and visited the Great Salt Lake in 1843; Peter Skene Ogden, a member of the Hudson's Bay Company, namesake of one of Utah's largest cities and representative of Utah's profitable fur trade from 1820 to 1850; and Brigham Young and Mormon pioneers entering the Salt Lake valley in 1847. Above, smaller paintings illustrate the raising of a banner on Ensign Peak, on July 26, 1847; a social gathering; the miracle of the gulls; completion of the transcontinental railroad; irrigation in the West; peace with the Native Americans; the Pony Express and stagecoach era; and the inauguration of mining.

On the walls, Georgian marble sections, cut and applied book-end style, contain fanciful illustrations of flowers, faces and animals. In a less prominent position, behind Young's statue, stands one of scientist Philo T. Farnsworth, inventor of television. Copies of both statues represent Utah in the United States Capitol in Washington, D.C.

The offices of the governor and lieutenant governor are also located on the main floor behind a glass partition that that features a beehive and the

House of Representatives chamber.

sego lily, Utah's state flower. Close by is the State Reception Room, or Gold Room, where the governor entertains visiting dignitaries. Utah marble, accented with gold, lines the walls. Other decorative features include imported mirrors and chandeliers, a ceiling painting entitled *Children at Play*, and a carpet with a beehive in its design.

From the main floor, two grand marble stairways, illuminated by barrel-vaulted skylights, lead to the wings on the third floor. They incorporate Georgian marble into their railings, balusters and newel posts, which are topped

with round brass and frosted lamps with eagle finials. Above, lunette paintings show Young and other pioneers arriving in the valley, and one year later, after the crops had been planted and irrigated. The east staircase leads to the Utah Supreme Court chamber. The court held sessions here from 1916 to 1998 before moving to a new facility south of downtown Salt Lake City.

The architect placed the House of Representatives chamber opposite the courtroom, on the other side of the rotunda. Ceiling panels of art glass provide partial light to the chamber. In one of the curved panels, divided by gilded strips and lion's heads, a painting shows Brigham Young examining a block of native granite that became a part of the Mormon Temple. Green and rose colors, accented with gold, predominate and blend with local brown-colored square marble columns. A brass railing with beehives incorporated into its design protects the public gallery. Light sconces and cherubs, or putti, flank the gilded clock above the speaker's desk. The House seal also incorporates the beehive. Other features include individual desks, electronic voting and the sego lily above the side entrance doors.

The Senate is smaller than the House and located on the north side of the building, onyx from central Utah lining its walls. Putti flank the clock in the round pediment of the marble arch, supported by marble pilasters on each side of the wooden backdrop for the Senate's presiding officer. Above the front desk hangs the Senate seal, also incorporating a beehive. A five-part mural, separated by marble pilasters, depicts Utah Lake, 40 miles south of Salt Lake City, near Provo. Other features include the original light standards, individual roll-top desks and marble consoles supporting the slightly projecting public galleries. Unlike many state Senates, Utah's votes electronically.

As seen throughout the capitol, Utah's history is dominated by the story of the Mormon settlers. They came to Utah to establish their vision of a perfect society on earth, with no division between between religious and secular life. From the beginning, the federal government tried to force them to conform to its standards of separation of church and state and to give up some of their religious beliefs and practices, especially polygamy. Their reluctance to renounce this practice is considered the primary reason for the state's late entry into the Union. As a condition of statehood, the federal government required a "no polygamy" provision in its constitution. It is the only state constitution to have one.

Detailing along the base of the barrel-vault.

Following statehood and a surge of economic development, Utah emerged into the mainstream of life in the United States. Yet there remains a commingling of government and religion. In 2000, the Utah state legislature became the only state in the United States to specifically create an office to help communities determine standards for controlling obscenity and pornography without violating the 1st Amendment of the U.S. Constitution. Additionally, alcohol consumption is discouraged by church leaders. This has resulted in the establishment of state-owned liquor stores for greater control, and laws that prohibit serving alcoholic beverages in restaurants. Meanwhile, as lawmakers increasingly pass laws to laws to encourage tourism, adherence to the ban on liquor is often an illusion, with customers, especially tourists, sometimes paying a small amount to "join" a restaurant club in order to be served.

In spite of Utah's Mormon background, its legislature played a pivotal role in repealing Prohibition. The ban on alcohol started in January 1920 with the passage of the 18th Amendment to the United States Constitution, which prohibited the sale of intoxicating alcoholic beverages throughout the country. Following nationwide practices, Utah lawmakers passed a law to enforce the ban. But from the beginning enforcement was a delusion. Not only were a number of distilleries uncovered, but the illegality of liquor and the determination of drinkers to obtain it by any means led to unprecedented corruption, bootlegging and racketeering.

Finally, the Depression brought a clamor for the repeal of Prohibition, with many believing it might lead to an economic recovery, along with more respect for law and order. After Congress adopted the 21st Amendment in 1933, abolishing Prohibition, the amendment required ratification by thirty-six states to become effective. In 1935, Utah's legislature became the thirty-sixth.

Georgia marble is used throughout the building.

ARKANSAS

ARKANSAS STATE CAPITOL

ORIGIN OF NAME: The Algonkian name for the Quapaw people, meaning "south wind."

CAPITAL: Little Rock

CONSTRUCTED: 1899–1915

ARCHITECTS: George R. Mann and Cass Gilbert

ADMITTED TO THE UNION: June 15, 1836 (twenty-fifth)

SENATE: 35 members

HOUSE OF REPRESENTATIVES: 100 members

The old Arkansas State House, the oldest surviving state capitol built in the area once covered by the Louisiana Purchase, dates from 1840. The new state legislature met and inaugurated its first governor in the building before its completion, in 1836. Based on a design by Gideon Shryock, the Greek Revival building consists of three blocks that were originally linked together by connecting colonnades. The center section, incorporating two pedimented porticoes supported by four fluted Doric columns, contained the state house. The courthouse and county building made up the flanking sections.

Today, inside the restored building, a cross corridor provides access to the porticoes and the now-enclosed colonnades. Two semicircular staircases rise to the second-floor legislative chambers. The Senate faces the Arkansas River, considered the front of the building, while the House overlooks downtown Little Rock.

After it became obvious that the old state house was too small for the growing state government and was rapidly deteriorating, lawmakers formed a state capitol commission in 1899 for the purpose of constructing a new one. The first chairman, George W. Donagney, untiringly supported completion of its construction. The commission selected plans submitted by architect George R. Mann, obtained a $1-million appropriation, and decided to build the new seat of state government on the slightly elevated site of the state penitentiary. The commission was the first of four to oversee construction. They worked alongside seven governors, two contractors and two architects.

From the beginning there was a disagreement as to whether Arkansas needed a new capitol and regarding problems from the initial limitation placed on construction costs. This led to political infighting, labor disputes, bribery, delay, scandals, lawsuits and trials. Even the preliminary survey for the foundation became controversial. Since the site was on the penitentiary

grounds, and prison laborers were assigned to construct the building, it was surrounded by a 20-foot-high wall. The survey was supposedly completed on a true east-west line, though Little Rock is not laid out on an east-west axis, but aligned with the Arkansas River. When the wall was later removed, the nearly complete capitol appeared slightly out of line with Capitol Avenue.

Another problem developed from the statutory requirement that Arkansas materials be incorporated into the capitol as much as practicable. Contrary to Donagney's preference, but in order to comply with the legislature's directive, white Arkansas limestone from Batesville, "Arkansas marble," was chosen for the exterior finish. This stone was used only to completion of the first floor. It was so hard that it wore out the equipment, making it too

Marble staircase leading to the Senate chamber.

The bronze front entrance doors to the Arkansas State Capitol.

expensive to quarry. In addition, the providers, eager to be compensated in a timely manner, tended to supply other projects before the reportedly slow-paying capitol commission. Indiana limestone was substituted for the native stone, with the result that the exterior of the capitol consists of two slightly different shades of stone.

By 1906, the walls to the second and third floors were completed, but the legislature refused to appropriate more money. The following year, Donagney ran on a platform promising to complete the capitol and was elected governor. Donagney began his term by instigating the dismissal of Mann on the grounds that he changed the architectural plan by eliminating eight columns on the west elevation and then ordered removal of marble from the interior walls without obtaining the commission's approval.

In 1911, Donagney won a second term and tried to finish the building. Although the legislature held its first meeting there, it refused to appropriate more funds until 1913, after Donagney's unsuccessful bid for a third term.

Completed two years later, the solidly built Neoclassical capitol's iron framework is covered with concrete, then stone. The lower floor is of rusticated Arkansas marble. The wings contain subsidiary domes indicating the location of the interior legislative chambers. To the east, Ionic columns, 3½ feet in diameter and 32 feet high, extend through the first and second stories. Four columns support a plain pediment placed above the entablature, which is pierced with round windows between mini pilasters above the entrance. Flanking sections contain four more columns. At the end of the wings, plain pediments jut above the balustraded roof, supported by two engaged Ionic columns and two plain pilasters.

The dome rises 230 feet above the ground from a square platform on the

Beneath the marble staircase.

roof, cornered by four low towers. Twenty-four detached Ionic columns surround the dome in front of tall, narrow openings covered with decorative iron and support a plain entablature with a balustrade above. The dome is marble with a columned lantern topped with a twenty-four-carat gold-leaf roof and finial.

Below the dome, the main entrance doors are solid bronze, 10 feet tall and 4 inches thick. They were purchased in 1908 from Tiffany's of New York. Especially sensitive to fingerprints, the doors are hand-polished every two weeks and were recently roped off. They now open only on ceremonial occasions such as the inauguration of a governor.

Inside in the rotunda hangs a Mitchell-Vance brass chandelier weighing two tons and containing sixty-four lightbulbs. Measuring 12 feet across and 14 feet high, it is the largest of three fixtures purchased when the capitol was constructed. Fluted Ionic columns and a stone balustrade surround the well. Above, a balcony railing encircles a walkway inside the marble dome.

Staircases, measuring ten feet wide and containing seventy-three steps lead from the rotunda's first floor to the third floor. Though working with a limited budget, Mann specified that the staircases be constructed of electroplated bronze over cast-iron. After Governor Donaghey instigated the firing of Mann, faulty fireproofing and weak floor construction led to a complete gutting of the interior. A new commission appointed Cass Gilbert in his place. Gilbert secured additional funding from the legislature and redesigned Mann's floors, leaving them in the locations Mann had designated, but substituting a heavier marble from Alabama. He also added Vermont marble to the walls and wainscoting.

Adding to the overall pristine marble appearance are the third-floor Ionic

Senate chamber with fabric swags hanging from the dome's skylight.

columns, which are made from Colorado marble. Lunette murals at end of the barrel-vault skylights over the grand staircases feature themes of Justice, War, Education and Religion..

The legislative chambers, located on opposite ends of the third floor, are circular in shape and contain stained-glass skylights and smaller-scale replicas of the rotunda chandelier. After the first session, the lawmakers asked Gilbert to fix the chambers' poor acoustics. He resolved the matter by draping curtains from the ceilings, not only for better acoustics but for added color. The Senate features a marble rostrum, Vermont marble walls, and studded leather doors.

The larger House is the only room in the capitol to feature not marble but scagliola columns with Corinthian capitals. Old photographs show the lawmakers sitting at individual tables. Today, ninety-nine Representatives sit at late 1960s laminate desks. The one hundredth member serves as speaker of the House. Elected by the other members for a two-year term, the speaker presides over legislative sessions from the large desk in front of the room. Next to the speaker sits the parliamentarian, a state employee who assists the speaker.

The Governor's Conference Room, situated next to the governor's private office, was restored to its 1915 appearance in 2000. The governor uses this

The House of Representatives chamber with its scagliola columns.

room to meet with staff, the press and members of the public. Its oak paneling and marble fireplaces are original, while the stenciling on the ceiling dates from a late 1940s restoration. When Governor Donaghey left office, he donated the walnut table in the center of the room to the state. The table was carved from a tree his father planted when he was a boy. The fireplace ornamentation commemorates Native Americans and early French explorers in Arkansas. A portrait of Donaghey, the first governor to serve in the capitol, hangs above the west fireplace, and a painting of the most recent past governor hangs above the east fireplace. Portraits of previous governors, including Bill Clinton, appear on the walls throughout the building.

The old Arkansas Supreme Court chamber is where the court convened until 1958, when it relocated to the Justice Building, on the southwest corner of the capitol complex. Now used as a meeting room, it was restored in 2001 to its early appearance. Although microphones, tables and carpet were added, many original details remain, such as the brass handrails and foot rails, the mahogany railing, the light fixtures and the ceiling fans. The green tiles on the ceiling illustrate symbols of Justice. The diamonds represent Arkansas's active diamond mine, the only one in the nation. Portraits on the walls portray territorial judges and supreme court justices.

The design of the dome on the Arkansas State Capitol is attributed to George Mann, but only indirectly. While most of the exterior is intact as Mann planned, the dome is not the one he included in his original design. Prior to beginning work in Arkansas, Mann submitted a design for the proposed Mississippi State Capitol in Jackson. Although Mississippi did not choose his design, the Mississippi Capitol Commission and Theodore Link, the selected architect, asked Mann's permission to build a dome similar to the one in his submission. Mann agreed. Subsequently, in 1909, after Cass Gilbert replaced Mann as architect of the Arkansas State Capitol, Governor George W. Donaghey visited Jackson. He was so impressed by the dome of the Mississippi Capitol that upon his return he asked Gilbert to duplicate it for the Arkansas Capitol. Reportedly and ironically, only after the dome was completed did Donaghey realize that he had endorsed the design of the architect he earlier insisted the legislature dismiss.

The Arkansas State Capitol.

WYOMING

WYOMING STATE CAPITOL

ORIGIN OF NAME: A Delaware Native word meaning "at the great plains."

CAPITAL: Cheyenne

CONSTRUCTED: 1886–1917

ARCHITECTS: David W. Gibbs

ADMITTED TO THE UNION: July 10, 1890 (forty-fourth)

SENATE: 30 members

HOUSE OF REPRESENTATIVES: 60 members

Archaeologists believe Native American tribes roamed the grassy plains of the Wyoming area more than ten thousand years ago. It wasn't until the nineteenth century that tribes such as the Shoshone, Cheyenne, Arapaho, Sioux, Blackfoot and Crow were forced to share their land with trappers, the military and settlers. Since the tribes sometimes reacted violently to the threat of European encroachment, forts were established to protect settlers and travelers, including those passing through on the Overland and Bozeman trails during the gold rush to California and, after 1849, to Montana. During this period, what is now Wyoming was part of the Oregon Territory (1848), Utah Territory (1850), Washington Territory (1853), Dakota Territory (1861), Idaho Territory (1863), Montana Territory (1864), and then the Dakota Territory again (1864).

The decision to build the Union Pacific Railroad through what is now the southern part of the state during the construction of the first transcontinental railroad affected Wyoming's future settlement. Coincidently, in 1867, gold deposits discovered at South Pass, on the historic route through the Rockies, brought prospectors to the area. Coal deposits also found along the railroad line led to the construction of mines to fuel the trains. Laborers, merchants, speculators, miners and adventurers soon filled the makeshift towns that sprang up along the tracks.

Grenville M. Dodge, chief engineer of the Union Pacific, selected a site that became the town of Cheyenne for the construction of machine shops and roundhouses. Cheyenne grew quickly into a frontier town with gambling houses, variety theaters, saloons and dance halls. Because of its growth, Cheyenne was named the seat of the territorial government after the Wyoming Territory was created on July 25, 1868.

In 1886, the Territorial Legislative Assembly authorized construction of the capitol at a cost not to exceed $150,000. It chose David W. Gibbs from Toledo, Ohio, to be the architect, and Adam Feick & Brothers, also from Ohio, as contractor. Gibbs designed Wyoming's only capitol in the Renaissance Revival style. The original building was similar in size and style to a courthouse (Gibbs had designed courthouses in Ohio), though Gibbs lifted the symbolic dome on an octagonal drum.

Three months prior to statehood, small wings, also designed by Gibbs, were added. Final wings designed by an unknown local architect, though consistent with Gibbs's earlier plans and containing the present House and Senate chambers, were completed in late 1917. The capitol's cost, including the additions, totaled $390,000.

The building's three-story exterior consists of sandstone from the quarries of Fort Collins, Colorado, and Rawlins, Wyoming. The foundation was to be made up of clear sand and concrete gravel, broken into the

Painted cast-iron column with stucco capital.

Under the Wyoming State Capitol dome.

size of hens' eggs. The capitol faces south and features a projected center portico covering the main entrance, which incorporates two groups of four Corinthian columns topped with a cornice. Above the cornice is an arch covered by a triangular pediment. Slight projections in the wings incorporate a modification of the portico, with Corinthian columns, cornice and pediment fronting the interior legislative chambers. Stone balustrades protect the portico, unite the end wing columns, and surround the double-columned drum below the dome. Less imposing entrances are located on the north and west ends of the building. The flat roof features a 24-carat gold-leaf-covered dome measuring 146 feet high with a 50-foot-diameter base.

Inside, the rotunda measures 30 feet in diameter and rises 54 feet from the floor to the stained-glass dome. The dome is mounted upon an arched ceiling decorated with painted swags and the state seal. Directly below and opposite the main entrance stands a statue of Chief Washakie, a warrior and chief of the Shoshone tribe who granted a right-of-way through Shoshone land in western Wyoming to the Union Pacific Railroad, aiding the completion of the transcontinental rail line. Off the rotunda, in the west hallway, stands a large preserved bison, an animal once common to Wyoming.

The hallway is 18 feet wide and extends the length of the wings. Where the hallways join in the rotunda, staircases ascend to the second-story hallways, and from the landing of the second story, box stairwells lead to the third floor. Throughout the building, cherry, oak and butternut are incorporated into the woodwork. Cherry, imported from Sandusky, Ohio, at the time of the original construction, predominates. The western half of the west wing, on both the second and third

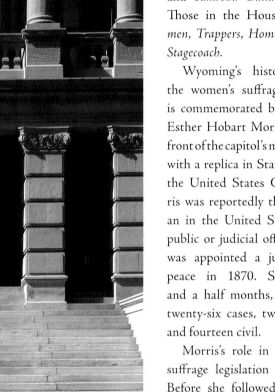

Statue of Esther Hobart Morris in front of the Wyoming State Capitol.

floors, is occupied by the Senate chamber, gallery, lobbies and anterooms. To the east, the House of Representatives wing is similarly designed. Both chambers have oak trim, Corinthian columns and stained-glass skylights decorated with the Great Seal of the State of Wyoming.

Four large murals dating from 1917 and reflecting Wyoming's history are found in each chamber. The Senate murals are entitled *Indian Chief Cheyenne*, *Frontier Cavalry Officer*, *Pony Express Rider*, and *Railroad Builders/Surveyors*. Those in the House are *Cattlemen*, *Trappers*, *Homesteaders*, and *Stagecoach*.

Wyoming's historic role in the women's suffrage movement is commemorated by a statue of Esther Hobart Morris located in front of the capitol's main entrance, with a replica in Statuary Hall in the United States Capitol. Morris was reportedly the first woman in the United States to hold public or judicial office when she was appointed a justice of the peace in 1870. Serving eight and a half months, she handled twenty-six cases, twelve criminal and fourteen civil.

Morris's role in affecting the suffrage legislation is less clear. Before she followed her saloon-keeping husband to Wyoming in 1869, she purportedly attended a Susan B. Anthony lecture in Illinois. Once settled in South Pass, she is said to have buttonholed state Senator William Bright at a tea party and persuaded him to sponsor a suffrage bill. No record of the conversation exists, but Bright, married to a suffragette, introduced the Women's Suffrage Bill, which passed the first legislature of the territory in 1869.

Later, the legislature required that women be allowed to vote as a condition for obtaining statehood, marking the first time in United States history that women were permanently granted suffrage. Not until 1920 and the

The House of Representatives chamber.

ratification of the 19th Amendment to the U. S. Constitution did the rest of the nation provide every woman with the right to vote. The Wyoming legislature passed other ground-breaking laws, including providing free, tax-supported compulsory education for children, and the granting to women of property rights, the right to hold office, and the right to receive wages equal to those of men, provided that the job and qualifications were the same.

There is no obvious rational for Wyoming's support of women's suffrage, though the general consensus is that women were enfranchised in order to meet the population requirement to become first a territory and then a state. Wyoming was and continues to be one of the most sparsely populated states. Other reasons may have been that the legislators wanted to be the first to do the inevitable because they knew other western territorial legislatures were

The Wyoming State Capitol.

considering suffrage reform, or that they hoped that the women's rights laws would attract more female settlers to the territory, or that the lawmakers respected women because they often performed the same tasks as men on the frontier, or that some believed women were as qualified to vote as newly enfranchised former slaves.

Soon after the territorial government was organized, the census taken in the summer of 1869 showed a population of 8,104, including women and transient Union Pacific construction crews. This met the five-thousand-persons territorial population requirement. The new territory's population was already down by half from the preceding year, when railroad-building was at its peak.

Nearly twenty years after granting women the right to vote, the territorial legislature asked Congress to pass legislation enabling it to draw up a constitution and apply for statehood. On November 5, 1889, Wyoming voters approved a constitution at a special election. Although there was some opposition in Congress to Wyoming's admission as a state (its population was still too small and there was the women's suffrage provision), on July 10, 1890, it was granted statehood.

Entrance lobby with statue honoring Chief Washakie.

WISCONSIN

WISCONSIN STATE CAPITOL

ORIGIN OF NAME: From the Native American word *Ouisconsin*,
 meaning "grassy place" or "gathering of waters."

CAPITAL: Madison

CONSTRUCTED: 1906–1917

ARCHITECT: George B. Post

ADMITTED TO THE UNION: May 29, 1848 (thirtieth)

SENATE: 33 members

HOUSE OF REPRESENTATIVES: 99 members

President Andrew Jackson signed the bill creating the Wisconsin Territory in 1836. At that time, it included all of the present state of Wisconsin, plus Iowa, Minnesota, parts of the two Dakotas, and "disputed" territory in northern Illinois. Most of the population clustered in the lead-mining region of southwestern Wisconsin, where Belmont was chosen the territorial capital. The legislature met there for one session, from October 25 to December 9, 1836, in a simple white clapboard building. Its timber, pre-cut in Pittsburgh, was transported by boat down the Ohio River to the Mississippi River, north to Galena, then hauled by wagon to Belmont.

Meanwhile, at least twenty other communities competed to be named the permanent capital. A former federal circuit judge and land speculator, James Duane Doty, purchased property on the isthmus between Lake Mendota and Lake Monona, hoping to cash in on the probable escalating land values if the territorial capitol was erected there. After Doty became territorial governor, it was not long before construction of the first capitol began on his land, in what became the city of Madison.

Because of the demands of the growing state government, a second Madison capitol was completed in 1869, serving until it was partially destroyed by fire in 1904. The lawmakers continued to meet in a section of the burned building while a competition was held to select a plan for the present capitol. In 1906, the building commission chose the design submitted by New Yorker George B. Post, architect of the New York Stock Exchange and building supervisor for the Georgia State Capitol.

Post's capitol, built in the Renaissance style, took eleven years to complete, starting with the west wing and continuing wing by wing. Because these four wings are oriented on the four cardinal compass points, radiating from the center area below the dome, there is no obvious front. At the end of each wing, a portico composed of Corinthian columns supports a pediment.

The tympanums of the pediments contain bas-reliefs reflecting the branch of government housed in the wing: in the Assembly wing, *The Unveiling of the Resources of the State*; in the Senate wing, *The Virtues and Traits of Character*; in the Supreme Court wing, *Liberty Supported by the Law*; and in the North Hearing Room wing, *Learning of the World*.

The outer dome consists of white Vermont granite blocks supported by steel. Topping it, about 285 feet from the ground, is a hollow bronze statue, *Wisconsin*, covered in 23-carat gold. Designed by Daniel Chester French, it represents the state motto, "Forward," and points southeast toward Washington, D.C. The female figure holds a globe with an eagle, symbolizing the spread of democracy to the world. Peeking out from her cap is the state animal, a badger.

While the style of the exterior is Classical, the building was modern from

Badgers are found in details throughout the capitol.

The Wisconsin State Capitol.

Interior view of the dome.

the beginning. Before studying architecture, Post received a degree in civil engineering, and he planned his projects to be technologically up to date. As a result, the capitol featured elevators, telephones, a telegraph, plumbing, a pneumatic clock system, and its own heat and power plant. In 1917, the Assembly chamber purportedly incorporated the first electric voting machine used by a legislative body.

The central rotunda dominates the interior. At its apex is a 34-foot-diameter mural called *Resources of Wisconsin*. The artist, Edwin H. Blashfield, described it as "a symbolization of Wisconsin enthroned upon clouds and wrapped in the folds of the American flag. She holds the escutcheon of the state with the coat of arms of Wisconsin upon it, and in her right hand a scepter of wheat. Around and below her are female figures, holding up specimens of the productions of the State, lead, copper, tobacco, fruit, a fresh water pearl…."

Below, mosaics composed of four hundred thousand pieces of colored glass, each about the size of a quarter, decorate the pendentives. Three figures represent the legislative, executive and judicial branches of government, while the fourth, Liberty, symbolizes the foundation of all power in a free country.

Off the rotunda, double marble staircases lead to the important rooms in each of the four wings on the second floor. Perhaps the most ornate of the rooms is the richly decorated cube-shaped chamber of the Wisconsin Supreme Court, measuring 42 feet by 43 feet with a 30-foot ceiling. Behind the original hand-carved mahogany bench and chairs stand small columns with carved capitals. The Italian white marble pilasters throughout the room contain rare purple veining. Also noteworthy is the German marble with symmetrical book-matched pattern covering the walls.

Four large murals painted in New York by Albert Herter represent significant legal events: *The Trial of Chief Oshkosh by Judge Doty*, *The Appeal of the Legionary to Caesar Augustus*, and *The Signing of the Magna Carta*. In the Magna Carta mural, the artist's son, Christian Herter, is shown with a dog. Christian Herter became governor of Massachusetts and secretary of state under President Dwight David Eisenhower. Behind the bench hangs *The Signing of the American Constitution*, depicting George Washington with Thomas Jefferson, Benjamin Franklin and James Madison, namesake of the capital. The artist's rendition is not entirely accurate because Jefferson was at that time serving as ambassador to France.

The circular upper chamber in the Senate wing integrates marble from Italy and France. The Senate retains its old-fashioned ambience. Its members sit at desks original to the room, there are no computers, and the clerk calls the vote. Behind the podium is a three-part mural by Kenyon Cox symbolizing the opening of the Panama Canal, *The Marriage of the Atlantic and Pacific*, an important event in the world at the time of the capitol's construction. To the right is Europe, with the goddess of peace during the First World War, and to the left, Mercury greeting the Pacific Rim nations.

View across the rotunda.

In another wing, the chamber of the Assembly is decorated with carved oak, in contrast to the mahogany-clad Senate. Another difference from the Senate is that since 1999 the Assembly permits the use of laptop computers and is paperless. Behind the speaker's platform is the mural *Wisconsin*, also attributed to Blashfield. A woman symbolizing Wisconsin is surrounded by women representing Lake Michigan, Lake Superior, and the Mississippi River, the bodies of water that border the state. The figure of Wisconsin is further surrounded by people of the past, though to the left is Future, who is protecting national resources, a somewhat revolutionary idea for that time. A badger is depicted to the left of the soldiers (painted over a soldier sitting on a rock). Reportedly, Post wanted a badger in the mural, but Blashfield did not know what one looked like, so he visited the New York Zoo to see one. The mural was restored in the 1990s, but afterwards the soldier started to show through faintly where the badger had been painted into the mural. The soldier is called the ghost of the capitol.

Below the mural stands Old Abe, a stuffed bald eagle commemorating one that flew freely in the old capitol. A mascot for Wisconsin soldiers in the Civil War and named after Lincoln, Old Abe reportedly survived thirty-nine battles before returning to Madison.

The North Hearing Room, the fourth important room located on the second floor, was designed for State Railroad Commission meetings, because the railroads were apparently heavily taxed to support the capitol's

The Governor's Conference Room.

The House of Representatives chamber.

building fund. Today, caucus meetings and public hearings convene there. On the walls, four murals by Charles Yardly Turner illustrate transportation themes: *Native Americans Striking the Trail*, *A Lake Trading Station*, *The Stagecoach*, and *A Modern Transportation System*. The last, completed in 1915, depicts an automobile, a steamboat, and a little white speck that represents an airplane. It was painted that way shortly after the Wright brothers' historic flight so that if the airplane failed it could easily be ignored or painted over.

Upstairs, the ornate Governor's Conference Room was designed after the lavish Doge Palace in Venice, Italy. The murals on the walls depict historic Wisconsin events. The floor is made from seven different woods and was laid without using nails. On the ceiling are paintings representing the "Virtues of Wisconsin."

The richly decorated modern capitol's price totaled $7.25 million in 1917.

In contrast, an eight-year renovation from 1993 to 2001 cost an estimated $70 million. The capitol features forty different exotic marbles and stones, along with African mahogany that is no longer available. Its grandeur is seen by some as an example of the ultimate respect for institutionalized authority. Others see it as architectural proof of agricultural Wisconsin's urbanity.

Wisconsin has a long and proud history of progressive legislation. As early as 1925, lawmakers, working amid the splendor of their capitol, provided pensions for the blind, aid to dependent children, and old-age assistance. The state was the first to enact unemployment compensation and comprehensive worker's compensation laws, to set a minimum wage and create a Public Service Commission. In 1984 Wisconsin became the first to adopt the Uniform Marital Property Act, followed by its groundbreaking welfare reform. Many states and the federal government have either adopted or adapted for their own use most of Wisconsin's progressive legislation.

Precious marble inlay surrounds the rotunda.

MISSOURI

MISSOURI STATE CAPITOL

ORIGIN OF NAME: From the Missouri tribe,
    meaning "town of large canoes."

CAPITAL: Jefferson City

CONSTRUCTED: 1913–1917

ARCHITECT: Tracy & Swartwout

ADMITTED TO THE UNION: August 10, 1821 (twenty-fourth)

SENATE: 34 members

HOUSE OF REPRESENTATIVES: 163 members

The capital of Missouri, named Jefferson City in honor of Thomas Jefferson, was initially built in an unpopulated area, as mandated by the state's first constitution (1820). St. Charles served as the temporary capital while the new city was established and its state house was constructed. Jefferson City assumed its capital duties in 1826, but its capitol building burned in 1837, and a fire, caused by lightning, destroyed the replacement structure in 1911.

In order to finance the third and present state capitol, a statewide special election was held to approve the issuing of bonds. Lawmakers appointed a building commission, which held a national competition to select an architect. From more than sixty-eight applicants, the commission chose the New York firm of Tracy & Swartwout. Evarts Tracy and Egerton Swartwout, former associates with McKim, Mead & White (Rhode Island State House), designed an American Renaissance capitol. As specified by lawmakers, it is constructed entirely of fireproof materials such as structural steel, concrete and native stone. Located on the south bank of the Missouri River, the building incorporates a symmetrical plan of two wings for the legislative houses, flanking a large central rotunda. Terraces with ornate lamp posts descend from the capitol to the river on the south side.

Missouri Carthage limestone covers the capitol's steel frame, which rests upon concrete piers. Its 134 columns comprise one quarter of the stone in the building. Thirty-two engaged, fluted Corinthian columns surround the exterior walls, while at each end of the building free-standing fluted columns support the north and south porticoes. The front portico contains a sculpted pediment with figures surrounding Lady Missouri representing the Spirit of Progress, Agriculture, Learning, Art, Commerce, Industry, Law, Order, Justice and Light. Originally, the riverfront portico was to have duplicated the front, but the architects later substituted a revised plan with a semicircular colonnaded porch.

Paired columns also support the large stone-covered dome. Behind plain columns, twelve arched stained-glass windows encircle the drum. Other features of the dome include pilasters; slightly protruding ribs; covered windows; anthemion; and round, covered bull's-eye windows. Atop the dome's columned lantern stands a bronze statue of Ceres, the Roman goddess of grain and agriculture.

After the completion of the building, lawmakers created the Capitol Decoration Commission when they discovered that the special Capitol Tax Fund contained a surplus. The commission's mandate was to use the extra money to decorate the building, but that also included paying for such practical matters as repainting, roof repairs, waterproofing the concrete terrace, installing a lighting system and fountains around the grounds, and furnishing its public spaces.

Missouri was the second state formed out of the Louisiana Purchase, and a bronze relief behind the capitol commemorates the signing of the 1803 treaty by which the United States acquired the land from France. France secured all Spanish possessions in North America after it conquered Spain.

N. C. Wyeth's paintings depict Civil War battles in Missouri.

The Missouri State Capitol.

That included the area now known as the Louisiana Purchase. Fearing the negative implications of a strong European power in control of New Orleans and the commerce of the Mississippi River, Jefferson authorized Robert Livingston, the American ambassador to France, to negotiate with Napoleon Bonaparte for the purchase of New Orleans. James Monroe was sent to Paris to assist him, resulting in not only the acquisition of the port city but also land that nearly doubled the size of the United States at that time. The sculpture shows Livingston, Monroe, and Napoleon's treasurer, Francois Barbe de Marbois, signing the treaty.

In commemoration of Jefferson's role in the land purchase, a 13-foot-tall bronze statue of him stands on a pedestal of granite in the center of the stairs leading to the main entrance on the capitol's north side. On either side of the stairway, reclining bronze figures symbolize Missouri's great rivers. The female figure represents the Missouri, while the male figure, the Mississippi River. Both are set on bronze bases decorated in low relief, representing Water and Nature.

The walls and floors of the capitol's corridors and rotunda are lined with native Carthage and Phenix marble. Embedded in the center of the 68-foot-diameter rotunda floor is a large bronze of the Great Seal of the State of Missouri. The Latin motto near its bottom translates to "Let the Welfare of the People be the Supreme Law," and two bears symbolize the strength of the state. Roman numerals represent 1820, the date the first constitution of Missouri was ratified.

Hanging from the interior of the dome and lighting the rotunda is a 9,000-pound bronze chandelier. The surrounding walls are decorated with colorful murals painted by Frank Brangwyn in his London, England, studio and shipped to Jefferson City, where they were attached to the contours of

The Missouri State Capitol rotunda.

the walls. Four figures, representing Agriculture, Commerce, Science and Education, encircle the center, along with the signs of the zodiac. Below, paintings of Missouri history show the eighteenth-century French landing, the coming of the pioneers, development, and modern times. Brangwyn filled the lower panels with illustrations incorporating themes of agriculture, science, education, and art.

Off the crypt, and separated from it by reddish columns from Graniteville, Missouri, corridors contain the History Hall and the Resources Hall of the state museum. Two curved marble stairways lead from there to the second or executive floor. As part of the governor's suite, the oval-shaped reception room overlooking the Missouri River is finished in oak with state seals carved in the frieze.

On the wall opposite a group of large windows are four panels, corresponding in size and shape to the windows. They contain paintings dedicated to education and literature, with portraits of Mark Twain; Susan Blow, a St. Louisan who in the 1860s adopted the ideas of Germany's Friedrich Froebel and opened a kindergarten; Major James Sidney Rollins, founder of the University of Missouri at Columbia; and Eugene Field, a writer of children's poetry.

In the corridors outside the governor's rooms forty-one lunettes, dating from 1920 through 1922, line the walls. They illustrate Missouri's resources and history. The lunettes were painted by many artists, including two by N. C. Wyeth that illustrate the Civil War battles of Wilson's Creek and Westport.

The grand stairway, 30 feet wide, starts from the entrance doors in the slightly protruding front portico and extends to the third or legislative floor. Covered by a skylight, the staircase is lined on either side by large columns of Phenix stone and is over 65 feet from the wall on one side to the wall across the stairway on the other side.

The House of Representatives chamber.

At the top of the stairway, niches hold bronze statues of Meriwether Lewis and William Clark. Hired by Jefferson after the Louisiana Purchase to find "the most direct and practicable water communication across the continent for purposes of commerce," the explorers departed on their journey from St. Louis on the Missouri River. In the rotunda and four smaller round rooms covered by shallow domes, artwork includes bronze busts of Missourians famous in the fields of sports, entertainment, science, literature, art, the military and business.

Opposite each other on this floor are the low-domed legislative chambers. In the Senate, the walls and Ionic columns consist of Carthage and Phenix stone. Sixteen columns front the 265-seat visitors' gallery, including four above the hand-carved rostrum. Art-glass windows extend above the walls, and the window behind the rostrum shows the landing of Hernando de Soto, the first European to set foot on Missouri soil. Other features include fabric swags, which replaced horse- and human-hair padding installed to cut down noise; original hand-carved native-walnut desks; ornate light standards and fixtures; and leather-covered doors with brass studs.

Narrow wall murals portray *Daniel Boone at the Judgment Tree*; *President Jefferson Greeting Lewis and Clark*; *Benton's Speech Promoting the West in St. Louis, 1849*; and *Blair's Pro-Union Speech at Louisiana, 1866*. Carved into the stone on either side of the rostrum are the admonitions "Nothing is Politically Right That is Morally Wrong" and "Free and Fair Discussion Will Ever be Found the Firmest Friend to Truth."

Carthage and Phenix stone also covers the walls of the House behind twelve New Hampshire granite Ionic columns that line the sides. Carved into the original mahogany speaker's dais is the guiding rule: "The Welfare of the People Shall be the Supreme Law." Above the rostrum the gallery is reserved for the press, while the three other galleries seat visitors. Behind the press gallery is a stained-glass window entitled *The Glory of Missouri in Peace.* It contains allegorical figures representing Missouri sitting on a throne surrounded by Commerce, Mining and Agriculture to her left, and Justice, Art and Science to her right.

Opposite the rostrum, a mural honors Missouri soldiers who fought in France during the First World War. Art-glass windows extend above the walls with the following words engraved below: "Liberty, equality, law, justice, fraternity, progress, honor, truth, virtue, and charity."

Across the hallway from the House of Representatives is its lounge, the most famous room in the capitol. A mural entitled *A Social History of the State of Missouri,* painted by Missouri native Thomas Hart Benton, covers the walls. After entering into a contract with the legislature in 1935 that provided him with complete artistic freedom, Benton spent eighteen months traveling the state, studying and sketching people. He prepared a 12-by-4-foot Plasticine clay model that contributed to the sculptural appearance of the mural's painted figures and its depth of space. During the subsequent six months of actual painting, Benton employed a tempera mixture, adding egg yolk to water and powdered paint. This ancient technique kept the colors bright. He also incorporated humor and detail into the active and often enlarged figures, and designed the scenes to flow easily from the beginning to the end.

The Senate chamber.

A student of American history, Benton believed that the frontier was the dominating force in shaping American life and culture. His mural reflects Missouri's role — good and bad. While such landmarks as the Nelson Gallery of Art, the St. Louis Cathedral, and a country church are easily identifiable, the mural mostly emphasizes everyday people. Three walls are cut by doors with wide marble surrounds. Benton expanded their frames and placed within the painted borders scenes of Missouri legends Huck Finn, Jesse James and "Frankie and Johnnie."

Starting on the north wall, background scenes show early settlers, the first capitol in St. Charles, a riverside baptismal ceremony, a slave being sold on the auction block, and early laborers. The east wall adds illustrations from Benton's past, such as political gatherings, farming, a courtroom, railroads and mining. Throughout, Benton painted faces of real Missourians, including his father giving a political speech before a small crowd. One spectator at the rally represents the friend who introduced the legislation commissioning the mural. At the edge of the crowd, a mother diapers her baby. The baby is now a businessman in Jefferson City. Benton's son modeled for the boy in an interior scene of a one-room farmhouse.

The south wall concentrates on city life and industry specific to Missouri, such as St. Louis beer manufacturing and slaughter houses in Kansas City. A dark cloud indicates industrial pollution. Benton was born into a family of lawyers and politicians. He was named for his great uncle, the first two United States senators from Missouri, and he believed politics played a significant and influential role in Missouri life. Benton knew Tom Pendergast, the Kansas City political boss, and painted him into the lower bottom corner. In spite of early criticism that Benton selected everyday people instead of Missouri's military and political heroes, his bold style of painting and his choice of commonplace subjects make the mural as vital today as when he completed it in 1936.

The House Lounge with murals by Thomas Hart Benton covering its walls.

OKLAHOMA

OKLAHOMA STATE CAPITOL
ORIGIN OF NAME: From the Choctaw words *okla humma*,
   meaning "red people."
CAPITAL: Oklahoma City
CONSTRUCTED: 1914–1917
ARCHITECTS: Solomon A. Layton and S. Wemyss Smith
ADMITTED TO THE UNION: November 6, 1907 (forty-sixth)
SENATE: 48 members
HOUSE OF REPRESENTATIVES: 101 members

The area that is now Oklahoma was the home to its earliest inhabitants, the Plains Indians, until 1825, when the United States declared the region a federal territory. Over the next half century, the federal government forcibly moved more than sixty tribes from the east and the northern plains to reservations in Native American territory in order to open up new land for European settlement. As part of President Andrew Jackson's Indian Removal Act of 1830, the Cherokee nation was forced to relinquish its lands east of the Mississippi and march under military escort to an area in present-day Oklahoma. Exhaustion, hunger and disease took the lives of almost a third of the Cherokees on what became known as the Trail of Tears. Later, under pressure from railroad executives, land speculators, settlers and others who sought free or cheap land for their own purposes, President Benjamin Harrison's government (1889–1893) rearranged tribal holdings, taking back millions of acres under Native American control and placing them in the public domain.

Since there were more land-hungry settlers and speculators than land, officials decided to offer the once-protected Native American land to home-steaders by a series of land rushes between 1889 and 1895. The first Oklahoma Land Rush began at noon on April 22, 1889, when an official's gun-shot signaled the opening of the territory. It was instantly transformed, as thousands of white settlers raced in wagons, on horseback, on bicycles and on foot across the borders from Texas and Kansas to claim homesteads. By nightfall, every one of the almost two million acres of offered land had been claimed. Local law-enforcement officials not only had a difficult time keeping out the "sooners," those who tried to sneak in sooner than was permissible, but also in maintaining order in the wild new society.

While the federal Homestead Act signed by President Abraham Lincoln in 1862, was meant to encourage settlement of the West, it did not apply to Oklahoma until the 1889 land rush. The law promised 160 acres of surveyed, unclaimed public land to families who would live on the land for five years. More than 1.6 million homesteads, covering millions of acres of land west of the Mississippi, were settled by 1890, and many more acres were granted to railroads or purchased by speculators through lottery and auction.

The Oklahoma Territory was created with Guthrie as its capital. It included the area that is today's state. In the eastern part were the Five Civilized Tribes, so called because these tribes came into contact with Europeans early and readily adopted many of their ways. Some intermarried with Europeans and became successful businessmen and farmers. Reacting primarily to political corruption, the tribes wrote their own constitution and codes of law, and sought separate independence or statehood, but Congress insisted the two areas be admitted together as one state.

Oklahomans approved a long and detailed constitution that adopted many progressive elements of the tribes' constitution. It provided, among other things, the initiative and referendum, an eight-hour workday for mines and public work projects, no child labor, and a prohibition on the sale of alcohol.

A special election was held to select a permanent location for the state capital in 1910. Oklahoma City prevailed over Guthrie, and a few years later, the legislature established the State Capitol Commission to oversee construction of a capitol. The commission constructed a building of reinforced concrete faced to the second-floor level with pinkish granite quarried in southeastern Oklahoma. Indiana limestone covered the remaining walls. Corinthian columns surround the Neoclassical building, with full columns supporting the south main portico and engaged elsewhere. The north and south facades contain projecting Corinthian porticoes with plain pediments, while the east and west have pilasters.

The initial plans for the capitol building included a high dome, but the $1.5 million appropriated by the legislature failed to cover its expense, and plans for completion of the dome were dropped.

While many efforts were initiated over the years to complete the dome, a cap remained over the rotunda. Finally, with Oklahoma's centennial approaching, the State Capitol Complex and Oklahoma Centennial Commemoration Commission initiated a private fundraising campaign to add contributions to public funds in order to build the dome. It was finally dedicated on November 6, 2002, Statehood Day. The $21-million

The Oklahoma State Capitol.

old-style Renaissance dome, created with modern materials, doubled the height of the capitol to 255 feet, about as high as a 26-story building.

At first, state officials thought a new dome could rest on the original support structure. When that proved unfeasible, structural steel and sixteen six-ton pieces of pre-cast concrete matching the capitol's limestone exterior were added for support. The new dome weighs approximately 2,500 tons. Concrete was substituted for limestone blocks not only because of cost but because skilled stonecutters like the ones who shaped limestone blocks nearly one hundred years ago were no longer available.

On June 7, 2002, a Native American warrior sculpture, *The Guardian*, became the last touch to the dome's cupola. It was by Enoch Kelly Haney, a state senator of Seminole and Creek descent whose family followed the Trail of Tears to Oklahoma. The bronze statue, not specific to any one tribe, stands 17 feet tall and holds a staff more than 22 feet tall.

Below the dome, eight winged lions accent the roofline. Long associated with power and authority, the lion is a fitting symbol for a seat-of-government building.

To the north, the Indian Flag Plaza flies the flags of the thirty-nine federally recognized tribes in Oklahoma, while the fourteen flags of the countries that at one time claimed Oklahoma fly to the south. Along with the flags, there is a bronze sculpture dating from 1929 of a cowboy on a horse rearing over prickly pear cacti. More recently, a bronze sculpture of a Native American woman was added. Entitled *As Long As the Waters Flow*, it honors the contributions of Native Americans to Oklahoma.

From the plaza, thirty-four broad steps lead to the second-story main entrance. A grand marble staircase climbs fifty-eight steps to the fourth floor, the location of both legislative chambers. Above the staircase, at the end of the barrel-vaulted ceiling, hangs a mural showing a soldier leaving his family to fight in the First World War. In 1921, Frank Phillips, founder of Phillips Petroleum, hired artist Gilbert White, then in Paris, to paint it as a tribute to Oklahoma soldiers who served during war. A separate

The Oklahoma Capitol is the only one in the United States with an oil field located beneath it. In the 1930s, when Oklahoma City's oil and gas fields became producers, the capitol grounds pumped twenty-four oil wells. They are approximately a mile and a quarter beneath the capitol. Oil companies such as Phillips Petroleum leased the wells for a fee and also paid royalties and taxes to the state treasury. Today, with oil production declining from earlier levels, the remaining non-operating rig in front of the south entrance stands as a historical monument to the discovery and development of the Oklahoma City oil fields.

Oklahoma's Hall of the Governors.

work, directly above, contains two Latin words, *Pro Patria*, meaning "for fatherland." White's painting is the only artwork by a non-Oklahoman artist in the capitol.

Below, in the center of the rotunda floor, is the Great Seal of the State of Oklahoma. Added in 1966, the large star represents Oklahoma, the forty-sixth state added to the Union, while forty-five smaller stars stand for each preceding state. Symbols on each point of the large star depict the Civilized Tribes of Oklahoma: the Cherokee, Chickasaw, Choctaw, Seminole and Creek. Green oak leaves encircle a cowboy and a Native American, symbolizing the joining of the Oklahoma Territory and Native American lands into one state, and beneath the leaves is inscribed the state motto: "Labor Conquers All." The tile seal mirrors the leaded stained-glass seal 190 feet above, filling the oculus.

The dome's coffered ceiling consists of reinforced plaster casts of recessed ornamental panels with 197 gold-leaf rosettes of varying sizes. The dome's colors are blue, for the Oklahoma sky, and gold, coral and reddish-brown, for its wildflowers. The windowed wall below the dome is encircled with sixteen pairs of faux-marble pilasters. Classical beige and cream are incorporated as a neutral backdrop in the dome, as well as throughout other areas of the capitol.

Full-length portraits of prominent Oklahomans appear on the fourth floor of the rotunda. They include Robert S. Kerr, former United States senator, Oklahoma's twelfth and first native-born governor, and co-founder of Kerr-McGee Oil Company; Sequoyah, who designed the Cherokee alphabet; Will Rogers, Cherokee descendant, journalist, humorist and actor; and Jim Thorpe, a member of the Sac and Fox tribes and winner of gold medals in the pentathlon and decathlon at the 1912 Olympic Games.

Above the portraits, four murals portray the history and development of Oklahoma: *Discovery and Exploration, 1541–1820*, showing Francisco Vasquez de Coronado's early exploration of the land; *Frontier Trade, 1790–1830*; *Indian Immigration from 1820–1885*, depicting the forced immigration of Native American tribes into the territory;

The Oklahoma state seal is woven into the carpet of the House of Representatives chamber.

and *Non-Indian Settlement, 1870–1906*, the rush for land by settlers during the Great Land Runs. At the north end is *Flight of Spirit*, commemorating five world-famous Oklahoma Native American ballerinas, and on the east side, *Oklahoma Black Gold*, referring to the significance of the state's oil and gas industry.

Off the rotunda, the House of Representatives was restored to its original appearance in 1999. During its restoration, sixteen windows along the north and south walls were uncovered and freshly painted, and gold paint was used to accent the hand-carved plaster ceiling. Local artisans recreated the origi-

nal design of the six skylights, which contained 234 panels of approximately 36,000 pieces of hand-cut glass in fifteen colors, held together by lead. Lamps copied from a surviving original were installed, along with ten vintage oscillating fans. The members' desks were reproduced based on the originals, and the state seal decorates their chairs. Portraits of previous speakers of the House hang along the walls, between pilasters with Ionic capitals, while above the speaker's desk are portraits of the president of the United States, the governor of Oklahoma, and the present speaker of the House.

On the other side is the Senate chamber, restored in to its original design

A replica of The Guardian *standing inside the capitol building.*

in 1993. At that time, windows were also uncovered and restored, including stained-glass panels from the original pattern. Paneling was removed to reveal Neoclassical scrollwork and ornamental plaster. Photographs of Senate presidents, who also serve as the lieutenant governor, also adorn the walls.

The Oklahoma Supreme Court fills the end of the western second-floor corridor. The court consists of nine justices who preside over civil cases, separate from the Oklahoma Court of Criminal Appeals, the highest state court of criminal appeals and also located on the same floor. The supreme court courtroom features mahogany woodwork imported from the West Indies and four large columns of Vermont marble that support a coffered ceiling. Both courts plan to move across the street when the new History Building is completed.

Interior view of the Oklahoma capitol dome.

IDAHO

IDAHO STATE CAPITOL

ORIGIN OF NAME: Unknown but may be derived from a Shoshone word meaning "sunup" or "light on the mountain."

CAPITAL: Boise

CONSTRUCTED: 1906–1920

ARCHITECT: John E. Tourtellotte

ADMITTED TO THE UNION: July 3, 1890 (forty-third)

SENATE: 35 members

HOUSE OF REPRESENTATIVES: 70 members

The first Euro-Americans to enter present-day Idaho were probably Meriwether Lewis and William Clark, explorers who crossed the Bitterroot Mountain Range on their expedition in 1805. Subsequent waves of trappers and traders came to the region for its wealth of wildlife. It was not until the 1860s that the town of Franklin became Idaho's first permanent settlement. Soon after the Territory of Idaho was officially recognized in 1863, Lewiston was named the first capital. Following Montana's formation as a separate territory the next year, the population growth shifted to the southwest and the capital moved to its present location in Boise. After President Benjamin Harrison signed the Idaho Admission Act in 1890, the Idaho legislature authorized the establishment of the University of Idaho in Moscow in order to compensate northern Idaho for the loss of the capital designation and all that went with it.

The first Boise state capitol was housed in a red-brick territorial building constructed in 1886. As the present capitol was erected, the old one was demolished to make way for the last wing. Today, the capitol stands as part of a governmental complex within a 4.69-acre park with large old trees. Three of the trees on the east side of the capitol were planted by visiting presidents of the United States: Benjamin Harrison (a water oak in 1891), Theodore Roosevelt (a rock maple in 1903), and William Howard Taft (an Ohio buckeye in 1911). Recently, the water oak was nearly cut down due to old age and disease, until a concerted conservation effort saved it. Today, a fence protects the much-diminished but still-surviving historic tree. Nearby stands an old Oregon Trail marker noting that the capitol faces a street that was once part of the pioneer trail.

In the act admitting Idaho to the Union, federal lands were also set aside to assist in the funding of a capitol. A building commission was created with power to issue bonds, negotiate and sign contracts, and approve architectural plans. An architectural competition was launched by the commission in 1905, and the Boise firm of J. W. Tourtellotte & Co. was chosen to implement its plan, which would incorporate Neoclassical characteristics patterned after the American Renaissance state capitols.

The first construction phase involved building the central block with the Renaissance dome and a three-story portico, with a pediment supported by four Corinthian columns. Flanking wings were subsequently completed. Its concrete foundation rests on river gravel 15 feet below the surface. The base course consists of Vermont granite rusticated in the shape of over-

The Senate chamber.

The brightly lit interior of Idaho's capitol dome.

sized logs, and the walls are of Idaho sandstone. Rectangular windows pierce the walls from the second to the fourth story, decreasing in size as they ascend toward the roof. The side entrances of the balanced legislative wings incorporate Ionic columns in slightly protruding pavilions. Above, a smooth parapet partially covers low domes, indicating the placement of the interior legislative chambers.

The dominant feature of the building, the dome, rises from the roof behind the portico's solid parapet. It incorporates a detached colonnade before frosted windows. The columns support decorative brackets, set between windows, which in turn support the terra-cotta-tiled roof. The elliptical windows encircling the lower portion of the roof allow additional light to flow into the rotunda below. The eagle perched on top of the dome stands 5 feet 7 inches tall on a triple pedestal of sandstone. Weighing 250 pounds, the eagle is solid copper covered in bronze.

The capitol's fireproof interior features four kinds of marble: Alaskan marble covering the floors, staircases and trimmings; Vermont marble on the walls; Georgian marble in trim and incorporated into the reddish pink inlaid floor patterns; and contrasting inlaid floor patterns of black Italian marble. Marble can sometimes be difficult to utilize because of its expense and weight. For those reasons, the eight large rotunda columns, 5 feet in diameter and 60 feet high, which bear the weight of the dome, are not marble but steel, and covered in pale-gray-and-white scagliola.

Idaho's old Supreme Court chamber is now a committee hearing room.

Flooded with natural light and open from the basement to the inner shell of the dome, the rotunda is ringed with balconies, which are outlined by electric lightbulbs set in gilt lilies. Cornices, ceilings and decorative elements such as the columns' Corinthian capitals, which feature acanthus leaves and egg-and-dart as well as dentil molding, consist of white plaster.

The rotunda is actually 80 feet square, though it appears curved. This is because of the location of the staircases in each of its four corners and the circular placement of the columns. The third and fourth floors contain circular colonnades, with a promenade in between. The colonnade on the fourth floor measures 60 feet in diameter, while the one on the third floor is 80 feet in diameter. In the center of the rotunda, on the main or second floor, is a large opening to the floor, about 25 feet in diameter and surrounded by a marble balustrade.

Except for the murals permanently installed on the fourth floor to commemorate Idaho's first one hundred years, the artwork of the building is located on the second floor. Especially prominent is an equestrian statue of George Washington, with all the pieces carved out of a single log of yellow pine. It was given to the Idaho Territory in 1869 and dedicated to its pioneers by its German sculptor, Charles Ostner. Ostner spent four winters under difficult conditions to complete the work (including working at night by the light of a pine torch held by his son). He supposedly copied Washington's face from his likeness on a postage stamp. The statue was displayed on the grounds until 1934, when the legislature repaired its weather damage, covered it with gold leaf, and moved it inside. In 1966, a glass case was added to further protect the statue.

Nearby stands a replica of the fourth-century BC *Winged Victory of Samothrace*, located in the Louvre Museum in Paris. This copy was donated to Idaho by France in appreciation for the state's role in helping France during the Second World War.

The House of Representatives, located in the east wing, features blue carpet, Ionic and composite marble columns supporting the mini-dome, new desks and chairs, with the state seal displayed above the speaker's desk. The Senate, in the west wing, features red carpet and a semicircular colonnade

The Idaho State Capitol at dusk.

at the front of the room. As in the House chamber, the ceiling is covered by a mini-dome supported by marble columns. Both chambers were renovated in the 1960s, and a planned restoration to return them to a more traditional style, complementing the exterior, remains on hold due to budget considerations.

The capitol's heating system uniquely taps natural geothermal springs 3,000 feet below Boise. Its heating plant, located about five blocks away, is connected to the building by a tunnel that transports hot water pumped through steam pipes from the springs.

The old Idaho Supreme Court chamber, now the Joint Finance and Appropriations Committee Hearing Room, contains original furnishings, including the dark green marble and mahogany bench in the front of the room that was once the seat of the supreme court justices. Also noteworthy are the Doric columns and the barrel-vaulted ceiling.

Not all laws that the court reviews originate in the capitol. The initiative process allows Idahoans to write or propose changes to state statutes, put them on the ballot, and ask voters to determine whether they should become law. In 1994, 59 percent of Idaho voters approved an initiative measure that limited the terms of all public officials, from Congress to the Idaho state legislature to local school boards. Later, the United States Supreme Court struck down the part of the law that restricted the tenure of Idaho's members in Congress, leaving the legislature to contend with the surviving limits imposed on state and local officials, law enforcement, school boards, county commissions and prosecutors' offices.

The state's term limits did not completely prevent elected officials from serving again, because even though an incumbent who held office for a certain number of years could not have his or her name appear on the ballot, they could still run a write-in campaign. In 1996 and 1998, the Idaho legislature asked voters to respond in a special ballot as to whether they wanted term limits to remain in place after the term limits for Congress were eliminated. Although it was a non-binding question, the majority of voters still said yes. The Idaho Supreme Court further ruled, in December 2001, that the Term Limits Law was constitutional. Despite citizens' support for term limits, in 2002 the Idaho legislature became the first state legislature in the United States to repeal them.

When a lawsuit was brought against this action, the Idaho Supreme Court unanimously upheld the legislature's repeal. The court held that once an initiative becomes law, it is on the same footing as laws initially created

The House of Representatives chamber.

by the legislature and subject to repeal or modification at any time. After a passionate debate, in November 2002, Idaho voters narrowly agreed with the legislature's repeal of term limits.

Those arguing against term limits included citizens in the more sparsely populated areas of the state, where local governments were not able to fill some elected offices because, for example, a single funeral director might be the only qualified county coroner. They also asserted that term limits take away the ability of voters to decide for themselves whether an otherwise will-ing and able incumbent should be kept in office. In addition, they argued that term limits restricted the amount of on-the-job experience office holders could attain, hindering leadership and empowering veteran legislative staff members and other non-elected officials such as lobbyists.

The central argument of the proponents of term limits is that new people bring new life and ideas to an entrenched system that supports the incum-bent. In spite of their setback, those in support of term limits vow to continue their fight.

One of four staircases in the rotunda.

WASHINGTON

WASHINGTON LEGISLATIVE BUILDING
ORIGIN OF NAME: Named for George Washington.
CAPITAL: Olympia
CONSTRUCTED: 1922–1928
ARCHITECTS: Walter R. Wilder and Harry K. White
ADMITTED TO THE UNION: November 11, 1889 (forty-second)
SENATE: 49 members
HOUSE OF REPRESENTATIVES: 98 members

In 1853, a bill came before the United States Congress proposing the area north of the Columbia River be separated from the Oregon Territory and be called the Territory of Columbia. Since there was already a District of Columbia but no state or territory named for the nation's first president, it was decided that the name of the new territory should be changed to Washington. As a result, on March 2, 1853, the territory separated from the Oregon Territory and was named Washington. It is the only state named for a president.

The following year, Olympia founder Edmund Sylvester set aside 12 acres for capitol grounds with views of Olympia, the Budd Inlet of the Puget Sound, and the distant Olympic Mountains. In 1856, the first capitol building was completed on the site of today's legislative building. The small two-story wood-frame building contained a front portico with columns supporting a balcony and a tower. The House of Representatives met on the second floor, and the Council (predecessor to the Senate) convened on the first. It was still in use at the time of statehood and the constitutional convention of 1889.

In 1893, following a nationwide competition that selected Ernest Flagg of New York as architect, work began on a larger capitol. Though the foundation was completed, construction work was interrupted because of a national depression and attempts to move the capital to another city.

In 1901, with a pressing need for space, the legislature decided to appropriate money to purchase the Thurston County Courthouse in Olympia's central business district and to build an addition for itself. The courthouse served as Washington's second capitol from 1903 to 1928. An example of nineteenth-century American Romanesque architecture, it incorporated rock-faced sandstone, arches, turrets and a tower. Architect Willis Ritchie added such innovations as steel framing and elevators. But after only ten years, lawmakers decided to resume construction on Flagg's 1893

building, and reauthorized plans to construct a larger building on the original grounds.

Flagg was called back to discuss changes in his plans, because even though a legislative mandate required that the already completed foundation be used, the original design was too small to meet increased state government requirements. To overcome this problem, Flagg, like Thomas Jefferson many years earlier in Virginia, suggested a group of buildings rather than one large building. This idea would also allow construction to continue uninterrupted as space was needed.

Although the capitol commission accepted Flagg's idea, it did not choose him as the architect. Instead, it invited two sets of designs in a new nationwide competition — one for a Temple of Justice and the other for a group

Bronze doors to the Senate chamber.

The legislative building dominates the Washington State Capitol grounds.

plan. This time the competition was won by the New York firm of Wilder & White. The principals of the firm, Walter R. Wilder and Harry K. White, worked together for many years as draftsmen for the firm of McKim, Mead & White (Rhode Island State House) before forming their own partnership in 1909.

The design of the dominant, domed Legislative Hall is part of the unified group of Classically designed buildings, including the Temple of Justice (1919), the Administration Building (1921), and the Insurance Building (1920). Initially, the legislative building was to be constructed on the foundation designed by Flagg, but it was decided to enlarge the building by extending the foundation 80 feet longer and 20 feet wider, and to double the size of the dome. Wilder & White also placed the legislative building in the center of the group of buildings in order to give the impression from a distance that there was just one broad base below a massive dome. The First World War delayed construction of the building until 1922. As a result, lawmakers stayed in the old capitol until 1928, when members of both houses marched in procession from the old building to the present one.

Another state office state office building was planned for the site of the governor's mansion, as well as a terrace behind the Temple of Justice, two grand staircases leading down the side of the hill to a manmade lake, and a landscaped walkway to a new railroad station near downtown Olympia. The lake was created, as was a park on its northeast corner, but the rest of the vision remains to be fulfilled.

The American Renaissance legislative building is the centerpiece of the Washington State Capitol group of structures. The exterior consists of a light-colored sandstone quarried from Wilkeson and native Index granite.

In 1940, George Talcott related the following story of the Washington state seal: "The Talcott Brothers were, in 1889 as they are today, jewelers in Olympia, conducting the oldest jewelry store in the state. A committee, a short time previous to statehood, appeared before my brother Charles at our store, with a design for the proposed seal, to be completed when the first legislature met in November 1889. The design submitted by the committee was a very complicated sketch depicting the port of Tacoma, vast wheat fields, sheep grazing in the valley at the foot of Mount Rainier, and a very good representation of the mountain itself.

"My brother told the committee that such a seal would be outmoded with the growth of the state. He picked up an ink bottle from his desk and drew a circle around its base. Next he placed a silver dollar in the circle and drew another or inner circle. Now he printed, between the two circles, the words, 'The Seal of the State of Washington, 1889.' Then he licked a postage stamp and pasted it in the center, saying, 'That represents the bust of George Washington.' His design was immediately accepted by the Legislature. The picture of Washington was copied from an advertisement of Dr. Jayne's Cure for Coughs and Colds!"

Over the years, many variations of the Talcott design were used. In 1967, a Gilbert Stuart portrait of Washington was accepted by the legislature and became the official Washington state seal.

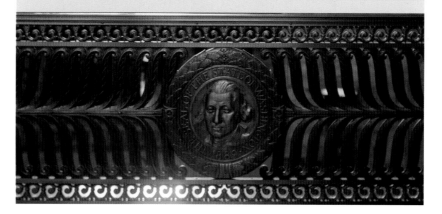

The roof is flat, though low gables extend to the east and west from the square base of a large central dome. The base rises above the gables and supports a circular foundation for a Corinthian colonnade. After a 1965 earthquake, twenty-two of the thirty windows in the colonnade section were filled with reinforced concrete to give the dome more rigidity. Above the columns, the 287-foot-high dome is made up of fourteen hundred machine-cut stones. A lantern, electrically illuminated from within and redesigned to make it lighter and stronger after a 1949 earthquake, tops the dome.

Colonnades cover all four elevations. The columns, 4 feet in diameter and 25 feet high, are similar to the unfluted type in other buildings in the group, and, with notable exceptions, the columns incorporate Doric capitals. The exceptions include columns over 30 feet high and paired pilasters encircling the ribbed dome, as well as those at the north and south entrances, which have Corinthian capitals.

The legislative building integrates more decorative carved stone than the other buildings in the group. In addition to the use of the more ornate Corinthian capitals on some of the columns, the roofline and the pediment of the main north entrance incorporate anthemion cresting. The gable ends contain dentil cornices, and bands of stone relief work appear around the dome and its base. At the four corners of the base, substituted for tourelles, are low, dome-shaped towers.

Except for the dome, most of the ornamental carving was done after the stone was in place. The column capitals of the north and south porticoes were put into place in a blocked-out raw state before American and Scottish stonecarvers shaped them using a combination of hand tools and sandblasting equipment.

Detail of guilloche-decorated wall sconces repeated in the nearby plaster wall decoration.

The principal entrance on the north facade integrates a broad flight of forty-two granite steps, symbolizing Washington as the forty-second state. Entry to the building is through bronze doors decorated with bas-relief representations of the first capitol and industrial activities in the state, such as logging and shipping. On the south facade is a porte-cochere supported by Corinthian columns. A large chandelier hangs within the porte-cochere.

The Olmsted landscape architecture firm, a successor to Frederick Law Olmsted's firm, designed the surrounding grounds. Planting began in 1931 and now includes over 120 varieties of trees, flowers, plants and shrubs. Particularly notable are the flowering Japanese cherry trees and a variety of rhododendrons.

Inside, flights of marble stairs lead to the rotunda from the south and north entrances. The innermost dome, almost 60 feet in diameter, rises 174 feet above the floor. Its drum is supported by an interior row of twenty-four 25-foot-high columns. They were originally to be made of marble, but as an economy measure it was decided to use marble only at the base of the dome. As a result, the columns and other interior finishes above them are plaster. The floors and walls of the rotunda are faced with Tokeen marble quarried in Alaska and transported to Tacoma by barge, where it was cut before being sent to Olympia. Though originally planned, there are no murals, but there is decorative molding around the base of the dome.

Embedded in the center of the marble floor is a bronze reproduction of the Washington state seal. With a diameter of four feet, it is surrounded by a wreath of oak leaves and acorns (symbolizing strength). Directly above the seal, hanging from the center of the inner dome on a 101-foot chain, is the largest chandelier ever designed by Tiffany of New York City. The bronze light fixture weighs five tons. In the corners of the rotunda are

The Washington Senate chamber.

A bronze light standard in the rotunda.

bronze light standards, reproductions of Roman firepots, also designed by Tiffany.

Stairs to the east and west lead up to the legislative chambers, located at opposite ends of the third floor. The House features walnut furniture, a ceiling decorated with eagles and rosettes, cream-colored Escolette marble imported from France, an ornate chandelier, and bronze doors with inner doors of leather with bronze nails. The Senate features mahogany furniture, a hand-carved rostrum, murals, and columns of Rose Fomosa, a dark-gray marble with rose highlights, from Germany.

To the south of the rotunda is the State Reception Room with parquet floors, fireplaces, a seven-foot-diameter table, and walls of cream and dark gray, and violet Italian marble. Two Czechoslovakian crystal chandeliers supplied by Tiffany light the room.

The state recently completed an extensive renovation and earthquake repair of the legislative building. Although it survived earthquakes in 1949, 1965 and 2001, after the latest one it was discovered that the dome had moved 34 inches and its surrounding columns six inches. As well as repairing overall earthquake damage, the renovation added steel reinforcement to the masonry dome; created additional office space underground; replaced air-conditioning, heating, plumbing, electrical and telecommunication systems; and increased accessibility for the disabled.

Financing for the construction of the capitol buildings came from the sale of the land given to the state when Congress admitted Washington to the Union. At that time, Congress authorized the new government to select tens of thousands of acres of unappropriated federal land within its borders. Well-timbered lands west of the Cascades were chosen, and with the development of highways and railroads, they appreciated in value. At first, revenue was derived from the sale of the land itself. But by the 1920s, lawmakers shifted from selling the lands to either selling timber rights or leasing the land for other production purposes. In addition, over the years Washington's land ownership has expanded in an effort to protect the state's long-term supply of timber.

The inner dome with large Tiffany chandelier.

ALASKA

ALASKA STATE CAPITOL

ORIGIN OF NAME: From Aleut word *Alyeska*, meaning "mainland" or "the great land."

CAPITAL: Juneau

CONSTRUCTED: 1929–1931

ARCHITECT: James A. Wetmore

ADMITTED TO THE UNION: January 3, 1959 (forty-ninth)

SENATE: 20 members

HOUSE OF REPRESENTATIVES: 40 members

Alaska is the northernmost and largest state, twice as large as Texas and almost one fifth the size of the other forty-nine states combined. Yet it is so sparsely populated that there is only about one person per square mile.

The first inhabitants of the area arrived thousands of years ago across a now-vanished Bering land bridge that connected Siberia and Alaska. In 1741, Vitus Bering, a Dane in the service of Russia, became the first European to reach Alaska. He claimed it for Russia, and the Russians established a base on Kodiak Island from which to hunt and trap. In 1804, Sitka became capital of Russian Alaska.

Over sixty years later, after the Civil War, the United States paid $7.2 million for 586,412 square miles of Alaska, about 2¢ an acre, negotiated by Secretary of State William H. Seward. Many ridiculed the purchase, calling it "Seward's Icebox" or "Seward's Folly." Others believed acquiring Alaska was part of America's manifest destiny — the belief that the United States was destined to occupy all the lands between the Atlantic and Pacific oceans. Late nineteenth-century gold discoveries led to an increase in its population, and Juneau, born as a gold-rush town in 1880, became the new capital in 1900. The move from Sitka reportedly involved three government employees and seven filing cabinets in one boat. After intense lobbying by Alaskans, Congress made Alaska a territory of the United States in 1912.

The Second World War brought military defense bases and more people to this strategically important territory, paving the way for statehood. Juneau remained the capital, though it was neither centrally located nor convenient. It clings to a mountainside along a narrow saltwater channel in the southeastern panhandle and can only be reached by boat or plane. Mountains, glaciers and rain forests prohibit construction of the normal network of roads.

Because of Juneau's lack of accessibility, discussions continue on the subject of relocating the capital. Juneau officials want to construct a larger capitol building to assure that the capital is not moved, as so often happened in the Lower 48 when populations shifted and the capitals followed. Attempts to relocate to more populated Anchorage or Fairbanks have so far proved unsuccessful, with those against relocation arguing that moving a governor, the legislature and state agencies would be too expensive and would leave Juneau a "ghost town."

Others claim that no matter where the capital is located it would be

Columns of Alaskan Tokeen marble on the portico of the state capitol.

The old Senate chamber is now a committee room.

difficult to reach. Furthermore, in recent years much has been done to make things easier: most of the legislature's work can be viewed on cable television or is available on its website; the Juneau airport incorporates state-of-the-art equipment to cope with bad weather conditions; and each citizen is entitled to one reduced fare each year to fly there for legislative business. There is also a movement by some government officials to build a 65-mile road to Skagway in order to connect Juneau to the Alaska Highway system via Canada.

At the time Alaska became a territory, Congress appropriated an amount for the purchase of the Juneau site that was adequate to buy only half the desired block of land. Fearing the building might be delayed indefinitely, the citizens of Juneau, correctly foreseeing state government as its largest employer, raised additional money, purchased the remaining land necessary and presented it to the government. The completed Federal and Territorial Building, designed by the office of James A. Wetmore, supervising architect of the treasury, lacks a dome or rotunda, but it became Alaska's capitol upon its admission to the Union.

The six-story box-like building is constructed of brick-faced reinforced concrete. The lower facade incorporates Indiana limestone, while the four columns of the slightly protruding two-story portico are composed of marble from the quarries at Tokeen, Prince of Wales Island, Alaska. They support a narrow balcony with balusters covering the entrance, which consists of three bronze-and-glass doors. Four two-story limestone pilasters, between windows, flank the entrance. Above, a string course and vertical rusticated stone separate windows, while horizontal panels incorporate a relief decoration.

The House finance committee room.

In 1969, the legislative chambers were gutted and modern-style narrow windows replaced the original ones of that section. First-level windows are framed in limestone with keystones. On the narrow strip of lawn before the sidewalk and street stands a replica of the Liberty Bell, which is rung annually on the Fourth of July.

Alaska is known for its natural resources, and references are visible throughout the capitol, such as the Tokeen marble prominent in the lobby. A narrow frieze contains symbols representing Mining, Lumber, Fisheries and Igloos. The igloos mistakenly refer to the houses of the Eskimo. In Alaska, igloos were only used as emergency hunting and fishing shelters. The state's interior is arid, and there is not enough snow for igloos, so the Eskimo lived in sod-and-driftwood structures called *barabarahs*.

The Alaskan Otters, sculpted from a 5,000-pound marble boulder from Haines, memorializes wildlife casualties of the 1989 *Exxon Valdez* oil spill, and stone-fired clay murals entitled *Harvest of the Sea* and *Harvest of the Land* depict fishermen on Alaska's coastal waters and Natives hunting in the state's interior.

Plain staircases and elevators lead to the second floor, which houses the functional legislative chambers, furnished with bench desks and upholstered chairs. The walls of the narrow hallway showcase the work of photographers Lloyd Winter and Percy Pond. Documenting Alaska during the period from 1893 to 1943, the black-and-white photographic collection consists of 1,200 mining photographs depicting operations and miners' living conditions, as well as 350 images of the southeastern Alaska Tlingit Natives.

The House of Representatives speaker's conference room is located on the second floor, along with the House majority caucus meeting room. During a 1980 renovation, they were refurbished to an earlier period. It was then that the territorial legislature granted citizenship and voting rights to any citizen born within its boundaries prior to Congress granting similar rights to the Lower 48 in 1923. Alaska's lawmakers remain sympathetic to the early Asian descendants that first settled Alaska, as well as to concerns for natural resources. For example, the Eskimo, who carve household utensils and everyday objects from walrus tusk ivory, are the only Alaskans allowed to own the scarce commodity. In November of 1998, lawmakers reaffirmed a ban on billboards in order to preserve the state's natural beauty.

Throughout Alaska's history, the benefits from its natural resources were controlled and primarily benefited outsiders. This started to change in the late 1960s when one of the largest deposits of oil in North America was discovered in the Prudhoe Bay area of the Arctic Slope. In 1969, the state held an oil-lease auction, with drilling rights going to the highest bidders. This earned the state over $900 million. Since the cost of living in Alaska is higher than almost anywhere else in the nation, in part because it is geographically isolated and so vast that providing basic services such as health care and transportation is extremely complicated and expensive, the young state immediately spent the money on much-needed services.

The doors of the Senate chamber incorporate Native symbols.

Construction of a privately financed overland pipeline to move the oil to the southern markets was delayed due to environmental concerns and Native claims to lands it would cross. Under the Alaska Native Claims Settlement Act of December 18, 1971, the Natives relinquished their title to all but about 44 million acres, and in turn received compensation of $962.5 million, environmental protection, and some individual grants.

After the 1972 oil crisis, construction of the costliest private undertaking in U.S. history began in 1974. The project involved building an 800-mile pipeline from Prudhoe Bay to the ice-free port of Valdez, on Prince William Sound. The engineering challenges of building the Trans-Alaska Pipeline included climbing two mountain ranges and crossing 350 rivers and streams.

Upon the pipeline's completion in 1977, an oil boom materialized. The collection of oil royalties led to an increase in state spending. Oil proceeds have not only paid for three quarters or more of the state budget and freed residents from paying state sales or income tax, they also made possible the creation of a state-managed public trust fund. The Alaska Permanent Fund, now the nation's largest trust, with over $25 billion, was established through a constitutional amendment approved by state voters in 1976. The amendment and its supporting statutes set aside at least 25 percent of certain mineral revenues paid to the state for deposit into a public savings account to be invested for the benefit of current and future generations of Alaskans.

The fund is invested in stocks, mutual funds and real-estate projects throughout the United States, with the annual earnings paid out as dividends to anyone who has lived in Alaska for at least a year. While it fluctuates with the economy, as well as with the price of oil, since 1982 the fund has paid an annual dividend of between $1,000 and $2,000 to each resident of Alaska six months of age and older who applies.

Today, oil is flowing down the Trans-Alaska Pipeline at a slower rate than previously. As oil revenues dwindle, many state leaders say that Alaska will not be able to meet its obligations unless lawmakers consider either an income tax or a sales tax — or perhaps dip into the Alaska Permanent Fund to forestall those alternatives. For many Alaskans,

The Alaska State Capitol.

extending drilling on the North Slope of the Arctic National Wildlife Refuge may be a way to extend their oil-fueled way of life for another decade or two. They further assert that new technology has resulted in more environmentally sensitive oil exploration. For others, further exploration is a controversial issue, one complicated by environmental concerns over caribou habitat and potential disasters such as that of the *Exxon Valdez* tanker spill.

The lobby of the governor's office.

WEST VIRGINIA

WEST VIRGINIA STATE CAPITOL

ORIGIN OF NAME: West was added to Virginia when this region refused to secede from the Union during the Civil War.

CAPITAL: Charleston

CONSTRUCTED: 1924–1932

ARCHITECT: Cass Gilbert

ADMITTED TO THE UNION: June 20, 1863 (thirty-fifth)

SENATE: 34 members

HOUSE OF DELEGATES: 100 members

Until June 20, 1863, the area now known as West Virginia was part of Virginia. During the Civil War, support for the Confederate cause by Virginians east of the Allegheny Mountains and along the Atlantic coast compelled the inland residents to form the new state of West Virginia.

According to its constitution, Wheeling was to be the capital until otherwise provided by the legislature. Seven years later, in 1870, the General Assembly moved the seat of government to Charleston, but by 1875, the fickle legislature decided that the capital should return to Wheeling. West Virginians in other parts of the state pressed for more stability, leading to legislation passed on February 21, 1877, which provided that the people vote for one of the three sites — Martinsburg, Charleston or Clarksburg. When Charleston prevailed, the seat of government returned there on May 1, 1885, ending the shipping of the state records and furniture up and down the Ohio and Kanawha rivers.

On January 3, 1921, after a fire swept through the Charleston capitol, completely destroying the building and its contents, a seven-member capitol building commission was created to erect a permanent fireproof one. The old site was sold and land was purchased on the banks of the Kanawha River, a mile east of the old capitol site. The commission selected Cass Gilbert as architect because of his proven track record of traditional architecture and his national reputation.

West Virginians' pride in their capitol is apparent throughout the vast documentation of the building's construction, along with rich snippets of history. One is that Gilbert, born in Zanesville, Ohio, designed the capitol on the site where his father, a brigadier general of the 44th Ohio Volunteer Infantry, fought during the Civil War at the Battle of Charleston. Another raconteur relates that at one point Gilbert decided to pull out of the project.

After Gilbert advised the commission of his decision, one commissioner reportedly said, in a typically proud Appalachian response, "We don't want someone from Ohio designing our capitol anyway." Whereupon Gilbert changed his mind.

With the popularity of American Renaissance capitols on the wane, Gilbert adapted Classical architecture to modern construction for this one, the last constructed in the American Renaissance style in the United States. The symmetrical U-shaped building consists of Indiana limestone over a steel frame. It incorporates a porticoed central section and two four-story wings that are attached to the center unit by a single-story connector. The three units were separately contracted, financed, built and inspected before starting the next phase. Gilbert directed construction from his New York office through letters and telegrams.

Ground was broken for the west wing on January 7, 1924. It was completed and accepted by the commission on April 14, 1925. The east wing's construction began in 1926 and was completed in December 1927. The main unit was not started until March 31, 1930, and was finished on February 10, 1932. The delay for the last section occurred because a special tax levy on all taxable property in the state needed to be passed by the legislature to pay for it, "not to exceed in any one year the sum of five cents or so much thereof

A view of the capitol from across the Kanawha River.

Square columns surround the well of the rotunda on the ground floor of the state capitol.

as may be necessary on the one hundred dollars valuation of said taxable property." The cost of the project was as follows: first, west — $1,218,171.32; second, east — $1,361,425.00; and third, main (the bid, in the Depression, was low) — $4,482,623.21. This totaled $7,062,219.53, plus $2,000,000 for the site, with a full payment of $9,134,000 completed on August 9, 1934. Gilbert responded to financial complaints, saying, "The recollection of quality lasts long after the price is forgotten."

The office wings measure about 300 feet long and 60 feet wide and incorporate slightly projecting central entrances with greater projections to the rear. Pilasters run between window arrangements on the upper three floors to support the surrounding cornice. As with the central section, the wings have a flat roof enclosed by a balustraded parapet. Carvings above the west-wing entrance are hand-chiseled from blocks of limestone and depict heads of mythological figures.

A 292-foot-high golden dome crowns the central section, which is just over four feet higher than the dome of the United States Capitol, though the Washington, D.C., dome, at 88 feet in diameter, is 13 feet wider than West Virginia's. Atop its lantern is a bronze staff with a golden eagle.

The gilding of the dome was controversial. Many felt that covering the capitol with gold leaf was simply too extravagant, especially in the middle of the Depression. But Gilbert believed the gilding was cheaper, at $23,700, than the marble covering of the capitols of Rhode Island and Minnesota by about $500,000.

Two-story-high Doric pilasters line the outer walls of the midsection, supporting the cornice. The main entrance on Kanawha Boulevard, protected by a Corinthian portico and mirrored on the opposite side by a similar entrance, is approached by a broad flight of steps. Solid limestone columns weighing 86 tons each support the portico with its plain pediment.

West Virginia's House of Delegates.

Inside, the spacious rotunda has pilastered walls of Vermont marble. Four arches rise to a carved frieze at the base of the drum, with lunette panels of blue-painted plaster. Gold-leaf bands decorate the walls of the drum and ceiling of the dome, painted in shades of blue, gray and rose. A row of narrow windows, covered with grilles, encircles the inner dome below tall, narrow windows divided by Corinthian pilasters. The floor of the rotunda features an open well and is inlaid with Italian travertine and white Vermont marble. A balustrade encircles the well, through which can be seen a colonnaded hall on the floor below.

Through the east and west arches, matching foyers lead to the House of Delegates and the Senate chambers, which are entered through marble columns weighing 34 tons each. Both foyer ceilings are covered with square coffered panels containing bronze-colored, plaster leaf arrangements representing such native hardwoods as red oak and sugar maple. The walls consist of white Vermont marble topped with a series of carved symbols for Agriculture, Art, Education, Engineering, Native Americans, Justice, Mining, Peace and Religion. Pedestals of black-and-gold Belgian marble support translucent Italian alabaster urns, which light the foyers.

Gilbert designed both chambers in a similar manner but with subtle differences befitting their legislative role. Rose-colored panels of acoustic plaster cover the walls of both rooms. Equal-sized public galleries framed by arches open on three sides of their chambers. Behind the galleries are small arched windows covered with decorative bronze grilles. Behind the dais is a fourth arch set with a blue panel. Above the dais hang gold-leaf clocks and replicas of the Great Seal of West Virginia, hand-carved in cherry. The state's Latin motto is *Montani Semper Liberi*, meaning "Mountaineers are Always Free."

Identical chandeliers of crystal hang on a brass chain in each chamber.

The Senate chamber.

The 1,500-pound fixtures contain ten thousand pieces of imported hand-cut glass and about three thousand pieces of beading. Adjacent to each, spacious offices accommodate the presiding officers and clerks and offer space that can be used for committees.

The most obvious difference between the chambers is that the Senate incorporates a domed ceiling topped with a small cupola, in the form of a paneled skylight with stained glass, while the House's ceiling is flat. There are two rows of coffers in the arches above the Senate's galleries, while the House has only one row. Carved eagles in the Senate have spread wings, while the wings of the eagles in the House are closed. The Senate continues the tradition of roll-call voting, but the House has adopted electronic voting. Walnut desks with leather-upholstered chairs are identical, though the Senate's desks are larger in size.

Back in the rotunda, double flanking stairways of white marble lead off the hallway on the south side to the Doric Hall on the ground floor. It contains fluted Doric columns and six crystal lights suspended on bronze chains.

The State Supreme Court.

A statue of U. S. Senator Robert C. Byrd.

In the center is a circular colonnade of sixteen square Doric piers that enclose the well in the rotunda floor. High above the well is the blue-vaulted ceiling of the dome. A chandelier hangs from it on a 54-foot brass-and-bronze chain, suspended 180 feet from the floor. Made of 10,080 pieces of Czechoslovakian crystal, the 4,000-pound chandelier is eight feet in diameter and is illuminated by ninety-six lights. A circular design on the floor has the same diameter as the chandelier far above.

The wings incorporate individual designs and functions. Both were designated as office buildings, but the east wing was specifically planned for the West Virginia Supreme Court and for the bank-like facilities of the Treasury. Gilbert personally designed the court chamber, including the walnut bench and other furnishings, but he did not include a bar because he wanted to symbolize that nothing stands between West Virginia's highest court and its citizens. The walls and columns are of white Vermont marble and feature bases of black Belgian marble. Burgundy-colored drapes line the sides of the room, and the cork floor is covered with a dark red carpet.

A rectangular opening in the ceiling consists of stained-glass lined with bronze carvings entitled *Scale and Balance* and *The Book of Law*. The frieze also incorporates quotes by Thomas Jefferson, "The true foundation of republican government is the equal right of every citizen in his person and property and in their management," and by Abraham Lincoln, "Firmness in the right as God gives us to see the right." From the bench, the justices can easily see Lincoln's quote located over the entrance. Gilbert later designed the Supreme Court of the United States, patterning its courtroom on this one, though in the larger Washington, D.C., chamber he added a double row of columns.

The capitol remains unfinished, most noticeably in the bare vaulted ceilings and wall panels near the rotunda, and the bare walls throughout the building, along with many empty wall niches. Gilbert originally specified that murals depicting state history be painted throughout, such as in the first-completed west wing, but money was not available during the Depression. Outside, the triangular pediments over the north and south entrances are bare and rough where he intended full-relief statues with historical references. According to Gilbert, "Whatever is done in the way of artwork will be done under proper guidance and direction and by artists of established reputation and experience and of real ability."

During the time between the completion of the east wing and the groundbreaking for the main section, criticism surfaced regarding the size of the building, covering 14 acres of floor space, with 333 rooms. At that time the number of office workers was relatively few, but today office buildings, including one designed by Gilbert's architect son, surround the capitol and are filled with state workers.

The West Virginia State Capitol.

NEBRASKA

NEBRASKA STATE CAPITOL
ORIGIN OF NAME: From an Oto Native word meaning "flat water."
CAPITAL: Lincoln
CONSTRUCTED: 1922–1932
ARCHITECT: Bertram G. Goodhue
ADMITTED TO THE UNION: March 1, 1867 (thirty-seventh)
UNICAMERAL: 49 Senators

The first Territorial Legislature of Nebraska met in Omaha in 1855, in a red-brick building owned by the Council Bluffs and Nebraska Ferry Company, the only brick building in the city at that time. It became the state's first capitol. The current Nebraska State Capitol occupies a four-city-block area that was designated Capitol Square in the original 1867 plat of Lincoln, named for the recently assassinated president. A second capitol, built between 1880 and 1889, became too small for government business, and a state capitol commission was formed in February of 1919 to oversee the planning and construction of a third capitol building to be constructed on the site. The commission initiated a national design competition, setting only general requirements in order to encourage originality and artistic expression. Some of the competitors included McKim, Mead & White, John Russell Pope, Tracy and Swartwout, and Bertram Grosvenor Goodhue.

The commission chose Goodhue's design as the winning entry. Goodhue began his career as a draftsman not as a formally trained architect, though he eventually became partner in an architectural firm that specialized in Gothic Revival buildings. In that style, Goodhue designed the Rockefeller Chapel (1918–1928) at the University of Chicago. Also recognized for reviving the Spanish Colonial style, he was exploring more innovative designs when he entered the Nebraska State Capitol competition.

Goodhue's plan stood out from the other proposals, which were for Renaissance-style buildings. It appeared smaller than the others, meaning it would probably cost less money to construct, and more modern because it broke with the traditional model of the United States Capitol by omitting pediments, columns, pilasters, porticoes and a dome. Instead, Goodhue incorporated twentieth-century steel-frame construction techniques in order to include a skyscraper tower. Unlike empty-spaced domes, the tower provided functional government office space. Still, the commission's choice of Goodhue's design was surprising at a time when the Neoclassical capitols

of Washington and West Virginia, with their dominating domes, were nearing completion.

Goodhue kept such Beaux Arts features as balance and symmetry, along with a few interior Italian marble columns, though their capitals incorporated agricultural images of cows and corn. He also followed the Beaux Arts tradition of integrating architecture and decorative arts through his collaboration with sculptor Lee Lawrie, mosaicist Hildreth Meirer, and painter Augustus Tack under the direction of a symbologist, University of Nebraska philosophy professor Hartley Burr Alexander.

All the sculpture of the capitol was designed by Lawrie, who worked closely with Goodhue. Since they both viewed sculpture as an integral part

Intricate ceiling mosaic in the unused Senate chamber.

The west side of the Nebraska State Capitol.

Nebraska's unicameral legislative chamber.

of the architecture, Lawrie's figures are not separate and free-standing but integrated into the building, partly sculptural, partly architectural.

Overall, Goodhue's design reflects the geography of Nebraska. The broad, low base replicates the flat landscape of the plains, and the tall tower rising from the base undoubtedly imitates grain elevators jutting up from the prairie horizon. The two-story-high square base, measuring 437 feet on each side, consists of a cross within a square, with four interior courtyards.

The courtyards provide natural light for the surrounding offices. This cross-within-a-square floor plan also allowed construction to begin in phases around the still-standing old capitol on a "pay-as-you-go" budget, so that government business continued uninterrupted and without the added expense of renting temporary facilities until the new offices were ready.

The 79-by-79-foot square tower rises 350 feet to form a slightly set-back platform for a 70-foot octagonal lantern. The main section of the tower is buttressed at the corners and incorporates long, narrow strips of windows running through each elevation. The lantern's sides contain square-columned loggias and support a traditional hemispherical dome covered in golden tiles. Eight abstract Native American thunderbirds in blue, red and yellow mosaic tiles encircle the base of the dome.

At the top of the dome, standing on a nearly 13-foot-high pedestal of wheat and corn, is Lawrie's male figure, *The Sower*, a tribute to the historical importance of agriculture for Nebraska. The bronze-and-reinforced-steel statue, 19 feet tall and weighing about 9 tons, also serves as a lightning rod for the capitol.

Although similar, the four sides of the building are differentiated by their entrances. On the north side, four bas-relief bison panels, two of bulls and two of cows with calves, flank the steps of the grand staircase leading to the second-story main entrance. A large stone arch featuring hand-carved coffers with motifs surrounds the doorway. Further decorations to the main entrance include a semicircular window; a bas-relief panel of settlers with their covered wagon pulled by oxen; the inscription "The Salvation of the State is Watchfulness in the Citizen"; and,

Nebraska's Hall of Fame includes Gilbert M. Hitchcock, publisher of the Omaha World Herald.

directly above the arch, the engraved words "Wisdom, Justice, Power, and Mercy, Constant Guardians of the Law." Four engaged figures on flanking towers of the entrance reiterate those legal attributes.

From this archway and encircling the outside base, Alexander's symbolic imagery depicts government and law from ancient times to modern Western democracies. Beginning on the on the north side is a series of eighteen bas-relief panels moving chronologically around the building. The first represents Moses bringing the law from Mount Sinai and the last is Nebraska's admission to the Union. The west facade, where the legislature meets, represents law in the ancient world with *The Judgment of Solomon* and *Plato Writing his Dialog on the ideal Republic*.

The south side highlights written and constitutional law. Above bas-relief panels, architecturally engaged sculptures of such great lawgivers as Moses, Charlemagne and Napoleon are carved between the arched windows and low towers. The supreme court chamber is located behind these windows, so it is

fitting that the relief panels illustrate the Declaration of Independence, the Magna Carta and the United States Constitution.

To the east, the spirit of law in the new world includes *The Signing of the Pilgrim Compact on the Mayflower* (1620), *Lincoln and the Emancipation Proclamation* (1863), *The Louisiana Purchase* (1803), and the *Kansas and Nebraska Bill* (1854). A frieze around the building contains the names of Nebraska's ninety-three counties.

Located on its original site, west of the west entrance, stands the *Lincoln Monument* by Daniel Chester French. It predates and is detached from the capitol. The monument consists of a bronze statue of Abraham Lincoln on a granite pedestal and a granite backdrop on which his Gettysburg Address is engraved. It was dedicated in 1912, with William Jennings Bryan of Lincoln the featured speaker.

Inside, life on the Nebraska plains is represented in Meiere's marble-tile floor and ceramic-tile ceiling mosaics. Her work unifies the public areas of the domed vestibule, foyer and rotunda, and contrasts with the muted tones of the stone exterior. The vestibule at the north entrance depicts farming, or *Nature's Gifts to Man on the Plains*. A mosaic sun, representing the source of energy and creation, fills up the marble floor, reminiscent of the mosaics from fifth- and sixth-century Christian churches. Symbols of the seasons, the signs of the zodiac, elements of agriculture and native animals surround the sun in the dome above. On the wall, murals illustrate a homesteader's campfire, the first furrow, and a house-raising.

Between the vestibule and the rotunda, the connecting foyer or corridor incorporates a cathedral-like nave. Its decorative theme, *The Life of Man on the Soil of Nebraska*, is illustrated in the mosaic floor panels, which suggest the natural foundation of life and its creation. The past, present and future of life on the plains, including its plant and animal life, are represented within the three medallions. On the walls, Venetian glass murals, added to celebrate the 1967 state centennial, depict *The United States Survey*, *The Blizzard of 1888*, *Tree Planting*, *The Coming of the Railroad*, *The Spirit of Nebraska*, and *Building the Capitol*.

In the rotunda, the decorative theme concentrates on the "Virtues of the State," which not only sustain society but are ideally embraced by every Nebraskan. Mosaic figures forming a celestial rose represent Temperance, Courage, Justice, Wisdom, Magnanimity, Faith, Charity and Hope. Fluted columns and pendentives depicting the agricultural activities of plowing, sowing, cultivating and reaping support the dome. The sun and representations of the four seasons can be seen on the inner dome. A frieze below incorporates inscriptions from Aristotle's *Politics* and Plato's *Dialogues*.

Wall murals added during the 1950s represent the work of society to achieve a virtuous and noble life: *Labors of the Head* (intellectual), *Labors of the Hand* (manual and industrial), and *Labors of the Heart* (humanitarian and artistic). In the center of the rotunda floor, the "Earth Mother" is surrounded by four smaller designs symbolizing Water, Fire, Air and Earth. They are encircled by a border decorated with prehistoric animal forms found in Nebraska.

On opposite sides of the rotunda, wooden doors lead to the legislative chambers. To the east, the doors of the old Senate chamber incorporate Native American symbolism, emphasizing the importance of corn. On the west, leading to the legislature chamber, Assyrian symbols on the doors illustrate the importance of trees in civilization.

The Senate chamber was abandoned in 1934 when Nebraska became the only state to adopt a unicameral legislature. At that time, the Nebraska constitution was amended to provide for a unicameral legislature of forty-three members, elected on ballots without a party affiliation. The first session of the unicameral legislature convened in 1937. It was instituted, in part, to enable the state to operate more efficiently, and because it is nonpartisan less pressure is put on members to vote along party lines. In 1965, the membership increased to forty-nine senators, elected from districts with an approximately equal number of residents. The members serve four-year terms, with half elected every two years, though they may only serve two terms in succession.

The capitol's north corridor.

The senators work under a gold-stenciled, walnut-beamed ceiling decorated to represent Native Americans and the pioneers that followed them onto the Great Plains. Above the front desk and flanking the electronic voting panel is a pioneer family carved into the limestone arch. The man with a shovel symbolizes Labor, and a woman with child represents Family. Multicolored marble columns support the public galleries. Fleur-de-lis represent French rule before the Louisiana Purchase. The seating is arranged by seniority.

South of the rotunda and at the end of the hall is the Nebraska Supreme Court. Its seven members meet monthly in a chamber featuring an eight-thousand-piece coffered walnut ceiling. Additional features include tile walls displaying three large handwoven tapestries that portray early commerce in the Louisiana Territory, and a bench with seventeen inlaid woods. Behind the bench, a concealed door made from walnut leads to the offices of the justices.

On the second floor is the governor's suite, which dates from 1927. The barrel-vaulted reception room contains oil-on-canvas murals by Tack that depict the rights and responsibilities of citizens and their government. The state's motto, "Equality before the Law," and a woman set in profile in a wreath appear above the fireplace. Images of bison, corn and wheat are inlaid or carved into the decorative details of the suite. Original green-covered velveteen seating surrounds the room.

Since its completion, there have been few alterations to the capitol, though the extremes of heat and cold in Nebraska's weather, have caused expansion and contraction of the exterior surface and have resulted in some cracking. In 1997, lawmakers authorized funds for an eight-year restoration. Among other projects, workers are constructing new stress joints at each floor level in the tower, repairing and restoring tower windows and the thunderbird mosaics, rebuilding the walls of the observation deck and turrets at the fourteenth level, properly cleaning the exterior limestone, and replacing the copper roofing around the base.

The rotunda with its Meiere floor mosaics.

LOUISIANA

LOUISIANA STATE CAPITOL

ORIGIN OF NAME: After France's King Louis XIV, by the explorer La Salle.

CAPITAL: Baton Rouge

CONSTRUCTED: 1931–1932

ARCHITECT: Weiss, Dreyfous & Seiferth

ADMITTED TO THE UNION: April 30, 1812 (eighteenth)

SENATE: 39 members

HOUSE OF REPRESENTATIVES: 105 members

Louisiana's state capitol conveys its rich history and diverse cultural influences, which are also reflected in its language, cuisine, folklore, government organization and laws. Until the Spanish arrived in the first half of the sixteenth century, a succession of Native American cultures inhabited the area of present-day Louisiana. In 1682, Robert Cavalier de La Salle reached the mouth of the Mississippi and claimed the land drained by it and its tributaries for France. The resulting French colony was ceded to Spain in 1763, returned to France in 1800, and sold to the United States for $15 million, or about 4¢ an acre, by Napoleon Bonaparte as part of the Louisiana Purchase.

Extending its western boundary from the Mississippi River to the Rocky Mountains and stretching from the Gulf of Mexico to the Canadian border, part or all of fifteen states were later formed from the Louisiana Purchase. In order to govern the vast area, Congress decided to divide it, creating the Territory of Orleans, covering about the same area as the present state of Louisiana.

New Orleans became the capital when the territory, renamed Louisiana, joined the Union. Donaldsonville briefly served as the capital during the War of 1812, but the seat of government returned to New Orleans. The legislature moved to Baton Rouge in 1850, where it remained until 1862. During 1861, Louisiana seceded from the Union and soon joined the Confederate States of America. After Louisiana fell to the North during the Civil War, Union forces maintained a capital in New Orleans while, Opelousas and Shreveport served as Confederate capitals. Following Reconstruction, the legislature adopted a new constitution in 1879 and Baton Rouge again replaced New Orleans as the capital. The General Assembly convened in the Gothic Revival capitol (1849–1932) designed by architect James H. Dakin. Following the Civil War, the Union troops used the capitol as a prison and later as a garrison for African-American troops. During this unsettled period, fires destroyed most of its interior, so when the seat of government returned, money was appropriated for the restoration of the castellated building.

Overlooking the Mississippi River, the Gothic Revival capitol is distinguished by its square and octagonal towers, along with its windows, shaped as circles or trefoils, rectangles or arches. It also retains its intact 1849 cast-iron fence. Each section was molded separately and made in such a way that it fits together without bolts. Decorative features include pineapples on the posts, quatrefoils that echo some of the capitol's windows, and fleur-de-lis. Inside, the spiral staircase and stained-glass dome, supported by a single cast-iron column that reaches to the basement floor, date from the restoration.

The abandonment of the old capitol began in 1928 with the election of Governor Huey P. Long. The legendary populist boss of Louisiana made the construction of a new capitol an issue in his campaign. Despite the lack of legislative support following his election, Long secured the services of the

The stained-glass dome of the old Louisiana capitol, now a museum.

The Louisiana State Capitol stands behind the grave of Huey Long.

The Louisiana Senate chamber.

New Orleans architectural firm Weiss, Dreyfous & Seiferth. The architects studied other buildings throughout the country for ideas and inspiration, including the Nebraska Capitol under construction in Lincoln. The image of such a building rising above southern Louisiana's flat countryside fascinated Long, who thought that a similar design would show the world that Louisiana belonged in the modern era. As plans for the new capitol progressed, Long's only instructions were that the tower concept be incorporated and that it be completed as quickly as possible in order that its dedication take place under his administration.

After Long successfully cajoled the legislature into authorizing the project, the state took advantage of cheap Depression-era labor and materials. As a result, the building cost 20 percent less than the low bid of $5 million. The excess money was spent on art, imported materials, furnishings and landscaping.

Completed in just fourteen months, the thirty-four-story capitol became the highest building in the South at the time, rising 450 feet above Baton Rouge and the Mississippi River. It also contained all the features of a modern office building, including one of the first central air-conditioning systems in the South. Electronic voting machines in both legislature chambers sent the results from the floor directly to the governor's office. Although Long never officially worked in the capitol, having moved on to the United States Senate even before it was dedicated, he continued to control Louisiana politics from there until he was fatally shot in a corridor outside the executive offices in 1935. Today, bullet holes in the marble and a plaque mark the spot of his assassination.

The tall capitol has a steel frame that is covered in white Alabama limestone set on a foundation of reinforced concrete. Above the high basement, the five-story base contains the central entrance and balanced wings. A central square tower rises from the base. The smooth, unadorned tower cuts away to an octagonal shape at the twenty-second floor. The transition is made by four engaged allegorical figures carved into the corners, representing Law, Science, Philosophy and Art. Above the twenty-sixth level, the tower returns to a plain surface before rising to the octagonal cupola with large pedimented windows on all four sides. Four flying buttresses, carved as eagles by Lee Lawrie, provide the transition from the cupola to the crowning aluminum lantern. The lantern sends out a beacon of light, symbolizing the light of truth, hope and faith.

While the tower reaches skyward in symbolic representation of the state's future and its spiritual underpinning, the base is a monument to Louisiana's history. Many sculptors and painters, incorporating various techniques and artistic periods, collaborated with the architects to tell the story of Louisiana

The bronze doors of the House chamber depict Louisiana's previous capitols.

through the building's decorations. Decorative details include free-standing sculptures, detailed carved friezes, bas-reliefs and allegorical murals. Cotton, sugarcane, magnolias, crawfish, raccoons, turtles, egrets, eagles, and especially pelicans (the state bird) are among the many motifs represented.

When one project required carvings of crawfish, the architects shipped live specimens from Louisiana to the artists' studio in New York.

The steps leading to the main entrance are each inscribed with the names of the forty-eight contiguous states, listed in the order of their admittance to the Union. The top step, engraved with *E Pluribus Unum* from the Great Seal of the United States, reads "One from Many" and symbolizes the interdependence of the states. Alaska and Hawaii were added to the top step after they became states.

The only free-standing sculpture in the capitol, designed by Lorado Taft, flanks the main steps. One half, *The Patriots*, consists of an armored soldier and the mourners of a warrior slain in battle. The other half, *The Pioneers*, depicts men and women who created the state out of wilderness. Both were carved in place from Indiana limestone by a team of workmen under Taft's supervision.

Located between the sculptures is a four-story portal that contains the building's main entrance. Bas-relief panels illustrating Louisiana's economy and natural resources surround the bronze-and-glass doors. Chiseled into the stone next to the entrance is a quotation by Robert Livingston, the American ambassador who negotiated the Louisiana Purchase. It reads: "We have lived long but this is the noblest work of our whole lives.... The United States take rank today among the first powers of the world."

At the top of the portal, two eagles, symbolizing the federal government, border the state seal, which incorporates a pelican in a nest. The pelican pricks its breast in order to nourish the young with her own blood. Above the eagles, and serving as the base for the vertical shafts that divide the tower windows, are six engaged figures with coats of arms representing the countries that ruled Louisiana. Native Americans face the four central figures of Spain, the United States, the Confederacy and France.

Between pilasters and encircling the wings, nearly six-foot-square stone relief busts of twenty-two historic figures are carved above bronze magnolia-decorated windows. The figures include William Charles Cole Claiborne, first governor; La Salle; de Soto; Andrew Jackson; Henry Watkins Allen, Confederate governor of Louisiana; Thomas Jefferson; Paul Tulane, founder of Tulane University; and John James Audubon, naturalist and illustrator who worked and lived in the state during the 1820s.

Decorative features continue in the two-story-high Memorial Hall, located between the House and Senate chambers. The light marble walls feature pairs of wide fluted pilasters, without capitals, executed in dark Italian marble. More than twenty types of stone, including two types of Mount Vesuvius lava imported from Italy, are incorporated into the hall's walls and floor.

Gold and oak-leaf stenciling covers the ceiling above a historical frieze. The bronze chandeliers, typical of fixtures in other parts of the building, weigh two tons each. The chandeliers are attached to steel cables anchored at the fifth-floor level. A pair of Sevre urns, a gift from France in 1934, flank the elevators. The bronze-relief-paneled elevator doors feature a bas-relief of the men who served as governors up to 1932, ending with Long.

Near the corners of the hall stand twice-life-size sculptures of four Louisiana governors. Carved from Georgian marble, they portray Sieur de Bienville; the first colonial governor, William C. C. Claiborne; Henry Watkins Allen; and Francis T. Nicholls, the first post-Reconstruction governor.

A bronze relief map of Louisiana occupies the center floor of the hall. The round plaque contains the names of its sixty-four parishes or local governmental entities. Each parish is depicted with a small star, while a large star signifies the state capital of Baton Rouge, with a miniature of the capitol tower in its center. Other symbols represent the state's agriculture, natural resources, industries and products, along with the Great Seal of Louisiana. A bronze railing protects the map.

Murals by Jules Guerin on the end walls depict agriculture in the state. They surround a pair of bronze doors that lead to the anterooms of the House chamber on the east side and the Senate chamber on the west. A free-standing marble-and-bronze staircase leads to a spectators' gallery on the Senate side. Bronze state seals hang above bas-relief doors to the anterooms and those that open from the anterooms to the chambers. On the doors are illustrations of additional events in Louisiana history, including representations of other buildings that once served as capitols.

The entrance to the capitol.

The size of the marble legislative chambers is the same, each one filling the end width of the base. The Senate seems smaller because of a marble colonnade consisting of engaged Ionic columns next to marble piers supporting the ceiling, which create aisles on either side of the room. The Senate features a hand-painted hexagonal coffered ceiling made from bagasse, a byproduct of sugar production. Its limestone-block walls feature Ionic fluted marble pilasters. Other features include a bronze railing, original walnut-inlaid desks and chairs, and a rostrum that is framed by columns and draperies, set in a semicircular space.

In the 1970s, bombs exploded in the Senate, causing extensive damage. A pencil that ricocheted from the floor of the chamber to the ceiling remains sticking out from the ceiling as a reminder of Louisiana's contentious state politics.

The House features fluted marble pilasters and a hand-painted ceiling. The frieze below the ceiling contains a Louisiana swamp scene, with pinecones, black-eyed Susans, magnolias and cattails. Original mahogany-and-walnut desks and chairs suffice as the members' offices. The wall behind the rostrum is paneled in walnut and contains an electronic voting board, clock and carved eagles. Cut into the walls on either side of the rostrum are grilles in the shape of sugar cane.

Upstairs on the fourth floor, the current press-conference room was originally constructed to accommodate the Louisiana Supreme Court, which preferred to stay in New Orleans. The governor's office occupies the old law library space nearby.

The Louisiana capitol's Memorial Hall.

DELAWARE

DELAWARE LEGISLATIVE HALL

ORIGIN OF NAME: Named after Lord De La Warr, the first governor of the colony of Virginia.

CAPITAL: Dover

CONSTRUCTED: 1931–1933

ARCHITECT: E. William Martin

ADMITTED TO THE UNION: December 7, 1787 (first)

SENATE: 21 members

HOUSE OF REPRESENTATIVES: 41 members

William Penn purchased the area that would become the state of Delaware, the "Three Lower Counties" of Pennsylvania, from the Duke of York around 1682. The Royal Charter of Pennsylvania omitted reference to the Lower Counties (New Castle, Kent and Sussex), and so they convened in their own separate Assembly, though at the same time as Pennsylvania's and usually in Philadelphia.

In 1704, with Penn's permission, the delegates from the Lower Counties seceded from the united Assembly and thereafter met as a single body at least once a year in the old courthouse at New Castle. Six members were elected by each of the three counties, and for seventy-two years all the laws for the Lower Counties were enacted by the Assemblies at New Castle. Although the government of the Lower Counties remained united in name with Pennsylvania under the executive branch, with the deputy governors visiting New Castle in order to approve or veto laws, in fact, they acted independently.

When the state government of Delaware was established under the first state constitution of 1776, the legislature became a bicameral body. The upper house, called the Legislative Council, consisted of three members from each county, and the lower house, the House of Assembly, included seven members from each county. Not until the second constitutional convention met in Dover in 1791 was a provision added to the constitution to popularly elect the governor.

The General Assembly met in New Castle in 1776 and 1777 before it decided, after rotating between sites in Wilmington, Lewes and Dover, to permanently meet in more centrally located Dover. From 1792 to 1875, the Delaware state government and the local county government coexisted in the same building, the Kent County Courthouse. In 1875, the county sold the building to the state and constructed the present Kent County Courthouse, on the south side of the Green. The former courthouse, now known as the old state house, continued as the seat of Delaware state government until 1932.

The old state house stands in the colonial section of Dover, on the east side of the Green, a square laid out in 1722 according to William Penn's 1683 plan. The Delaware Supreme Court building, the Kent County Courthouse, private homes, and former private homes converted for state or professional office use surround it. It was outside the old state house that the Declaration of Independence was read and King George's portrait was burned in July 1776. Close by, at the Golden Fleece Tavern, Delaware became the first state of the Union when it ratified the Constitution on December 7, 1787. The date is celebrated as a state holiday.

Delaware became the first state by ratifying the U. S. Constitution on this site in 1787.

Delaware's Legislative Hall.

Topped with an octagonal cupola and a Palladian window above a center door with a fanlight, the old state house, built in the Georgian style, was altered and enlarged over the years. Between 1972 and 1976, it was restored to its eighteenth-century appearance. Today it serves as a historic-structure museum owned and maintained by the state of Delaware, and contains a ceremonial office for the governor.

By the late 1920s, state officials realized that the Delaware government could no longer function in the old state house, regardless of efforts to save it through remodeling. As this was a period of conflicting architectural trends, the many varied proposals to replace it pitted traditionalists against proponents of the Art Deco and Moderne styles. A governor-appointed commission decided, somewhat controversially, on plan for a group of government buildings meant to recreate the architecture of Colonial days, circa 1750. The group was to be built behind the Green in a large open space in order to open up a new area of Dover for development.

The buildings comprising the Delaware Capitol Buildings Complex harmonize with the old state house. The Legislative Hall is the only state capitol in the United States in the Georgian Revival style. The original section of Legislative Hall, the first building in the plan to be erected, was constructed entirely of handmade brick in order to match as closely as possible the bricks of the old state house. The red bricks sharply contrast with the building's white woodwork trim.

Symmetrical, restrained and modest, the hall features a simple central wooden door below a window with a balcony. In the pediment above is a round painted relief of the state coat of arms. The roof, with dormer windows protruding, is surrounded by a balustrade and crowned by a three-tiered cupola.

The old state house faces the historic Green.

Legislative Hall was expanded twice, first in 1968–1970 with the addition of 45-foot wings giving each member an office in addition to their desk in the chambers, and again in 1994, when wings were added to the east end for hearing and caucus rooms and additional office space. The facade remains unchanged, the Colonial architecture maintained, though there is some disagreement as to whether the 1932 entrance facing the Legislative Mall or the 1994 entrance looking toward Court Street is now the main entrance.

The interior has an eighteenth-century-style lobby, which includes a colonnade, a staircase, and reproduction chairs and sofas. The Senate and House chambers flank the lobby. In both chambers, murals depict ten historical state events commemorating the two-hundredth anniversary of the United States Constitution and Delaware's ratification of it as "the First State." Commissioned in 1986, the murals are painted in acrylic on 8-by-4-foot panels. An interior renovation was completed in 1997.

Throughout the building the use of blue color, broken pediments above doorways, deep soffits and wood trim and furnishings further replicate the Colonial period. The executive offices, located on the second floor, are used by the governor and lieutenant governor when the General Assembly is in session. The governor's office is furnished with antiques and reproductions of the eighteenth-century Georgian period including mahogany Chippendale mirrors decorated with gold-trim eagles and a variety of tables, including a tilt-top, tea, card, and a maple-top table. The furnishings were obtained by a committee in 1933 headed by Henry Francis du Pont, of E. I. du Pont de Nemours and Company, and well known for the large antique collection in his home at Winterthur.

Over one hundred years ago, in 1899, the Delaware General Assembly passed one of the most well-known statutes in the United States, the General

The Senate chamber.

Corporation Law. The law streamlined the creation of corporations by taking the power to grant charters or incorporate companies out of the hands of the legislature. Today, the law controls the internal affairs of thousands of American corporations, including more than half of the Fortune 500 companies as well as half of the companies traded on the New York Stock Exchange, even though their headquarters are located elsewhere.

Revenue generated from initial filings and the ongoing yearly fees make up about one third of total Delaware government revenues collected for the state, stabilizing the small state's economy. In addition, the incorporation of so many businesses creates related jobs, not only in state government but in the corporate services industry, including the companies, law firms and accountants that handle the paperwork and act as local registered agents. Although other states, eager to emulate Delaware's success, have tried to copy its statute, businesses continue to prefer incorporating in Delaware. Its law was thoroughly revised in 1967 and stays flexible through smaller, incremental changes.

The Delaware Chancery Court provides another advantage for corporations. Unlike nearly all the other states that merged their chancery or equity courts with other courts, Delaware's was preserved. It hears cases involving trusts and estates, fiduciary matters, disputes involving the sale

The House of Representatives chamber.

of land, questions of title to real estate, and contractual matters, but has no jurisdiction over the criminal or tort actions that often result in case backlogs. The Chancery has evolved into the court of choice for corporations when they are seeking quick resolution of corporate disputes, injunctive relief or other equitable type remedies.

On the two-hundredth anniversary of the Delaware Court of Chancery, United States Supreme Court Chief Justice William H. Rehnquist wrote:

"Corporate lawyers across the United States have praised the expertise of the Court of Chancery, noting that since the turn of the century, it has handed down thousands of opinions interpreting virtually every provision of Delaware's corporate law statute. No other state can make such a claim. As one scholar has observed, 'The economies of scale created by the high volume of corporate litigation in Delaware contribute to an efficient and expert court system and bar.'"

The Delaware governor's office.

NORTH DAKOTA

NORTH DAKOTA STATE CAPITOL

ORIGIN OF NAME: From the Sioux word meaning "friend" or "ally."

CAPITAL: Bismarck

CONSTRUCTED: 1932–1934

ARCHITECT: Holabird & Root

ADMITTED TO THE UNION: November 2, 1889 (thirty-ninth)

SENATE: 49 members

HOUSE OF REPRESENTATIVES: 98 members

When Congress established the Dakota Territory in 1861, it included the area covered today by both Dakotas as well as much of Montana and Wyoming. Its territorial capital at Yankton moved to Bismarck in 1883 after settlement patterns changed with the advancing Northern Pacific Railroad. Bismarck also offered 160 acres of land to the territorial government to be used as a capitol building site and as a source of revenue through the sale of residential building lots.

Although efforts were made to bring Dakota into the Union both as a single state and as two states, it was not until late 1889 that both North Dakota and South Dakota were separately admitted. When signing the statehood papers, President Benjamin Harrison reportedly covered their names so that no one would know which one was admitted first. In the end, because of its alphabetical position, North Dakota claimed the thirty-ninth-state status.

Because of limited funds, construction was completed only on the middle section and not the proposed dome of the 1883 capitol, then center of territorial government and later the first state capitol. The growth that came with statehood meant wings had to be added in 1894 and in 1903. This construction in stages resulted in an eclectic red-brick building that was not particularly popular with North Dakotans. Its fate was determined on December 28, 1930, when the capitol caught fire and was almost totally destroyed. Part of its north wing was salvaged and served as the capitol until completion of the present one.

Soon after the fire, the Capitol Act was passed authorizing the formation of the board of state capitol Commissioners to oversee the construction of a new capitol. Working within the financial limitations of insurance money from the first capitol and a frugal Depression-era budget, the commissioners first toured Baton Rouge, Louisiana, and Lincoln, Nebraska, along with the state capitols of Colorado and Wyoming, and then decided to deviate from the traditional domed capitol design by choosing a new and more efficient style. They hired the Chicago architectural firm of Holabird & Root, well known for their commercial skyscraper and public buildings, to work alongside North Dakota associate architects.

The most striking design feature of the capitol, completed in 1934, is the nineteen-story-high administrative tower, which houses the business activities of the state. The legislative function is carried out in the semi-circular-shaped chambers next to the tower. To conserve energy resources, the legislative wing was designed so that it can be closed off from the everyday activities of the state offices.

However, ongoing funding shortfalls resulted in alterations to the plan, such as the elimination of a proposed statue on the southern steps and of the decoration of the metal panels between the windows, omissions that

Assembly Hall lies between the legislative chambers.

The House of Representatives chamber.

made the capitol appear even more like a commercial building. Yet, with its vertical lines and uncluttered spaces, the building kept its Art Deco roots, and its more austere look transformed it to a transitional building with links to the International style, an architectural style that later dominated commercial construction.

From 1977 to 1981, in order to make the capitol larger and more symmetrical, the Judicial Wing and State Office Building was constructed at the same level as the legislative wing. Some critics believe that the addition, returning the building to a more traditional symmetrical shape centered around the tower, diminished the original, more dramatic, asymmetrical look. But the addition was designed to emphasize the coequal balance of the three branches of state government, and the legislative and judicial wings now flank the central executive tower. Moreover, the four-story east section not only blends with the original construction but expresses its own time period.

Light-colored Indiana limestone covers the building's steel framework above a base of Wisconsin black granite. Between the windows in the tower, aluminum panels, treated with baked-on enamel, give the effect of perpendicular stripes and accentuate the vertical lines of its walls. Eighty-two broad stone steps lead to the bronze-and-glass entryway.

Between the revolving doors stand six bronze columns, weathered to a black finish. Separated by the columns and sitting on the bronze canopies on top of glass panels, bas-relief sculptured bronze figures of a blacksmith, a farmer and his family, a woman with three children, a hunter and his family, and a Native American, symbolize North Dakota's history.

Memorial Hall, three stories high and only 26 feet wide, serves as a memorial to First and Second World War veterans. Sunlight pours into the

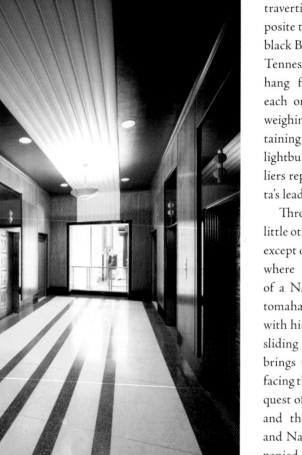

The second-floor elevator lobby.

corridor-like space through a wall of plate-glass windows set in bronze, lighting the Art Deco interior of smooth polished marble, wood and brass surfaces. Bronze bas-relief representations of miners decorate the panels above the revolving entry doors. In front of the windows stand six fluted bronze columns that rise to the ceiling.

The walls are of Yellowstone travertine from Montana and, opposite the windows, highly polished black Belgian marble. The floors are Tennessee marble. From the ceiling hang five cylindrical chandeliers, each one measuring 12 feet long, weighing more than a ton, and containing over one hundred electric lightbulbs. These bronze chandeliers represent wheat, North Dakota's leading agricultural product.

Throughout the building there is little other visual art ornamentation except on the bronze elevator doors, where there are representations of a Native American with raised tomahawk, and a hunter or settler with his musket, one on each of the sliding doors. Closing the doors brings them almost together, each facing the other to illustrate the conquest of the West by the white man and the struggle between whites and Native Americans that accompanied development. Other relief decorations, side by side, include a train and a settler in a covered wagon, a hunter and a buffalo, cows, a miner and a farmer, wheat and corn, and a rancher and his wife. Repeated Art Deco motifs and details such as the lines and ribbing found on pillars, walls, ceilings, doors, and window and elevator frames are found throughout.

West of Memorial Hall is the Legislative Assembly Hall, only 25 feet wide. The House, on the south side of the hallway, and the Senate across from it form a complete circle. Art Deco fixtures such as the three-tiered lotus-blossom wall sconces light the corridor meeting area. The lower parts of the walls are paneled in rosewood. Recessed alcoves, with

Memorial Hall.

canopies of rosewood with curly maple wood incorporating a Greek key design, contain leather couches.

The House chamber measures 60 feet from the front of the speaker's desk to the south wall and 120 feet east to west. American chestnut panels the walls of the House chamber, and its ceiling is made of blue plaster. A bronze railing 10 feet from the windows sets off the original walnut desks of the

members from the rest of the room. Inside the railing are semicircular platforms, each lower than the next, on which desks are located. A second-floor gallery with plain bronze railings seats over two hundred visitors.

The Senate, with fewer members, meets in a smaller chamber. Part of the space on the outer edge of a circle is set aside by a railing, fashioned in Art Deco style, for a lounge and committee rooms. Walls are lined with paneling of English oak with horizontal bronze bands at 8-foot intervals. The rostrum and furniture are made of American oak, and set in a curved niche for the lieutenant governor's desk. Fluted brass columns support a gallery, which seats 186 people and also incorporates bronze Art Deco ornamentation on its railing. Senators have no office except their desks. The telephones underneath their desks do not ring; they flash.

East, past the high-speed elevators, the Judicial Wing and State Office Building offers a transition to new materials, colors and designs. In the North Dakota Supreme Court chamber, there are no murals on the walls; the African mahogany woodwork and dark wool wall fabric contribute to the austere, uncluttered space. The lectern is raised so that attorneys can see eye-to-eye with the five justices sitting at the bench.

The floor of the skylighted Judicial Wing and State Office Building atrium is a gray-and-white veined marble, accented with a black terrazzo of mostly small black and a few white marble chips set in dark gray concrete. Other features include limestone walls, and balconies with bronze and stainless-steel railings around the upper stories.

Overall, the capitol's clean and uncluttered appearance reflects the geography of North Dakota. Part of the vast open plains, it is a predominantly agricultural state, and farming is both directly and indirectly the major source of income. North Dakota's farmers are the leading producers of hard red spring wheat, a premium crop used in bread and rolls. Recently, farmers are facing a dilemma that the North Dakota legislature is seeking to address.

It stems from wheat developed by a biotechnology giant, Monsanto. The wheat is protected from the Roundup herbicide, allowing farmers to use the herbicide to kill weeds without harming their wheat. But the wheat is

The Supreme Court chamber.

a genetically modified organism (GMO), that is, it carries new traits added using techniques that alter the molecular or cell biology of the crop by artificial means.

Proponents of GMO say that by 2050 the population of the Earth is predicted to exceed 9 billion people but the land necessary to feed that many people at today's rate of production will not be available. Consequently, the alternative is to obtain higher levels of productivity from the land that is available. Since this biotechnology allows the production of crops that have increased resistance to weeds, insects, pests and disease, GMOs result in increased yields and increased efficiency for farmers. Proponents further argue that food made from GMO wheat was tested and found safe by the United States Food and Drug Administration and the Environmental Protection Agency.

However, North Dakota lawmakers considered a bill that would make it the first state to ban the planting of genetically modified crops, reflecting a growing concern about such crops in the state. This is because genetically modified wheat poses risks of unknown dimensions to the state's economy and agricultural industry, and to public health and environmental safety. Farmers planting GMO crops may also be at risk for the damage they may cause to neighboring farmers, and they also fear losing the ability to export their crops to countries in European Union, Asian and Middle Eastern markets where consumers refuse to accept genetically modified wheat and governments strictly regulate GMO.

In 2001, North Dakota lawmakers considered, and, after extensive hearings, rejected a two-year ban on genetically engineered wheat seed, instead calling for further study of the issues surrounding it.

The North Dakota State Capitol.

OREGON

OREGON STATE CAPITOL

ORIGIN OF NAME: Uncertain, perhaps from the French word *ouragan*, meaning "hurricane," an early name for the Columbia River.

CAPITAL: Salem

CONSTRUCTED: 1936–1938

ARCHITECT: Francis Keally

ADMITTED TO THE UNION: February 14, 1859 (thirty-third)

SENATE: 30 members

HOUSE OF REPRESENTATIVES: 60 members

Before Lewis and Clark's expedition in the first decade of the nineteenth century, Spain, England and the United States sought control over the area that is now Oregon. After, in 1818, the United States and Great Britain agreed to a joint occupancy treaty that permitted citizens of both countries to settle and trade there. The next year, under the Treaty of Florida, Spain relinquished its claim to sovereignty over the region to the United States.

During the 1840s and 1850s until the provisional government was established in about 1860, thousands of people crossed the boundary of the United States at Missouri and Iowa and traveled 2,000 miles on the Oregon Trail to eventually settle in Oregon country. Unlike the earlier fur traders, most of the settlers moved west to farm the rich land in the Willamette Valley, and to build homes and communities. As a result, by 1848, Oregon became a territory encompassing all the land west of the Continental Divide between 42 and 49 degrees north latitude. Oregon City became the first territorial capital, until it was removed to Salem in 1850. Three years later, when Congress created Washington Territory to its north, Oregon's present boundaries were established.

Oregon's first capitol, erected in 1854, was destroyed by fire shortly after its completion, forcing officials to meet throughout Salem in temporary quarters. In 1872, the legislature authorized construction of a second one. The Classical capitol, which stood from 1873 to 1876, incorporated a large copper dome, two-story porticoes with Corinthian columns, and wings. Fire also destroyed it on April 25, 1935, when the strong draft created by the stair and elevator wells, the rotunda, and the dome-supporting girders caused the flames to spread rapidly. Only furniture, records and equipment from the first floor were saved, because the rapid advance of the fire prevented the removal of anything but a few records and articles from the floors above.

After the fire, the Works Progress Administration offered to cover forty-five percent of the cost to replace the capitol. It was the only federally assisted capitol project in the United States. A nationwide architectural competition was announced, and since it was during the Depression, received many entries. Francis Keally of New York won with a plan that balanced traditional and modern styles.

Keally's design is distinguished by its angular and unadorned smooth-surfaced elevations. The fireproof structural system combines reinforced concrete with steel framing and hollow clay tile. Above a granite base, white Vermont marble covers the exterior of the building. Made up of three blocks with identical east and west wings, the building incorporates 17-foot-high windows separated by pilasters that indicate the traditionally balanced

The governor's reception room.

The Oregon State Capitol.

House and Senate chambers above the first floor. The pavilions of the central block slant slightly toward the entry wall and lead visitors to the main entrance, reached by two flights of low steps.

The central area is decorated with bas-relief depictions of an otter, a beaver, and an eagle over a sunburst field above the inscription "State of Oregon." Separating the steel multi-paned casement windows from the three sets of revolving glass-and-bronze doors are bronze panels with cast-bronze bas-reliefs of a sheep, horse and steer, the three-masted schooner *Columbia*, and a stag, buffalo and doe.

In the place of a traditional Classical dome, a large flat-topped ribbed lantern rises above the roof on a series of set-back marble-faced pedestals. From there the main section of the tower rises approximately 43 feet to the parapet, which is recessed and adds 6 feet in height. The marble pedestal for the gilded 23-foot-high bronze *Oregon Pioneer* statue extends up another 18 feet.

The capitol was constructed and furnished within its $2.5- million budget and within three years. The site of the new capitol had expansion possibilities and so, beginning in 1975, 189,199 square feet of office space and hearing rooms were added to the capitol's south elevation. The addition, completed in 1977, cost $12.5-million. The integrity of the capitol's design was kept intact by block-like wings of comparable scale, compatibly styled, and covered in matching Vermont marble. Yet it remains subordinate and distinguishable as an addition by its set-back from the original building.

Flanking the main entrance, at the base of the front steps, stand marble sculpture slabs. On the west side are *The Covered Wagon* and *Lewis and Clark Led by Sacagawea*. The east side has maps outlining the Old Oregon Trail and the routes of Lewis and Clark. On the Capitol Mall and in its sur-

rounding parks are hundreds of trees, shrubs, flowers, fountains, statues and monuments. A giant sequoia tree over 120 feet tall stands near the capitol, along with a Douglas fir "Moon Tree" that grew from a seed taken to the moon by *Apollo 14* in 1971. Also included are fluted column fragments from the old capitol's portico and a statue of Dr. John McLoughlin, the Hudson's Bay official who first governed the Oregon Territory.

The main entrance leads to a fireproof interior. Since the capitol was partially funded by the federal government, its materials were chosen from sources throughout the United States to try to provide jobs to the many unemployed at that time. The rotunda, halls and lobby areas are lined with rose travertine marble from Montana. The floor and staircases are of Phenix gray marble from Missouri, with Vermont black marble used as borders. Because of the lack of hardwood in Oregon, wood was also imported.

The rotunda, which is 55 feet in diameter, extends approximately 106 feet from the floor to the roof of the interior dome, where thirty-three gold-leaf stars cover its ceiling, signifying that Oregon was the thirty-third state to join the Union. Below, a large bronze replica of the Oregon state seal, which incorporates the shape of a heart because Valentine's Day in 1859 was the date when Oregon became a state, lies embedded in the center of the rotunda floor.

The House of Representatives chamber.

Above the marble wainscoting hang four 11-by-26-foot canvas murals by Frank H. Schwarz and Barry Faulkner, paid for by 1930s Federal Art Program. The Depression-era art depicts Oregon historical events: Captain Robert Gray at the mouth of the Columbia River in 1792; Lewis and Clark on their way to the Pacific in 1805; the first women to cross the continent by covered wagon, welcomed by Dr. John McLoughlin in 1836; and the first wagon-train migration in 1843.

The rotunda, with Depression-era murals on surrounding walls and a bronze state seal embedded in the floor.

From the top of the murals to the base of the dome, the smooth rotunda wall surface is unadorned except for eight octagonal medallions, illustrating subjects found in the Oregon state seal. The 25-foot-wide marble stairs lead to the second floor, where the east and west wings contain the Senate and House chambers.

Each chamber is a triple-height space unencumbered by structural col-umns, and features wood-paneled walls and matching wood furniture — golden oak in the House and walnut in the Senate. Around the upper perimeter, names of Oregonians and others prominent in the history and development of the state are inscribed.

The practically identical rostrums are raised on marble platforms set into niches. In the House of Representatives niche, Faulkner's mural depicts the 1843 Champoeg Meeting, capturing the moment when, according to tradition, in a tie vote to decide whether to join British Columbia or the United States, Joe Meek convinced two French Canadians to switch their vote for the United States. This led to the first provisional government in the region.

The painting *News of the Admission of Oregon into the Union*, by Schwarz, hangs in the Senate. It shows a horseman riding from Oregon City to Salem, bringing the news of Oregon's admission to the Union. It took over a month for word to come from San Francisco by way of Portland to Oregon City, and an additional thirty hours, with no road and bad weather, before it finally arrived in Salem on March 17.

The carpeting in the chambers was reproduced in Ireland, in 1986, from the original design. In the Senate the pattern alternates wheat sheaves and chinook salmon motifs, symbolizing the state's agricultural and fishing industries. Within the House, the Douglas fir pattern (Oregon's state tree) is set on a diagonal grid.

The architect placed the governor's suite, with a reception room, ceremonial office, and private office, between the legislative chambers. Also incorporating black walnut, the reception room contains sofas and chairs that are original to the room, along with a circular table donated to the state by the architect. The table features a five-column base and an inlaid design of the old capitol, created from forty different types of wood. The ceremonial office contains photographs of past governors and artifacts from Oregon's past, including a desk and chairs saved from the earlier capitol. Especially precious is the china from Captain Robert Gray's ship, the *Columbia*. Gray reportedly named the Columbia River after his vessel.

The governor's office, as well as the first-floor galleria, benefit from a 1975 law requiring that one percent of all state building construction and renovation budgets be set aside for the acquisition of visual art for public display.

The entrance to the capitol.

As a consequence, twentieth-century works of art are installed there and throughout the capitol.

Oregon lawmakers not only actively promote the visual arts, but Oregon is well known as a progressive and environmentally sensitive state. In 1902, the "Oregon System" set forth the nation's first initiative, referendum and repeal laws, which allowed citizens to enact and repeal legislation as well as remove undesirable officials from office. During the 1906 election, Oregon voters became the first in the nation to elect a United States senator directly. Its 1929 legislation, the Oregon Reforestation Act, considered the beginning of environmental law, requires timber companies to replant logged-out areas. In 1971, lawmakers adopted the nation's first bottle-deposit law, banning nonrefundable bottles and cans. Later, a statewide ban on aerosol sprays containing fluorocarbons was enacted. The state also declared its Pacific coastline the property of all Oregonians and further restricted land use in order to prevent sprawl, as a way to preserve farms and forests.

While other states, in varying numbers and degrees, followed Oregon's groundbreaking legislation, the state remains the only one that authorizes doctors to assist terminally ill patients in committing suicide. The law attempts to balance the desires of some critically ill patients to end their lives peacefully against fears that suicidal people or the families of the severely handicapped might abuse it.

It is the state's intention that Oregon residents have the ability to end their lives in a humane and dignified manner rather than suffer a slow and agonizing death. Although many insist that doctor-assisted suicide is incompatible with the physician's role as a healer, the law has survived many attacks, including a constitutional challenge in the courts, a voter initiative to repeal it, and failed legislation in Congress to override it. For now, the court protects an area of state regulation from federal incursion or attack by agreeing that only states can regulate their own doctors.

The Senate chamber.

ARIZONA

ARIZONA LEGISLATIVE BUILDINGS
ORIGIN OF NAME: From a Native American word, *arizonac*, meaning "small spring."
CAPITAL: Phoenix
CONSTRUCTED: 1957–1960
ARCHITECT: Associated State Capitol Architects
ADMITTED TO THE UNION: February 14, 1912 (forty-eighth)
SENATE: 30 members
HOUSE OF REPRESENTATIVES: 60 members

The United States acquired the land that is now Arizona by the terms of the Treaty of Guadalupe Hidalgo at the end of the 1846–1848 war with Mexico. In 1850, Congress created the New Mexico Territory out of New Mexico and most of what is now Arizona. Four years later, the terms of the Gadsen Purchase provided land for a rail route across the southern part of the territory, and in 1863, Congress divided the New Mexico Territory, creating the Arizona Territory.

The territorial capital moved back and forth between Prescott and Tucson until 1889, when lawmakers permanently established it in Phoenix. Territorial offices and the legislature were at first housed in municipal buildings, until an alfalfa field west of downtown was selected for the site of the capitol. A bond issue and an appropriation by the legislature funded its construction. The capitol, constructed as nearly as possible of Arizona materials with a tufa-stone exterior, served as the territorial center from 1901 to 1912. It also was the site of the Constitution convention before it became the state capitol when Arizona was admitted to the Union.

An addition extending west from its center was completed in 1920. In the 1930s, with help from the federal government, another west wing that parallels the original building and forms the letter H was added. Today, the building serves as a museum of territorial and state government history.

By 1957, most Arizonans believed something needed to be done about the state's antiquated seat of government, with its pressing need for more office space and such modern conveniences as air conditioning. However there was almost complete disagreement as to what to do about it. Some wanted a skyscraper-type design, while others wanted to enlarge the capitol and add a Renaissance dome on a drum with a grand entrance staircase leading to the porch, fronted by the Ionic colonnade above today's entrance. Adding to the confusion was a design proposed by longtime Arizona winter resident Frank Lloyd Wright, submitted to the "people, not the politicians" of Arizona. The controversy tweaked national interest, and *Life* magazine devoted a page to the capitol design dilemma.

Wright submitted plans for a new capitol building, called "Oasis," to be built in the desert hills of Papago Park, outside Phoenix. Planned for the hot Arizona climate, it reflected an ancient Native American thunderbird, with the governor's office as the head, followed by the supreme court, then offices in the outspread wings, and the balanced chambers and public ceremonial spaces in the body and pointed tail. These branches of government were to be housed in individual hexagonal buildings, and the rest of the capitol would flow from them on an axis shaded, except for the solidly roofed wings, by a

Arizona's Executive Tower.

The Arizona legislative buildings flank the old capitol, now a museum.

giant canopy of pierced concrete. This 400-foot cover would break the fierceness of the Arizona sun and act like a greenhouse to permit exotic plantings. The roof resembled a tepee balanced by a pair of tall steeples and centrally crowned with a cupola.

Wright's plan was rejected for many reasons. First, people wanted to reserve Papago Park for recreational use. Second, his plan was limited to housing only the legislature, the governor, and the supreme court, inefficiently leaving most of the government departments at the old site, and the distance from Papago Park to the metropolitan center as well as from the other state buildings was too far and inconvenient. Third, the state constitution specified that the capitol must be located in Phoenix, and the park was outside the city limits. Moreover, a clause in the original deed for the land on which the capitol is located provides that it revert to the owner or estate of the owner in case it is no longer used for the capitol. And then there was its controversial design.

Finally, after years of debate and controversy, an agreement was reached for construction of separate legislative buildings north and south of the capitol. The Wright design summarily dismissed, the buildings were a compromise between advocates of keeping the capitol, although enlarging it, and those favoring a twenty-story skyscraper.

The legislative buildings, made up of reinforced steel, concrete, aggregate sand and gravel, are faced with Arizona tufa stone, like the nearby capitol though in a more modern way. Constructed in the plain and unadorned International style, reflecting the taste of the time, they incorporate flat overhanging roofs and rectangles with spans of glass. The glass is screened by pre-cast concrete sunbreaks, or screens, pierced with exposed stone aggregate, which serve as a decorative sun shield on the outside on all four sides of each unit. The provenance of the screen design is unknown, but some officials suggest it may represent a modified A, representing Arizona. As the sun shines onto the building, filtering through the screen, shadows outline the A design on the interior. The three-story-plus-basement structures contain 80,160 square feet each and are connected by a 200-foot-long underground walkway tunnel.

The main entrances to the utilitarian buildings face each other across the legislative mall area of grass and concrete. Glass panels extend the entire height of the building's entrance side, while on the other three sides the glass only extends along the upper two floors. The door handles of the four central Senate entrance doors bear the Arizona state seal. Inside both buildings, the first- and second-floor lobby wall panels are of Ozark marble from Arkansas, and terrazzo covers the floors. The state seal is embedded in the Senate lobby floor.

Today, lawmakers have their own offices, but when the legislative buildings were constructed they had only a desk in the chamber. Because many of the agencies had been crammed into the old capitol or in rented spaces outside the complex were moved into the buildings, legislators were limited

Wright's plea to the citizens of Arizona

The cramped urban accommodations of the Nineteenth Century as now seen in the officially approved Capitol for Arizona should not be allowed to date the State. That design for the proposed Capitol is completely out of date in this middle of the Twentieth Century. Arizona, youngest of the United States, is also youngest in geological time. Therefore outlines are sharpest and colorful; contours most picturesque. Her terrain is unique in the world: destined, in spite of obtuse insistence upon industry and agriculture, to become the playground of these United States of America. The tendency of parrot-and-monkey politics "à la Los Angeles" — quantity at expense to quality — will delay this consummation but cannot destroy Arizona's destiny. Therefore no more Nineteenth Century building for Arizona to go with the mortgage already foreclosed upon her landscape by the "developer," the pole-and-wire men and political slaves-of-the-Expedient. When the state of Arizona builds her Capitol, the establishment should signify, develop and herald her unique character. Therefore:

1.   The plan I respectfully submit is a simple commodious arrangement of her official family: the Senate, the Assembly, and the Chief Executive suites — all provided conveniently with ample offices, committee rooms, lounges, attractive refectory and a Great Hall for the people in which the history of the State would be adequately memorialized. Television and Radio are integral features of the Capitol. This officialdom is related to the Arizona public in convenient ways, simple, becoming and direct — the whole spacious and dignified in design: all to be executed in materials characteristic of the State and by the latest methods of economic modern-technique.

2.   I present a true Twentieth Century economical building of a character suited to grace Arizona landscape as seen, for instance, in unique Papago Park — a park near enough to an urban center to be convenient but yet be unspoiled by mediocrity — its appropriate use thus heightening its beauty. The park and the Capitol together as here presented make a harmonious circumstance of which future Arizona will have good reason to be proud.

3.   These preliminary drawings indicate a high, wide, sheltering crenellated-canopy of modern structure — like a great tree, filtering sunlight over subordinate but beautiful buildings and gardens standing together beneath the canopy in harmonious relation to this hexagonal domed shelter and to each other. All stand beneath and together in green gardens, fountains playing, pools reflecting. Great vistas of beauty are everywhere: useful function perfected no less — but more so when thus sheltered and standing high and wide in Arizona landscape out in the Valley of the Sun. Stone, copper, plastics employed in the great ferro-concrete system of construction that now constitutes the Twentieth Century body of our world. A sheltered air-conditioned spaciousness — all on one level: no elevator service needed. A new freedom — this — that would stand in modern times for Arizona as the Alhambra once stood in Spain before our continent was discovered.

Codicil

I can see why you, the citizens of Arizona, need to appoint certain men to arrange and look after your mundane affairs — just as you need police. But I am totally unable to see why those men should choose the buildings that will characterize your spirit — no more than those same officers should appoint the ministers of your churches or the man who will design your homes.

Citizens of Arizona — the State is your home! Your spirit should there find appropriate expression. To build an already dated New York monstrosity to stand up to present Arizona to posterity seems to me a crime punishable by you — yourselves. Hoping to save the State — I love the State — from this threat by rousing you to action, I have put on paper definite outlines of an edifice more suitable to the character and beauty of our Arizona and its landscape, at a cost not much more than one half that of the official aberration by which you are now threatened. This would leave ample opportunity for fine sculpture, great murals in painting and stained-glass, and furnishings of the highest possible quality suitably employing the artists of this region.

Frank Lloyd Wright
Arizona February 17th, 1957

Winged Victory atop the old capitol dome.

to the two upper floors, and had no private offices. After construction of the Executive Tower (1971–1974) west of the old capitol, state business was moved to its nine floors. There also are the offices of the governor, secretary of state, treasurer, mine inspector and the Department of Administration.

Within the House of Representatives building, the functional chamber features wall paneling of walnut veneer, plain-style desks with sequence-matched walnut veneer, a large visitors' gallery extending across the rear, and solid turquoise-colored carpeting, chosen because turquoise is the state gem.

The wall behind the speaker of the House's desk is made of polished rainbow granite from Minnesota. The original electronic voting panels were removed, and now a screen comes down over the granite to display voting results. When walnut veneer could not be replaced after the electronic voting panels were removed, plywood painted to simulate walnut veneer was substituted. Originally murals were planned to decorate the room. The artist was paid, apparently before he completed the work, but they were never delivered.

The detail on the speaker's desk, members' desks, and below the gallery is the same modified A that appears on the sun screens outside and is

The Senate chamber.

The House of Representatives chamber.

repeated around the railing of the large visitors' gallery in the back of the Senate chamber. Other features in the Senate include wooden strips above concrete walls, and blue carpeting incorporating stars with the state seal. The desks for the president, secretary of the Senate and individual members are made with quarter-sliced, book-matched walnut veneer. Battens on the front of the Senate platform desks are of premium-grade walnut. The fronts of those desks are decorated with bronze state seals, and a bronze seal hangs on the polished Italian travertine marble wall behind the president's desk. The Senate also votes electronically, with a screen coming down from above

the president's desk. Portraits of past presidents of the Senate hang round the room.

In 1967, a long-range planning program conceived of the Arizona Capitol Complex, including Wesley Bolin Plaza, as a corridor of city, county, state and federal government offices facing downtown Phoenix. At the eastern edge of the plaza, since December 7, 1976, rests an anchor and thirty links of its chain, lifted from the battleship USS *Arizona*. In the shape of an inverted T, it measures 10.5 feet tall and 8.5 feet across. The 1,202 sailors and Marines who died on the ship are named on plaques at the base of the memorial.

Inside the copper dome of the old capitol museum.

NORTH CAROLINA

NORTH CAROLINA STATE LEGISLATIVE BUILDING
ORIGIN OF NAME: After King Charles I of England.
CAPITAL: Raleigh
CONSTRUCTED: 1960–1963
ARCHITECT: Edward Durell Stone
ADMITTED TO THE UNION: November 21, 1789 (twelfth)
SENATE: 50 members
HOUSE OF REPRESENTATIVES: 120 members

The state of North Carolina claims that its state legislative building, which houses both the House of Representatives and the Senate, is the first building constructed exclusively for the use of a state legislature in the United States. When the representatives and senators moved to their new quarters in 1963, the state's governor and lieutenant governor and their staffs remained behind in the historic state capitol, completed in 1840 to replace North Carolina's first State House, destroyed by a fire in 1831.

Architects Ithiel Town, Alexander Jackson Davis and, in 1835, Scotsman David Paton designed the 1840 capitol by integrating elements copied from ancient Greek temples. The building brought together porticoes, a dome, a central public space, legislative chambers located opposite one another, and spaces for all the state government offices. The east and west facades have identical central pedimented porticoes, supported by Doric columns on rusticated piers. From a low hip roof, hidden by a solid parapet, rises the octagonal drum of the copper-covered dome, crowned by an iron anthemion cresting.

Inside the cruciform-shaped building, four halls intersect at the rotunda. Staircases off the rotunda lead to the second floor, where the chambers formerly occupied by North Carolina's Senate and House of Representatives are preserved, along with most of the original furnishings. The Senate chamber contains a shallow dome resting on pendentives. Fluted Ionic columns support galleries behind each arch.

On the other side of the floor, the House of Representatives chamber features a semicircular colonnade with a row of four columns behind the speaker's desk and below an elliptical half dome. In front of the original rostrum stands a table for newspaper reporters, where the Secession Ordinance of 1861 was reportedly signed. The portrait of George Washington (circa

1818) by Thomas Sully, after Gilbert Stuart, was saved from the burning first state house.

During the 1990s, the entire capitol was restored to its 1840–1865 appearance. Today its integrity remains intact, but for many years it was clearly inadequate, lacking offices and meeting rooms and providing cramped legislative chambers. Before 1959, however, all proposed remedies involving additions and modifications of the landmark building met strong opposition. In that year, the General Assembly established a seven-man commission of business leaders and lawmakers to select an architect and a site on which to erect a new legislative building. They chose Edward Durell Stone from New York. Stone worked in the International style and was noted for his design of the United States Embassy in India. Later, he completed the

The Vietnam Memorial on the capitol grounds.

North Carolina's state capitol.

John F. Kennedy Performing Arts Center in Washington, D.C., in 1968; the Standard Oil Building in Chicago in 1974; and the Florida Capitol in 1977.

The site selected for the North Carolina legislative building encompasses a two-block area, one block north of the old capitol. Five copper-covered concrete pyramids project from its broad, overhanging roof. It sits on a 340-foot-wide podium of native granite; the podium's terrace made of square concrete blocks, contains two large, saucer-like fountains flanking the main entrance. Before the entrance is the state seal, embedded in the terrace floor. Made of stone mosaic, it measures 28 feet in diameter. The architect devised the podium not only as a practical means for providing a level base for the building, constructed on irregular ground, but also to provide a convenient and out-of-sight place for parking.

Though not an imitation of Classical architectural style or of earlier state capitols, the legislature building incorporates some Classical characteristics, such as scored white marble (suggestive of Classical fretting), the Greek key, a white Vermont marble facade, and the grand proportions of the House and Senate chambers and the staircase. Some standard capitol architectural symbols include a domed rotunda — albeit pyramidal — and balanced legislative chambers. The legislative building is surrounded by a colonnade of square columns that are faced with white Vermont marble and reach from the terrace to the roof of the second floor.

The three-story building has an interior organization that eliminates corridors and substitutes garden courts to provide meeting and waiting areas as well as move traffic. This arrangement reflects Stone's philosophy: "I am concerned more with spatial than with structural drama."

The podium forms the base of the first floor, and the garden courts are its the four corners. Most committee rooms and offices of this floor are entered from the courts. Although each garden court is somewhat different from the others, they are all landscaped, with tropical plants and trees, three of them with fountains, and all contain seating space for visitors.

A statue of George Washington dressed as a Roman in the rotunda of the capitol.

The two legislative chambers occupy the east and west wings of the second floor. Following a traditional capitol relationship, they are directly opposite each other across the rotunda. The round Senate and the rectangular House of Representatives can be entered from the rotunda through large bronze doors. The rotunda, located at the exact center of the floor, is open through the third floor to the height of one of the five concrete pyramids.

Both chambers are also covered by a pyramid, with their ceilings 45 feet above the floor. As in the rotunda, the structural ribs of the roof form the coffered ceiling. Within the coffered pattern, geometric patterns are outlined in gold. The sides of each chamber open onto mezzanines of the first-floor garden courts and provide access to the members' office.

The chambers are furnished with red carpeting, brass chandeliers and walnut contemporary-style furniture, with smooth leather upholstery, designed by Stone and manufactured in North Carolina, a leading producer of furniture. The brass chandeliers in the chambers and above the main staircase are 8 feet in diameter and weigh 625 pounds each. The 12-foot-diameter chandeliers of the rotunda weigh 750 pounds.

Also on the second floor are the legislative library and a small chapel. Between the entrances to the chapel hangs the painting *The Baptism of Virginia Dare*, by William Steene. Virginia Dare was the first child born to English

The Senate chamber in the State Legislative Building.

parents in North America and her baptism on Roanoke Island, August 24, 1587, was the first-known baptism of a child in the English colonies.

A single, grand, red-carpeted staircase covered by a pyramid leads visitors directly from the first-floor entrance to the rotunda mezzanine on the third and top floor. From there they can enter the cantilevered House and Senate galleries, go to a large auditorium (also topped by a pyramid) for public hearings, or step outside onto the four corner roof gardens, where bubble skylights tucked into the landscaping allow light to filter into the corner courts below.

Since much of the building is glass, from the inside there are glimpses of flowers and shrubbery outside. Among the indigenous trees on the grounds, the terrace, and the roof are sugar maples, crabapples, magnolias and pines.

On the first and second floors, two tiers of small offices for the lawmakers are placed along the perimeter. A nearby legislative office building, constructed in the 1980s, houses the remaining members along with other legislative services.

Stone built into the State Legislative Building advances in engineering and architecture available in the 1960s, such as reinforced concrete, air conditioning, a generous use of large plates of glass and the latest technology equipment. At the old capitol, legislators had to wait in line to use a telephone, but each member of the General Assembly received his or her own telephone in their own small office in the new building.

The entire project cost approximately $6.2 million, land costing $890,000, construction $4.6 million, furnishings and equipment $430,000,

The governor's office in the capitol.

landscaping $75,000 and architect's fees $240,000. Of that, $4.5 million was financed by bond issue and the remainder by direct appropriation. The low cost, even in today's dollars, is attributed to simple finishes, the simple structure of cast-in-place concrete, and the close calculation of profit margins by the contractors for the prestige of the job.

Working from this legislative building, North Carolina lawmakers, like their peers in other states, struggle with a myriad of issues. Especially pressing are the problems resulting from the state's recent rapid population growth, economic success and unregulated development, particularly along the Atlantic coast. Many advocate addressing these issues by with "smart growth," with its emphasis on protecting natural resources, preserving open space, and revitalizing existing urban cores while containing urban sprawl.

Others, especially in the environmental community, advocate better im-

plementation of North Carolina's premier land-use regulation, the Coastal Area Management Act (CAMA). This statute was passed in response to the 1972 enactment by Congress of the Coastal Zone Management Act, which requires states to keep their coastal regions healthy by establishing programs to protect, preserve and manage orderly development of the country's fragile coastal resources.

CAMA created the Coastal Resources Commission to help manage and regulate population growth, expanding industrial development, and recreational pressures in North Carolina's twenty coastal counties, to protect the state's coastal land and waters that make it economically, esthetically and ecologically rich. The program continues to evolve in an effort to balance the constitutional protections of private property owners and the environmental protection of this sensitive area.

The entrance to the Legislative Building.

NEW MEXICO

NEW MEXICO STATE CAPITOL
ORIGIN OF NAME: Named by the first Spanish settlers
in honor of Mexico.
CAPITAL: Santa Fe
CONSTRUCTED: 1964–1966
ARCHITECT: W. C. Kruger
ADMITTED TO THE UNION: January 6, 1912 (forty-seventh)
SENATE: 42 members
HOUSE OF REPRESENTATIVES: 70 members

In the heart of Santa Fe, across from the Plaza, stands the Palace of the Governors. It is often referred to as the oldest continuously occupied public building in the United States. Originally built in 1610, before the pilgrims landed at Plymouth Rock, it is the location of nearly four centuries of government — Spanish, Mexican and American. Today, the low adobe-style building houses the New Mexico State History Museum, and its long verandah is reserved for Native American artists selling jewelry, black Pueblo pottery, and textiles.

Easterners began coming to Santa Fe and the New Mexico area with the opening of the Santa Fe Trail in 1821. After the Mexican War of 1846–48, it became an American territory. In 1885, New Mexicans passed a bond issue to fund construction of a new territorial capitol south of the Santa Fe River. Finished the following year, the three-story yellow sandstone building, with two small domes, was decorated with columns, hand-carving and stained glass. It lasted only a few years, burning to the ground on May 12, 1892.

After a decision that Santa Fe and not Albuquerque would remain the capital, a new territorial capitol was completed in 1900. In an apparent attempt to fit in with other states and territories, the capitol was constructed in a Greek Revival style with a central dome and six columns supporting a triangular pediment, and finished in marble imported from Indiana. It was a popular building, and in 1903 when President Theodore Roosevelt stopped in Santa Fe to honor the Rough Riders who had served in the Spanish-American War, the capitol was decorated in his honor. Among other things, a larger-than-life portrait of the President hung under the portico, flanked by large American flags. Many New Mexicans believed that the completion of the Classical capitol and its recognition and acceptance contributed to their achieving statehood.

Shortly after statehood, however, attitudes changed and it was no longer fashionable to copy the architectural styles of the rest of the nation. Many in Santa Fe began to recognize and build in an architectural style native to New Mexico. During the 1950s the dome and columns were removed from the capitol in an effort to redesign it in an indigenous style. It was covered with brown stucco and a flat roof, though some interior features such as the columns and the interior glass dome remain. Renamed the Bataan Memorial Building in honor of New Mexicans on the Bataan Death March during the Second World War, it is now a state office building.

In 1966, the state constructed its current capitol, a building that retains the old territorial character and blends with the surrounding buildings, yet appears modern. Local architect Willard C. Kruger looked to the area's Native American past for architectural inspiration, while adding such historical state capitol features as a rotunda and balanced legislative chambers. He designed the building in the traditional adobe or territorial style, which blends with the distinctive architecture of the historical buildings of Santa Fe (made up of hundreds of interrelated buildings composed of common materials drawn from the surrounding natural environment) and New Mexico's four cultures — Native American, Spanish, Mexican and Anglo.

The Palace of the Governors.

The New Mexico State Capitol rotunda.

Nicknamed the "Merry Roundhouse," it had a round shape inspired by the ancient sun sign of the Zia Indian Pueblo. In response to criticism that it was too modern, architect W. C. Kruger defended the concept: "A round shape is very old in the history of New Mexico, having its origin in the pueblo Kivas, which were round ceremonial rooms or meeting places for the leaders of the tribes just as the legislative building is a meeting place for the leaders of the state."

The capitol building is entered from four equally spaced projecting bays meant to simulate the sunrays that appear in the Zia symbol. A symbol of life, the Zia also appears on the state flag. Other architectural features include sloping, adobe-colored plaster and stucco walls, small window openings, brick coping edging the roofline, and a flat roof.

The circular interior consists of four levels. The first level, which is underground, contains balanced chambers for the House of Representatives and the Senate, along with legislative offices and lounges. The legislative chambers are wedge-shaped, with curved walls at the front and rear. The materials in the chambers were selected for optimum sound reception; the rear and side walls consist of vertical strips of walnut every six inches with acoustical panels in between. The wall behind the podium is accented in the center with an aluminum cast of the state seal. The legislators' desks are continuous curved sections of walnut and formica, each holding file drawers and microphones.

At the second level are the entrances. Pieces of turquoise embedded in the lock plates adorn the bronze doors. This blue semiprecious stone is sacred to southwest Native American tribes, and is the official state gem of New Mexico. A central rotunda, 49 feet in diameter, rises 60 feet to a small domed skylight. Balconies circle the third and fourth levels.

The New Mexico Senate chamber.

The focal point of the rotunda is the state seal set in the terrazzo floor. Composed of bronze divider strips with marble chips and native turquoise, it forms the design of American and Mexican eagles. Extending outward from the circular seal in four directions are the rays of the Zia sun symbol. Plaques in the shape of the state were sandblasted into the marble walls on the north and south sides.

The third level houses Senate and House committee rooms and offices for individual legislators and their staff. The fourth level is devoted to the governor's suite, the offices of the lieutenant governor, secretary of state and other executive officers.

Most of the marble used as in the capitol was quarried in New Mexico. The native marble and travertine covering the walls, pillars and stairwells in the rotunda and public lobbies, and marble chips used as aggregate in the terrazzo floors came from quarries west of Belen, on the Laguna Reservation. The marble comes in two colors — Mescalero, a reddish brown true marble variety that covers most of the pillars and occurs in the panels below the third level of the rotunda — and the lighter beige Temple Cream, which faces the walls and the stairwells in the first, second and third levels. The only out-of-state marble used is the black marble from Minnesota that forms the window sills throughout the building.

Contemporary art by artists who live and work in New Mexico fills the building. In 1991, the New Mexico legislature created the Capitol Art Foundation to collect, preserve and promote the appreciation of works of art that reflect the diverse history, cultures and art forms of the people of New Mexico, and to exhibit the works in and around the capitol.

For years, artists and others have flocked to New Mexico in order to enjoy the high elevations, wide-open spaces, dry climate, blue skies and

The New Mexico State Capitol.

star-filled clear night skies. But toward the end of the twentieth century, city lights from brightly lit gas stations, grocery stores and streetlights, as well as other building lights, slowly started blotting out the stars, making them appear dimmer. Called "light pollution" or, as astronomers refer to it, "sky glow," it erased some stars from the sky for millions of people, especially in New Mexico's inevitably growing urban areas. After a state preservation agency named New Mexico's night sky one of its most endangered historic places, noting the significance the heavens hold for Native Americans, and as part of the growing effort by preservationists, astronomers and environmentalists to bring back the black night skies and brightly shining stars, New Mexico's legislature passed the Sky Protection Act in 1999. The law regulates outdoor night lighting fixtures while

Aquacia stands outside the Secretary of State's office.

promoting safety, conserving energy, and preserving the environment for astronomy. All outdoor light fixtures are to be shielded or hooded so that the light they emit is directed at the ground and wasteful lighting is also reduced by exchanging low-pressure sodium lamps for now outlawed mercury-vapor outdoor lighting fixtures. The statute includes exemptions for oil, gas and industrial facilities, as well as farms, ranches and livestock feedlots, and some other businesses have been permitted to continue with their current lighting for now, allowing for a gradual replacement. Even with these limitations, the law is considered an important step toward reducing the glare toward the sky. Some counties and municipalities are enacting more stringent ordinances because, as one proponent put it, "What matters is if our children can see the stars when they go out at night and get a sense of the infinite."

This underground passage between the capitol and its annex serves as a gallery.

HAWAII

HAWAII STATE CAPITOL

ORIGIN OF NAME: After Hawaii Loa, who is said to have discovered the islands, or Hawaiki or Hawaii, the traditional home of the Polynesians.

CAPITAL: Honolulu

CONSTRUCTED: 1965–1969

ARCHITECT: John Carl Warnecke with Belt, Lemmon and Lo

ADMITTED TO THE UNION: August 21, 1959 (fiftieth)

SENATE: 25 members

HOUSE OF REPRESENTATIVES: 51 members

The state of Hawaii consists of a chain of volcanic and coral islands nearly 1,600 miles long. Although most of them are tiny, Hawaii, Maui, Oahu, Lanai, Kauai, Niihau, Kahoolawe and Molokai make up the main islands. As the most southern state and the only oceanic state, Hawaii lies about 2,400 miles southwest of the continental United States.

As early as AD 750, the Polynesians from the South Pacific inhabited the islands that today we call Hawaii. The first Westerner known to visit, in 1778, was the British navigator Captain James Cook. Not long after, around 1810, Kamehameha I unified the disparate tribes of the archipelago into a single kingdom. For the remainder of the nineteenth century, missionaries and American businessmen increasingly asserted themselves in Hawaiian economic and political affairs. Although Queen Lili'uokalani tried to reclaim native Hawaiian control over governmental operations in 1893, she was overthrown by commercial interests working in coordination with the United States minister to Hawaii, controversially acting with military support. President Grover Cleveland refused to recognize the resulting provisional government, but five years later, President William McKinley signed a congressional joint resolution annexing Hawaii. It became the Territory of Hawaii in 1900.

The success of agribusiness, including the plantation-style production of sugar and later pineapple, the rise of United States military installations (especially after the attack on Pearl Harbor), and the introduction and growth of air travel and tourism propelled Congress to offer Hawaiians statehood. A majority of the citizens voted to accept the proposal.

Iolani Palace, located in Honolulu on the island of Oahu, became the first state capitol. Constructed on the site of an earlier palace, it was the official residence of King David Kalakaua from 1882 until his death. His sister and successor, Queen Lili'uokalani, lived there until the overthrow of the monarchy. After an unsuccessful attempt to restore the kingdom in 1895, the palace became the queen's prison for nine months.

Later, during the time the palace served as the state capitol, King Kalakaua's bedroom was turned into the governor's office, the Senate met in the state dining room, and the throne room became home to the House of Representatives. After the state capitol was completed the palace was restored, and it now functions as a museum.

Iolani Palace is the only royal palace in the United States.

The Hawaii State Capitol.

Soon after the Hawaii became a state, the former territorial governor and first governor, William F. Quinn, appointed a capitol advisory committee to determine a building site, select an architect through a competition with ties to Hawaii, and work with the architect to construct a building reflecting Hawaii. Since being chosen architect of a state capitol remained a special honor, the competition drew at least twenty-two architects, including Minoru Yamasaki, I. M. Pei, Richard J. Neutra, and John Carl Warnecke. Warnecke, from San Francisco, prevailed. His resume included the development of a master plan for the expansion of California's state capitol in and many federal buildings in Washington, D.C. In order to meet the committee's criteria for having a local architectural connection, his firm entered into a partnership with Belt, Lemmon and Lo of Honolulu for the duration of the project.

But before construction began, a controversy erupted over the selection of the Honolulu downtown site. Some wanted to remove the capitol from the center of the city because land elsewhere was cheaper. Considerations included downtown accessibility; efficiency of operation between the state, city and federal governments and the nearby financial-commercial district; and the preservation of historic values. Today, the capitol is situated in the middle of what was once known as the Civic Center and is referred to as the Capitol District. The district includes the city hall, the state court building, the state library, Iolani Palace, the federal building, and the state, city and county office buildings.

The capitol building, constructed of reinforced concrete and structural steel, and built in the international style, measures 360 by 270 feet and is approximately 100 feet high. From the beginning, the consensus was that the capitol should not be just another office building, but should epitomize the state and its people. The architects focused on designing a place that would reflect Hawaii's island setting, tropical climate and local character. The result is a symbolic capitol that represents the geological formation of the Hawaiian Islands rising out of the sea. It stands for both a volcano and an island, surrounded by a reflecting pool representing the Pacific Ocean.

The basement entrance from the capitol's parking garage.

Forty fluted columns, evoking the palm trees that were so important to the early Hawaiians as a source of food and building materials, form the perimeter of the building and support the roof and overhanging office floors. The roof incorporates a crater-like opening, like the throat of one of the volcanoes that built the islands, instead of a covered dome.

Broad steps lead to four grand doorless entrances that bid *Aloha*, welcome, to visitors, and funnel them into a rotunda that is open to the sky, symbolizing a government that is open and accessible to everyone. This design is ideally suited to the gentle, tropical Hawaiian climate, with the sun, rain and trade winds free to enter. A six-hundred-thousand-piece ceramic mosaic, *Aquarius*, on the rotunda floor, represents the changing colors of the Pacific Ocean. On opposite sides of the lobby, large windows enable visitors and passersby to view legislators at work inside the volcano-shaped legislative chambers.

The cone-shaped chambers, constructed from coarse brick made of cinder from Hawaii's volcanoes, also represent the geological origin of the islands. The House of Representatives is decorated in earth tones, and a large tapestry featuring two coconut palms and a pineapple hangs behind the speaker's podium. The chandelier represents the sun and is made from copper and brass, elements of the earth.

In contrast, the decor of the Senate is blue-green, the color of water and sky. Here the chandelier represents the moon and consists of 630 shells, hand picked for size and shape, polished and put together with aluminum,

The governor's ceremonial office.

an element of the ocean. The blue tapestry depicts the ever-present Hawaiian rainbow and ancient voyaging canoes.

The governor's office is located on the top floor. There 700-pound Koa wood doors, made of material taken from native tropical rain forests, are visible from most places in the capitol. Welcoming signs encourage visitors to enter. In the reception area, cabinets contain Hawaiian artifacts.

The governor's office bears the influence of one-time Honolulu resident, Jacqueline Kennedy Onassis. A friend of Warnecke, she visited the construction site, where she suggested altering the blueprints by adding height to the ceiling, from three panels to four. She believed that the governor's office was the most important room in the most important building in the state, reflecting the history and culture of the Hawaiian people, and should be more imposing and elegant than originally designed.

Also on this floor and scattered throughout the building are offices for the seventy-six lawmakers. These members of the General Assembly reflect Hawaii's ethnically diverse population. During the nineteenth century, large plantation owners welcomed laborers from China, Japan, Korea, the Philippines and Portugal to assist in the hard work of harvesting sugar. Most easily assimilated into Hawaiian life, though through the years there was a growing concern for the welfare of Hawaii's aboriginal people.

Since the annexation of Hawaii, over a million acres of public land formerly owned by the monarchy and passed from one government entity to another was ceded to the United States. When Hawaii became a state, the United States government granted it title to all the public lands except those set aside for federal use, and Hawaii assumed responsibility for administering the land. In 1978, when Hawaii adopted a new constitution, it created a state agency known as the Office of Hawaiian Affairs (OHA) to administer programs for the betterment of Native Hawaiians and Hawaiians from the

Senate chamber detail.

Reverend Joseph Damien de Venster cared for victims of leprosy.

millions of dollars generated from the lands. Native Hawaiians are defined by state law as those with 50 percent Hawaiian ancestry. Hawaiians are those with any degree of descent from original residents, including Native Hawaiians. Almost one quarter of the state's residents claim descent from the people living in the islands when Captain Cook and his crew became the first Westerners to land in Hawaii.

OHA's responsibilities include the administration of two public trusts: the first is comprised of part of the proceeds from the ceded lands, which must be used "for the betterment of the conditions of Native Hawaiians," and the second is money appropriated by the state legislature and administered for their benefit. Programs include personal loans and grants, small-business loans, educational funding, health programs and homesteading rights.

The Hawaiian constitution also provided that OHA be managed by a board of trustees, all of whom "shall be Hawaiians," to be chosen in a state-wide election in which only Hawaiians (as defined by state law) could vote. In 1996, this limitation on voting was challenged in court by a caucasian rancher whose ancestors arrived in Hawaii in 1831. The state argued that the restriction was not discriminatory, but rooted in historical concern for the Hawaiian peoples. The United States Supreme Court overturned the restricted voting provision on the basis of the 15th Amendment, which provides that the right to vote "shall not be denied or abridged by the United States or by any state on account of race, color or previous condition of servitude." The court saw discrimination and reverse discrimination as the same thing, and the election of the board of trustees is now open to all Hawaiian registered voters.

In the place of a traditional rotunda, Hawaii's capitol is open to the sky.

NEVADA

Nevada Legislative Building
Origin of Name: From the Spanish word for "snow clad."
Capital: Carson City
Constructed: 1968–1970
Architect: Graham Erskin
Admitted to the Union: October 31, 1864 (thirty-sixth)
Senate: 21 members
Assembly: 42 members

In 1859, gold prospectors discovered the Comstock Lode, with its precious minerals, in the hills east of Carson City. The area that is now Nevada was then a part of Utah, and since 1854 called Carson County. Mormons made up the majority of the population in the large county until word of the gold and silver discovery sent Californians and others into the region. The newcomers renounced allegiance to Utah and its leader, Brigham Young, and instituted a temporary government.

Soon after, on March 2, 1861, the Territory of Nevada was organized from the western part of the Utah Territory, including Carson and neighboring Humboldt counties, and Carson City was named the capital. This organization took place under the presidency of James Buchanan, two days before the inauguration of Abraham Lincoln.

Throughout the territorial period, Lincoln named Orion Clemens of Iowa as secretary of Nevada. Clemens traveled west by overland stage accompanied by his younger brother, Samuel, arriving in Virginia City in 1862. Writing for the local newspaper, Samuel Clemens poked fun at territorial politicians while reporting on the legislature and, at this time, started signing his name as Mark Twain. He also wrote about his overland journey from Missouri to Nevada in the book *Roughing It*.

Then, even before Nevada achieved the required population for statehood set by the Northwest Ordinance, Civil War politics apparently encouraged Lincoln to support Nevada's admission to the Union on October 31, 1864. At that time, Nevada was smaller than it is today. Soon afterward its boundary extended east, and in 1867, Nevada added its southern tip, including Las Vegas, today its most populated area, from the Arizona Territory.

Nevada's statehood brought three pro-Lincoln electoral votes during the following election and gave him the support of two more senators and a member of the House of Representatives. These votes and wealth from the new state contributed to ending the Civil War, and supported the Lincoln-backed proposed 13th Amendment (abolishing slavery) and his policies for reconstruction of the southern states after the war. Nevada was nicknamed the "Battle Born" state because of its entrance into the Union near the end of the Civil War and the "Silver State" for its rich mineral deposits used by the federal government for, among other things, making silver coins.

Following statehood, the Act to provide for the erection of a state capitol was signed on February 23, 1869. The two-story native-sandstone Italianate building, completed in 1871, features rusticated quoins and window surrounds, arched windows, and walls three feet thick. The portico contains fluted Doric columns of painted metal, and its pediment incorporates a wooden cornice and a plain tympanum of sandstone. The roof is crowned by an eight-sided, windowed cupola, 30 feet in diameter and 120 feet above the ground. An 1875 fence installed to keep out roaming cattle surrounds the capitol.

In 1905, an octagonal extension constructed in the building's architectural style and of the same material was added to the east side of the capitol to serve as its state library. It now houses the state controller's office. North

The south stairway in the capitol.

The Nevada State Capitol.

and south wings, with larger chambers on the second floor for the Senate and Assembly, were added in 1915.

Inside the old building, decorative features include Alaskan marble wainscoting and floors, and a decorative frieze depicting the industries and resources of Nevada. Official paintings of past governors line the halls, a sign that the governor and other officials still maintain their offices there, though a museum replaced the old Senate chamber. From 1977 to 1981, the capitol was rebuilt to make it earthquake and fire proof. At that time, the original dome was replaced with a fiberglass copy.

The capitol's rehabilitation followed the construction, to its south, of a legislative building where lawmakers moved in 1971. This building's original appearance was geometric, with a central three-story section containing a lobby and offices flanked by semicircular wings housing the legislative chambers. Vertical beige-and-brown aggregate sections, divided by strips of white stucco, covered its exterior walls. Narrow white pre-cast concrete panels projected beyond the windows, allowing some light inside the building, at the same time protecting the building from the nearby busy highway. Inside, special features, not part of the capitol, included public and private lounges for both the Senate and Assembly, a first-aid room, a communications center, press rooms, offices for the legislative officers, and a multi-purpose auditorium seating three hundred people.

In answer to Nevada's population growth and the need for more space, in 1995 the legislature appropriated money to double the size of the legislative building by adding a five-story rear addition. At the same time, it also received a Postmodern exterior face-lift. The panels over the windows were removed and the walls resurfaced with concrete and covered with a pinkish tan-colored stucco. An arcade of plain engaged columns was added around square window openings on the third story.

The 1995 addition to the Nevada Legislative Building.

A small dome, indicating in a traditional way that the building houses the state's legislature, was also added on the front, above two-story levels of columns that support a panel with the words "Nevada State Legislature." Beneath the dome, at the entry level, is a small circular glass vestibule. It opens into the lobby, featuring terrazzo floors and stairways with steel balustrades that date from the 1970 construction. After a runaway car rammed into the front door, granite blocks were placed at the sidewalk in front of the entrance. Sign on the lawn outside the semicircular chambers identify the interior location of the Nevada State Senate and the State Assembly.

A white-painted hallway, displaying historical photography, connects the legislative chambers. The square Senate has blue carpeting and wood-paneled walls decorated with two silver Great Seals of the State of Nevada. Six lights in the ceiling repeat the shape of the windows in the nearby old capitol. An electronic voting board hangs above the podium. The members' bench desks have granite tops.

The Assembly features eleven large light fixtures and wood paneling, and state seals hang from the walls. In front of the clerk's desk stand four chairs reserved for the pages. The chief clerk of the house sits directly in the center of the large curved desk; other occupants include the history clerk, document clerk, assistant chief clerk, media clerk, journal clerk and recording clerk. Behind, and slightly higher, is the desk for the speaker of the Nevada State Assembly.

Above the speaker hang a gavel, a clock, and a large portrait of Lincoln. For many years there was an effort to commemorate the state's appreciation of the role Lincoln played in helping Nevada become a state. On March 12, 1915, a bill was passed "to provide for an oil painting of Abraham Lincoln for the state capitol building, in commemoration of the fiftieth anniversary of Nevada's statehood." A sum of $1,300 was appropriated for that purpose, and after viewing many portraits, the committee chose one by Charles M. Shean of Brooklyn, New York. On

The Nevada Legislative Building.

Sunday, March 14, 1915, in the Assembly chamber, the 59-by-44 inch portrait in a gilded frame was ceremoniously unveiled, and since then hangs whenever the Assembly convenes. However, in the early 1950s, a buildings and grounds employee was preparing the capitol for an upcoming legislative session when he heard three shots coming from the Assembly chamber. The shots were fired by teenagers with a .22-caliber derringer into the Lincoln portrait — one in the lapel of his black coat, one in the left elbow and one in the right forearm. The culprits were never caught and the custodian repaired the damage by pasting paper over the holes. The paper remained until the painting was restored in the 1980s.

Today, the legislative building is a part of the capitol complex, in the heart of Carson City. The campus-like setting includes the capitol, the supreme

The 1905 octagonal rear extension to the capitol.

The restored Supreme Court chamber in the capitol.

court, and the state library and archives building. Officials contend that the renovated stucco, almost adobe-like covering of the legislative building blends better with the other buildings.

The stucco is also a reminder that Nevada is the most arid state in the United States and remains largely uninhabited. The federal government owns more land in Nevada (about 87 percent), mostly national forest and military land, than in any other state except Alaska. Because of this, the state's taxable resources are limited. In an effort to raise revenues, in 1931 the Nevada legislature lowered the residence requirements for divorce to six weeks and legalized gambling. Gambling in Nevada dates back to the days of the mining camps and fits to the state's libertarian leanings. Lawmakers also saw the opportunity to encourage and stimulate business, severely suffering in the nationwide Depression. They succeeded, and people flocked into the state, not only to gamble, but also to marry and divorce. Nevada soon became the gambling and entertainment center of United States.

In 1945, dissatisfaction with the lack of regulation prompted lawmakers to take control over gambling by setting up the Nevada Tax Commission to regulate gambling and to issue state licences. State powers were further tightened in 1947 and 1949, but despite these efforts, organized crime infil-

trated the casinos and resorts in Las Vegas and surrounding Clark County during the 1950s and 1960s.

As a result, Congress pressured the Nevada legislature to further strengthen gambling-licence regulations. Fearing that the federal government might take control of gambling in the state, and wanting to keep its share of taxes, in 1955 lawmakers created a Gaming Control Board to act as the enforcement and investigative unit of the Tax Commission and to eliminate the participation of undesirable elements in Nevada's gambling industry.

After Nevada passed the Corporate Gaming Act in 1969, publicly traded companies, with more stringent business practices, moved to Nevada and they now dominate casino operations. There may be compelling social and economic arguments against gambling, but gaming revenues continue to be a popular alternative to raising taxes. Seven mega resorts opened during the period from 1990 to 1996, and the Las Vegas metropolitan area became the fastest-growing region in the United States. This rapid growth has made Nevada the fastest-growing state in every decade since the 1960s. Thanks to this ongoing growth, interests such as real estate, banks and retailing may soon challenge the domination of gambling in the state's economic and political sectors, providing a long sought-after balance.

The Senate chamber in the Legislative Building.

Florida

Florida State Capitol

Origin of Name: Attributed to Spanish explorer Ponce de Leon, from *Pascua Florida*, meaning "feast of flowers."

Capital: Tallahassee

Constructed: 1972–1977

Architect: Edward Durell Stone

Admitted to the Union: March 3, 1845 (twenty-seventh)

Senate: 40 members

House of Representatives: 120 members

Soon after the United States acquired Florida from Spain in 1821, the former Spanish provinces of East Florida and West Florida were combined to form one territory. The earlier provincial capitals of Pensacola and St. Augustine were the only towns of importance in the territory, so in 1822 the first legislative council, a unicameral body with members appointed by the president of the United States, met in Pensacola. A second session followed the next year in St. Augustine. But travel conditions were so difficult that the legislative council decided to select a more centrally located site between the towns for a capital, where Congress agreed to set aside land for the territorial government.

The council then met in the first capitol, a log cabin located on the southeast corner of the present capitol grounds, and passed a law to symmetrically lay out a town with Capitol Square at the center. The lawmakers financed and constructed a permanent capitol building through the sale of town lots, and in 1824 named the town Tallahassee, proclaiming it the seat of government.

The small two-story frame building that replaced the log cabin served as the capitol. In 1838, Congress created a bicameral legislature, and its members served in the constitutional convention that led to statehood. They also began construction of the surviving third capitol of Florida (1839–1845). A three-story Greek Revival building with white stucco walls, it incorporates a six-columned Doric portico on the east and west elevations, with pediments containing an off-white bas-relief rendition of the Florida state seal. This building was the scene of the secession convention of 1861 that withdrew Florida from the Union, and it was the site of the constitutional conventions of 1865, 1868, 1885 and 1968. It also attracted national attention during the 1876 disputed presidential election when the Florida Canvassing Board awarded four Republican electors to Republican Rutherford B. Hayes, who promised to end federal occupation in the South, thus ensuring his election as President of the United States.

In 1902, the capitol received its first addition, and a dome to replace its wooden cupola. Three further enlargements included extending the porticoes after adding east and east wings in 1923, a 1936 north-wing addition and, in 1947, a south wing. Every time a move was made to expand the capitol, there was also an effort to remove the seat of government from Tallahassee.

After fighting off a challenge from Orlando to replace Tallahassee as the capital when the present capitol was built in 1977, it was decided to tear down the old one. But because of its historic significance, preservationists won a battle to retain and restore the capitol as it had existed in 1902, when

The House of Representatives chamber.

The Florida State Capitol.

all of Florida's state government business was combined under one roof.

The decision to build the fourth capitol immediately behind the old one allowed construction to proceed while government operations continued. Following its completion, the legislature approved demolition of the 1923, 1936 and 1947 additions of the old building and construction of a plaza area between the old and the new capitols. Now the old capitol serves as a museum, the Florida Center of Political History and Governance.

When it came time to build the present capitol in Tallahassee, the lawmakers reportedly pushed through an authorization so expensive and so big that Floridians would never consider moving the capital again. The architect, Edward Durell Stone, was instructed to design a capitol reflecting a modern Florida, not one representing the antebellum magnolia-and-honeysuckle traditional style with columns and a dome. Stone responded with a sleek high-rise office building, designed in the International style.

Today, the Florida State Capitol consists of a complex of five connected structures, with a reinforced-steel concrete-and-glass skyscraper in the center. The twenty-two-story tower rises 307 feet above the main entrance and is flanked by two buildings with slightly protruding domes that mark the locations of the legislative chambers. Connected to the other buildings, but closer to the old capitol, are the five-story House and Senate office buildings, completed in 1973. Louvers cover the windows of all the buildings, a Stone architectural trademark that adds to the sleekness of the tower facade.

At the time of its construction, the capitol incorporated the very latest in building technology, materials and equipment. Technological features include special fireproofing and computerized smoke detectors, a heating system that uses heat from warm bodies and lights, only using fuel during extremely cold weather to heat the building; a sophisticated security system; and a diesel-driven emergency generator. Solar screens and the louvers on the windows help keep out the sun and decrease the reliance on air-conditioning.

The Senate chamber.

The first five floors and the observation deck on the twenty-second floor of the capitol are open to the public. The governor and cabinet members occupy offices on the plaza level, and the legislative chambers are located on the fourth floor. A system of stairways and private corridors leads to elevators without passing through the public areas, separating officials from the public.

Terrazzo covers the floors, and travertine marble from Italy covers the walls of the halls in the public places. This marble is also found around handrails and facings of the elliptical rotundas on the plaza level and the fourth-floor meeting area between the House and the Senate chambers. An opening in the ceiling rises to the fifth floor, where there is access to the visitor galleries.

The plaza entrance leads to a three-story, oval-shaped rotunda featuring a balcony with a railing and balustrade of plain strips of marble. On a raised platform in the center of the floor is the fifth design of six modifications of the Great Seal of Florida, cast in bronze and mounted on terra verde marble from Italy. Featured in the seal are rays that symbolize the Sunshine State; the sabal palmetto palm; a steamboat; a Seminole woman; and orange blossoms, the state flower. The smaller medallions refer to nations that governed Florida at one time, including Spain, France, Great Britain, the Confederate States of America, and the United States.

The old Florida capitol sits adjacent to its modern counterpart.

Above, on the fourth floor, is the Senate, a round chamber with a circular, domed ceiling formed with trapezoidal acoustic panels. Over the main entrance of the Senate floor, behind a glass wall, is the press gallery. No glass separates the visitors' gallery from the floor. The portraits hanging below the gallery commemorate past Senate presidents. Ebony wood imported from Africa, is used in the wall paneling, the rostrum and members' desks. The seats in the Senate are assigned by districts. There are electronic voting panels on the front wall.

The House of Representatives is octagonal; its domed ceiling formed by triangular sections of acoustical panels. Other features include a faux-alabaster-and-glass 15-foot-wide chandelier, blue carpeting with a woven state seal and a large overhead screen to show the text of bills and amendments, flanked by two electronic voting boards.

Dark wood paneling lines the wall behind the speaker of the House's rostrum, flanked by engaged columns. Portraits of former speakers hang on the balcony railing wall, which slightly protrudes over the chamber and is supported by columns. On the walls beneath the balcony and surrounding the room, painted murals depict Florida's history, from a prehistoric sunrise on the east wall to a space-shuttle launch, and two underwater scenes.

The public galleries contain hardwood pews; inch-thick, bullet- and shatter-proof glass separates the spectators from the House for safety and sound proofing. The speaker of the House, selected by members of the majority party, determines the seating arrangement on the floor.

The House originally had teak wood, imported from southeast Asia, throughout the room. But during 1999 and 2000 it was renovated to a Colonial Revival or more traditional look and the Scandinavian-styled teak was removed and replaced with mahogany desks and leather chairs. One justification given by the House leadership for renovating the chamber was that it was designed in the 1970s at the time of the state's battles over reapportionment, for fewer members than the 120 that now sit there. Smaller desks and lower chairs make it less crowded.

The members in the Senate and House of Representatives are apportioned on the basis of population, and the constitution requires the legislature to redraw the boundaries of the legislative districts every ten years in response to the United States census. The new plans must be approved by the state supreme court, and if the legislature fails to produce an acceptable plan, the supreme court will step in to do so.

This was not always the case. Florida's 1885 constitution gave each county the right to send roughly equal representatives to the legislature. But as the populations of some counties grew faster than others, this geographic system gave small counties almost the same number of votes as larger, more populated counties. The inequality continued as Florida's population grew substantially, especially in urban areas.

Following the Second World War, one third of the Florida population was electing a majority of the Senate. In the 1950s and 1960s, those in

Reconstructed staircase in the old capitol.

power, mostly from North Florida and controlling the Senate, were reluctant to yield it to urbanites, who mostly favored reapportionment. In fact, by the early 1960s a majority of the Florida House of Representatives could be elected by about 14 percent of the population, and a majority of the Florida Senate could be elected by about 12 percent. Such misrepresentation led to, among other things, "pork-chop counties," with 18 percent of the population paying 15 percent of the taxes but receiving 30 percent of state disbursements.

Finally, in 1962, the United States Supreme Court's decision in *Baker v. Carr* established the principle of one person, one vote. This meant that each senator or representative should serve roughly equally populated districts. Although that case involved Tennessee's legislature, it set a standard that all states must meet. The Florida legislature tried redistricting in 1965 and 1966 but failed to meet the standard, leading to three trials, collectively referred to as *Swann v. Adams*, where the United States Supreme Court issued three rulings on Florida's reapportionment plans.

By the last case, in January 1967, the court invalidated previous legislative elections and ordered the lower court to draw a plan that incorporated the principle of population-based equity and ended the small counties' domination of the Florida Senate. Since 1972, it is population, not county boundaries, that determines the legislative districts.

An exhibit in the old capitol museum summarizes the issue: "Imagine if the old system had not been replaced. Under the 1885 constitution, if you live in a county with many people, like Miami-Dade County, you would have two senators, one for about every 1,000,000 people in 2000. But if you live in Liberty County, you would have one senator for about 7,000 residents.... *Swann v. Adams* matters to you because it guarantees that your vote for state legislators counts the same as every other person voting. Each senator serves about the same number of people today."

The interior dome of the old capitol.

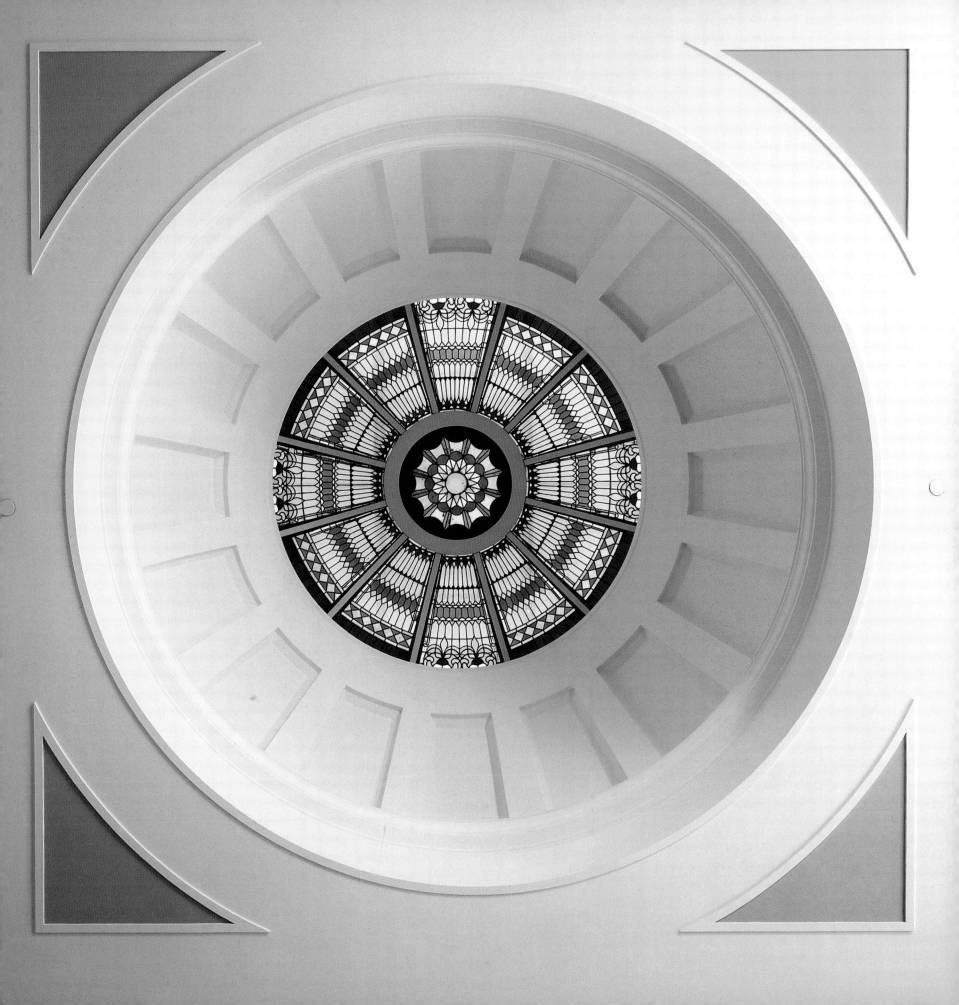

ALABAMA

ALABAMA STATE HOUSE

ORIGIN OF NAME: From the Choctaw language, meaning "thicket-clearers" or "vegetation-gatherers."

CAPITAL: Montgomery

ADAPTED FOR LEGISLATURE 1985–1986

ARCHITECT: State of Alabama

ADMITTED TO THE UNION: December 14, 1819 (twenty-second)

SENATE: 35 members

HOUSE OF REPRESENTATIVES: 105 members

Huntsville served as the first Alabama capital for less than a year; after that the role went to Cahaba from 1820 to 1826, and Tuscaloosa from 1826 to 1847. In 1846, lawmakers decided to make Montgomery the permanent capital, on the condition that the people of Montgomery agree to pay for the construction of the capitol building and for all the expenses involved in moving the government records from Tuscaloosa to Montgomery. They agreed, and the top of Goat Hill, at the head of Dexter Avenue, Montgomery's main business street, was chosen as the site for the capitol.

The first capitol, completed in 1847, burned just two years later. Using its foundation, the second dates from 1852 and stands today surrounded by matching white state office buildings. The three-story capitol building features large windows and a portico with six Corinthian columns supporting a flat roof. A large clock juts from the roof of the portico, and above, detached Corinthian columns circle the windowed drum, supporting the white metal dome.

Inside, a pair of cantilevered stairs spiral up from the vestibule to the rotunda. They are attributed to Horace King, a freed slave, engineer and bridge builder who became the first African American to serve in the Alabama legislature after the Civil War. Murals, dating from the 1930s, surround the inner dome and convey events from the state's history. They are titled *Hostile Meeting of de Soto, Spanish Explorer, and Tuscaloosa, Indian Chieftain — 1540*; *France Establishing First White Colony in Alabama Under Iberville and Bienville, Mobile, 1702–1711*; *Surrender of William Weatherford, Hostile Creek Leader to General Andrew Jackson, 1814*; *Pioneer Home-seekers led into Alabama Wilderness by San Dale — 1816*; *Governor William W. Bibb and Committee Drafting the First State Constitution at Huntsville — 1819*; *Wealth and Leisure Produce the "Golden Period"* of Ante-Bellum Life in Alabama — 1840–1860; Secession and the Confederacy, Inauguration of President Jefferson Davis 1861; and *Prosperity Follows Development of Resources, Agriculture, Commerce, and Industry 1874–1930.* On one side of the rotunda is the Senate chamber, now a museum, and on the other the House, still used for ceremonies and press conferences.

After the election of Abraham Lincoln as President in November 1860, the Alabama Secession Convention invited other seceded southern states to send delegates to Montgomery in February 1861. South Carolina, Mississippi, Florida, Georgia and Louisiana joined Alabama and met in the capitol's Senate chamber to form the Confederate States of America, with Montgomery as its capital. Texas also seceded, but did not attend. The confederation also unanimously elected Jefferson Davis as its president, and on February 18, 1861, he was inaugurated at the top of the steps on the west portico of the capitol, where today, a six-pointed brass star marks the spot.

The current House of Representatives chamber in the state house.

The rotunda of Alabama's capitol.

The permanent Constitution of the Confederate States of America was adopted in the Senate chamber on March 11, 1861, a month before Confederate guns fired on Fort Sumter. The Confederate Congress continued to meet in Montgomery until the capital was moved to Richmond, on May 22, 1861, following Virginia's entrance into the Confederacy.

Initially, and during this Civil War period, the capitol was square-shaped. It was extended to the east in 1885–1886, and restored and further expanded by plans prepared, in part, by Charles F. McKim from 1903 to 1912, with north and south wings incorporating Ionic porticoes on three sides. McKim, of the architectural firm, McKim, Mead & White, was the son of Yankee Abolitionists, yet he reportedly persuaded the Alabamans to save their historic capitol from demolition and preserve it as a shrine to the memory of the Confederate States of America.

From 1989 to 1992, another east addition was added, completing the shape of an H, with a portico similar to the one on the west. The governor and staff, along with the secretary of state, secretary of treasury and lieutenant governor, keep offices in the capitol, but in 1986 state legislators moved to the old Highway Building across Union Street. At first, lawmakers moved across the street temporarily so that the old capitol could be restored. The plan was to use the 1961 renovated Highway Building for large committee rooms. But the legislators grew fond of their office suites and the latest technology, and decided to remain in the Highway Building. A new building was later constructed for the Highway Department, and the building where the lawmakers convene is now called the Alabama State House.

The whitewashed exterior of the state house has pilasters lining the walls between rectangular windows from above the ground floor to a string course dividing the middle section from the upper floors. Above the three double-door glass entrances is a map of Alabama and the words "Alabama State House."

Elevators in the small lobby provide access to the House of Representatives, located on the fifth floor. Marble columns dominate the functional and high-tech chamber. The beige-and-cream woodwork and furniture, including the podium, were made by Alabama prison labor. Over the speaker's desk hangs the seal of the House of Representatives. The visitors' gallery, on the sixth floor, is separated from the chamber below by floor-to-ceiling glass.

The red color scheme of the House chamber, including red carpet and red leather chairs, extends even to legislation – if a bill originates in the House, its cover is red. But if a bill originates in the Senate, the cover is blue: the seventh-floor Senate has blue carpeting and light gray toned furnishings with blue leather chairs. The visitors' gallery can be reached on the eighth floor, which was added when the building was adapted in order to give height to the Senate chamber. Here, no columns are necessary.

The Senate votes by roll call, and senators need permission to speak, though they can do so for one hour, in contrast to the House, where members can only speak for ten minutes. Behind the Senate podium, a clock is flanked by the Great Seal of Alabama, showing its river system, and the Alabama Senate seal. This clock can play an important role in legislative calendar. For example, if the budget is not completed within the mandated 105 days of a regular session, the clock is stopped before midnight.

The power of the Alabama state legislature flows from its 1901 constitution, the longest and most detailed constitution in the world, containing 315,000 words and 706 amendments (and counting). It was designed to consolidate power in the hands of an alliance of large planters and industrialists

A spiral staircase in the capitol.

The historic Senate chamber in the capitol.

who were reacting to a late-nineteenth-century reform movement, and gave more power to the legislature, than to the people.

With the help of federal reforms, Alabamans have made some progress toward correcting the constitution's worst features. Court rulings on reapportionment gave urban areas fairer representation, women received the vote in 1919 by constitutional amendment, African Americans procured the right to vote through the federal Voting Rights Act of 1965, and the following year the United States Supreme Court ensured the right to vote for all poor people of Alabama when it struck down the poll tax.

The Alabama constitution has been amended many times because it deprives local and county governments of home rule and instead operates local government through the slow, cumbersome process of constitutional

The current chamber of the Alabama Senate in the state house.

amendment. For example, if a community wants to set up an elected Board of Education, the constitution must be amended. If a county wants to simplify how it licenses real-estate agents, the constitution must be amended. Even mosquito control has been put to a statewide referendum.

Currently, consideration of local bills accounts for about half the legislature's workload, and about 75 percent of the constitutional amendments affect only specific cities and counties. However, there are signs that a movement for constitutional reform is gaining some momentum. Alabama's "Golden Period," pictured in the capitol's rotunda, may not be relegated to its past but may in fact be a part of its future.

The Alabama State Capitol.

PHOTOGRAHER'S NOTES AND ACKNOWLEDGMENTS

The photography for this book was done with 4x5 view cameras, with two exceptions: The George Washington statue in South Carolina and the Blaine House in Maine. Those two were shot on 120 film with medium-format cameras. The first because I was too lazy to carry all the equipment over there, and the second because I had to dodge traffic. All of the photographs were made with color transparency film of ISO 100. The lenses used ranged from 47mm to 14 inches in focal length. All of the photographs were made with available light.

I have no way to count the number of people without whom this book would not have been possible. To all of you, my thanks. Below, I'd like to single out more than a few for acknowledgment:

I want to thank Susan Thrane. The work she did was difficult and time-consuming, but she and I shared the joys, the hardships and, ultimately, the rewards of traveling to each state capitol.

My family has been a steady source of help, humor and an occasional swift kick in the butt when it has been needed. My father Bill, has shared with me the benefits of a lifetime of experience in making things look good—his touch is gentle, but unerring . My mother Jane, (the source of most of the butt-kicking), has given steady support and assistance, as well as passing along to me a stubborn streak that has served me well more often than not. My brother Dan, who has been over the sometimes rocky ground of publishing many times, has never failed to offer me his experiences as a guide. His critical eye as a photographer is a standard and a goal for me. My brother Bill was always there to answer questions when the computer froze, crashed or just plain bewildered me. By working out there on the leading edge, he has been able to point me in the right direction. To my sisters-in-law, Cheryl and Kathy, my nephews, Nate, Joe and Lawrence, and my nieces Brigitta and Margaret: you have always showed interest in this project and my travels, and if you weren't interested, you've faked it with real conviction.

Sister Angela Ann Zukowski has been a great help in looking beyond the simple content of the images and finding meaning in them. She also made arrangements for me to connect with some outstanding people at Chaminade University in Honolulu, making the completion of the photography a reality.

My "other family," Tom and Carolyn Speshock and their flock of kids in Portales, New Mexico, have been a steady point of reference for a wandering spirit.

Friends scattered across the country have let me stay in their homes, shared their meals and given companionship after a long day's drive or an even longer day of photography. Some helped carry equipment and even contributed ideas for shots. I hope I've got all of you here. If not, I'm sure you will forgive me: Sue and Tom Armstrong, Kendra and Brian Bunch, Andrea Carlson, Diane and Gilberto Cintron, Ron and Paul Dick, Scott and Tina Edwards, Barb Foster, Art and Danae Goss, Steve Hoglund, Paul and Grace Merchant, George and Darlene Quinn, Kristine and Bill Riley, Tom Rose, Colleen, David and Emily Taylor, George Nathan Taylor, Susan and Bill Thrane and Sara Wilfong

My car got really sick one week into the longest photo expedition for this book, from late August to early October of 2004. Darrell Mayabb was the hero of the saga. First, he and his wife, Sharon, welcomed me into their home in Denver. Then, he connected me with friends of his who offered advice on all things mechanical, which got me (and my car) back to Ohio on schedule and with all the photographs in hand. Thanks especially to Don Spalding in Denver and Skip Landon in Sacramento.

Beyond the elected officials who serve the people of their states, there are the staff and support workers who keep things running inside these buildings. These are the clerks and sergeants-at-arms, the secretaries, janitors, curators, tour-guides, door keepers and security guards. Without fail, these people were helpful to me and concerned with how their buildings would be portrayed. At almost every stop, someone would ask, "Other than ours, which is your favorite?" To all of you, thank you for your time and for sharing your knowledge about the buildings where you work. Your contribution is immeasurable.

Noel Hudson, our editor at Boston Mills Press, has patiently walked me through the layout and design of this book. With input from Kathy Fraser, we somehow made it through the end of several months of back and forth e-mails and phone calls. Kim Sullivan at Firefly Books has been a joy to work with on color proofing and other arcana of book production.

Finally, two wonderful women. First, my big sister, Sarah Ryterband. She provided me with not only the means to get this done, but with a reason. Thank you for believing I could do this.

And Mariann. You have carried the burden of this work as much as I have. Literally too: in Frankfort, Charleston, Salt Lake City, Santa Fe, Cheyenne, Montgomery, Raleigh, Jackson, Lincoln, Topeka and Honolulu. But I know that the real weight has been late nights, missing weekends and weeks-on-end, and my obliviousness to non-state-house matters. You stood by me anyway. I love you. Now that spring is here, let's go to a ballgame and sit in the sun for a while.

Tom Patterson

The doors to Nebraska's unused Senate chamber.

SELECTED BIBLIOGRAPHY

Acton, Lord Richard, and Patricia Nassif Acton. *To Go Free: A Treasury of Iowa's Legal Heritage.* Ames: Iowa State University Press, 1995.

Alaska Blue Book 1993-1994, 11th ed. Department of Education, Division of State Libraries, Archives & Museums.

Anderson, Leon W. *The State House Concord, N.H. Sesquicentennial 1819-1969.* Concord, N.H.: Evans Printing Company, Inc., 1969.

Andes, Roy H. "A Triumph of Myth Over Principle: The Saga of the Montana Open Range." *Montana Law Review* 56 (University of Montana), no.2, (Summer 1995).

Andrews, Judith M., ed. *A History of South Carolina's State House.* Columbia S.C.: South Carolina Department of Archives and History, 1994.

Archer, Ryan M. "Searching for the Montana Open Range: A Judicial and Legislative Struggle to Balance Tradition and Modernization in an Evolving West." *Montana Law Review* (University of Montana), (2002).

Beyle, Thad L., ed. *State Government, Congressional Quarterly's Guide to Current Issues and Activities 1998-1999.* Washington, D.C.: Congressional Quarterly, Inc., 1998.

Blackman, Seth. "Long Gone Town Jobs." *Vermont Life* (Spring 2000): 24–28.

Bodenhamer, David J, and Robert G. Barrows, eds. *The Encyclopedia of Indianapolis.* Bloomington: Indiana University Press, 1994.

Brodeur, Paul. *Restitution, The Land Claims of the Mashpee, Passamaquoddy and Penobscot Indians of New England.* Boston, Mass.: Northeastern University Press, 1985.

Browne, William H., ed. "An Act for Advancement of Trade, 1693," *Archives of Maryland*, Proceedings and Acts of the General Assembly of Maryland (October 1678-November 1683), Baltimore, 1889, p. 612.

Bryan, John M. *Creating the South Carolina State House.* Columbia, S.C.: University of South Carolina Press, 1999.

Burbank, Jeff. *License to Steal.* Reno: University of Nevada Press, 2000.

Campbell, Rutherford B. Jr. "Racing Syndicates as Securities." *The Kentucky Law Journal* (University of Kentucky) 74, no. 4 (1985–86).

The Capitol of Texas, A Legend is Reborn. Atlanta, Ga.: Longstreet Press, Inc., 1995.

Carmon, Michael D. *Under the Copper Dome, The Arizona Capitol 1898-1974.* Arizona Capitol Museum, The Museum Division of the Arizona State Library, Archives and Public Records, Phoenix, Arizona, 2001.

A Century of Pride, The Arkansas State Capitol. Little Rock, Ark.: The Arkansas State Capitol Association, 1983.

Coel, Margaret. *The Colorado State Capitol*, 1st ed. Colorado General Assembly, 1992.

Cohan, Zara. "A Comprehensive History of the State House of New Jersey and Recommendations for its Continuation as a Historic Site." Thesis presented to the Faculty of the Department of Fine Arts, Newark State College, 1969.

Congressional Record, Proceedings and Debates of the 92nd Congress, Second Session, Senate, "National Arbor Day," Volume 118, Number 56, April 11, 1972.

Cummings, Abbott Lowell. *Ohio's Capitols at Columbus.* Columbus, Ohio: Ohio State Architectural and Historical Society Library, 1948.

Curry, Daniel Park, and Patricia Dawes Pierce, eds. *Monument: The Connecticut State Capitol.* Hartford, Conn.: Old State House Association, 1979.

The Daily Standard, Celina, Ohio, September 3, 1923.

Damron, Bob. "Building the Capitol." *Goldenseal* 8, no. 2 (Summer 1982).

Davis, Zan. *Advanced Worker's Compensation in Arkansas.* Eu Claire, Wisc.: National Business Institute, 1996.

Dedication of the Remodeled State House Concord, New Hampshire, October 25, 1910. Concord, N.H.: The Rumford Press, 1911.

Delaware Journal of Corporate Law 20, (1995): 965.

Department of the Interior, National Register Inventory Nomination Form, Virginia.

Dodson, E. Griffith. *The Capitol of the Commonwealth of Virginia at Richmond, Portraits, Statuary, Inscriptions, & Biographical Sketches.* Richmond, Virginia, 1937.

North Carolina's historic State Library.

Dolan, Catherine, J. "*Kildon v. Baldwin Piano & Organ* - The Tide Has Turned for Legitimate Carpal Tunnel Syndrome Claims in Arkansas Workers' Compensation Law." *Arkansas Law Review* (University of Arkansas) 53 (November 2, 2000).

Donaghey, George Washington. *Building a State Capitol*. Little Rock, Ark.: Parke-Harper Company, 1937.

Donnelly, Loraine B., and Evelyn T. Cray. *California's Historic Capitol*. Sacramento, Ca.: California Capitol Enterprises, 1995.

Duckworth, W. A. *Capitol of Iowa*. 1913, N.A.

Echoes (Ohio Historical Society) 2, no. 10 (October 1963).

Edelman, Nancy. *The Thomas Hart Benton Murals in the Missouri State Capitol*. Jefferson City, Miss.: Missouri State Council on the Arts, Missouri Department of Natural Resources, 1997.

Ehlert, Willis J. *America's Heritage: Capitols of the United States*, 6th ed revised. Madison, Wisc.: State House Publishing, 1999.

Fielder, Mildred. *The Treasure of Homestake Gold*. Deadwood, S. Dak.: Dakota Graphics, 2003.

Furnas, Robert W. *Arbor Day*, Lincoln, Nebr.: State Journal Company, 1888.

Gadski, Mary Ellen. "The Tennessee State Capitol: An Architectural History." *Tennessee Historical Quarterly* (Tennesee Historical Commission) XLVII, no.2 (Summer 1988).

Garrett, Ruth A. (for The League of Women Voters of Wyoming). *A Look at Wyoming Government*, 6th ed. Gillette, Wyo.: LWV Publications, 1998.

Getting to Know Georgia, A Guide for Exploring Georgia's History and Government. Atlanta, Ga.: Office of Secretary of State, June 2002.

Gibbs, D. W. & Co. *Specifications for the Erection and Completion of a Capitol Building for Wyoming Territory to be Located in Cheyenne*. Toledo, Ohio: Bardull Brothers, 1886.

Goodsell, Charles T. *The American Statehouse, Interpreting Democracy's Temples*. University Press of Kansas, 2001.

Goodsell, Charles T. "Old Capitols in the New Century." *State Legislatures* 26, no. 7 (July/August 2000): 54–58.

Gray, Virginia, Hanson, Russell, and Herbert Jacob, eds. *Politics in the American States*, 7th ed. Washington, D.C.: Congressional Quarterly Books, 1999.

Gregory, William. *Message to the General Assembly, January Session, 1901*. Providence: E. L. Freeman & Sons.

Guide to Exterior Art and Symbolism, Nebraska State Capitol. Lincoln, Nebr.: State of Nebraska Department of Administrative Services, Building Division, 1995.

Guide to the Kansas State Capitol. Topeka, Kansas: Kansas State Historical Society, 2002.

Haynes, Anne M. "Tension in the Judicial-Legislative Relationship: *DeRolph v. State*." *The University of Toledo Law Review* (University of Toledo) 32, no.4 (Summer 2001).

Hedge, David M. *Governance and the Changing American States*. Boulder, Col.: Westview Press, 1998.

Henshaw, Harry Preston III. "Tax Update: The 1993 West Virginia Legislature." *West Virginia Law Review* (West Virginia University Law Center) 95, no.4 (Summer 1993).

Herndon, Dallas T., ed. *The Centennial History of Arkansas*, Vol. 1. Chicago-Little Rock: The S. J. Clarke Publishing Company, 1922.

Hitchcock, Henry-Russell and William Seale. *Temples of Democracy: The State Capitols of the USA*. New York: Harcourt, Brace Jovanovich, 1976.

Hitchings, Sinclair H. and Catherine H. Farlow. *A New Guide To The Massachusetts State House*. John Hancock Mutual Life Insurance Company, 1964.

Hoobler, James A. "William Strickland, Architect." *Tennessee Historical Quarterly* (Tennessee Historical Society) XLV, no.1 (Spring 1986).

Indiana Clipping File, Indiana State Library, Indianapolis, Indiana.

Indiana Magazine of History. Department of History at Indiana University in cooperation with the Indiana Historical Society 80 (December 1984):329–347.

Indiana's State House. Indianapolis, Ind.: Indiana Historical Bureau, 2000.

Johnston, Norman J. *Washington's Audacious State Capitol and Its Builders*. Seattle: University of Washington Press, 1988.

Kansas Capitol Square, Kansas Secretary of State Ron Thornburgh in collaboration with the Kansas State Historical Society.

Katz, Ellen D. "Race and the right to vote after *Rice v. Cayetano*." *Michigan Law Review* (University of Michigan) 99, no.3 (December 2000): 491.

Kearnes, John. "Utah, Sexton of Prohibition." *Utah Historical Quarterly* (Utah Historical Society) 47, no. 1 (Winter 1979): 5–21.

Kubly, Vincent F. *The Louisiana Capitol, Its Art and Architecture*. Gretna, La.: Pelican Publishing Company, 1995.

Lambert, Kirby, Burnham, Patricia M., and Susan R. Near. *Montana's State Capitol The People's House*. Helena, Mont.: Montana Historical Society Press, 2002.

Lautaret, Richard, comp. *Alaska Historical Documents Since 1867*. Jefferson, N.C.: McFarland & Company, Inc., 1989.

League of Women Voters of California. *Guide to California Government*, 14th ed. Sacramento, Ca., 1992.

Ledbetter, Calvin R. Jr. *Carpenter from Conway, George Washington Donaghey as Governor of Arkansas 1909-1913*. Fayetteville, Ark.: The University of Arkansas Press, 1993.

Luberoff, David, and Alan Altshuler. *Mega-Project, A Political History of Boston's Multibillion Dollar Artery/Tunnel Project*. Boston, Mass.: A. Alfred Taubman Center for State and Local Government, John F. Kennedy School of Government, Harvard University, 1996.

Luebke, Frederick C., ed. *The Nebraska State Capitol*. Lincoln, Nebr.: University of Nebraska Press, 1990.

Lyman, Edward Leo. *Political Deliverance, The Mormon Quest for Utah Statehood*. Urbana: University of Illinois Press, 1986.

Lyon, Elizabeth and Anne Mack. "Business Buildings in Atlanta: A Study in Urban Growth and Form." an abstract of a PhD dissertation submitted to the Faculty of the Graduate School of Emory University, 1971.

MacManus, Susan A., ed. *Reapportionment and Representation in Florida: A Historical Collection*. Tampa, Fla: University of South Florida, 1991.

Major Public Lands of Washington. Olympia, Wash.: Washington State Department of Natural Resources, 2000.

Marlowe, Lynn G. *California State Capitol Restoration*. California State Capitol Museum Volunteer Association, 1988.

"The Massachusetts State House," published by William Francis Galvin, Secretary of the Commonwealth State House Tours, and Government Education Division, 2000.

Massie, Michael A. "Reform Is Where You Find It: The Roots of Woman Suffrage in Wyoming." *Annals of Wyoming* 62, no. 1 (Spring 1990): 3–21.

Mathias, Frank F. "John Randolph's Freedmen: The Thwarting of a Will." *Journal of Southern History* (Southern Historical Association) 39 (1973): 263–272.

Maxfield, Marilyn. *"The Nevada Lincoln" A History of the Portrait in the Nevada Assembly Chamber*. Carson City, Nev.: Nevada Legislative Counsel Bureau, 2003.

McNichol, Dan. *The Big Dig*. New York: Silver Lining Books, 2001.

Melhouse, James C. "Construction of North Dakota's New Capitol, 1931-1934." *Plain Talk* (State Historical Society of North Dakota) 1, no.3 (Summer 1970).

Miller, B. Michael. "Capitol Ideas." *New Mexico Magazine* 69, no.1 (January 1991).

Miller, Sam. *Capitol - A Guide for Visitors*. Historic Tallahassee Preservation Board, Department of State, State of Florida, 1982.

Minnesota Historical Society. *Art Treasures in the Minnesota State Capitol*. St. Paul, Minnesota: Minnesota Historical Society, 1998.

Missouri's Capitol. Jefferson City, Miss.: Missouri Department of Natural Resources.

"The Missouri State Capitol." *Architectural Record* CXI (February 1927): 105–126.

Morris, Allen. *The Florida Handbook*, 26th biennial ed. Tallahasse, Fla: The Peninsula Publishing Company, 1997–1998.

Museum Council of New Jersey. *Public Art in New Jersey During the Period of the American Renaissance*. Wayne, N.J.: William Patterson College, 1990.

National Register of Historic Places Inventory — Nomination forms.

Nebraska Blue Book, Clerk of the Legislature, State Capitol, Lincoln, Nebraska, 2002-2003.

Nevada Gaming Commission and State Gaming Control Board. *Legalized Gambling in Nevada, Its History, Economics and Control*. Carson City, Nevada: Nevada Gaming Commission and State Gaming Control Board, 1963.

The News and Observer, Raleigh, North Carolina, February 3, 1963.

Nicandri, David, and Derek Valley. *Olympia Wins: Washington's Capital Controversies*. Olympia, Washington: Washington State Capitol Museum, 1980.

Nicoletta, Julie. *Buildings of Nevada*. Oxford: Oxford University Press, 2000.

North Dakota Blue Book 2003-2005, Bismarck, North Dakota.

"North Dakota Legislative Council (Interim Study) Report on Issues Relating to Genetic Modification of (transgenic) products," Agriculture Committee of the North Dakota State House of Representatives, 2003.

Nye, Mary Greene. *Vermont's State House*. Montpelier, Vt.: Vermont Publicity Service, 1936.

The Ohio Statehouse. Columbus, Ohio: Statehouse Education & Visitors Center, May 2002.

Ohman, Marian M. *The History of Missouri Capitols*. Columbia, Miss.: University of Missouri-Columbia, Extension Division, by the Curators of the University of Missouri, 1982.

Oklahoma Almanac, 48th ed. Oklahoma City, Okla: The Oklahoma Department of Libraries, revised 2001–2002.

Oklahoma Tourism & Recreation Department. *The Oklahoma State Capitol*. Oklahoma City, Okla.: Oklahoma Today Custom Publishing, 2003.

Olson, Thomas. "(Not a) Learned Treatise on Adverse Possession." *Hennipen Lawyer* (Hennepin County Bar Association) 68, no. 8 (August 1999): 4–6.

O'Sullivan, Thomas. *North Star Statehouse, An Armchair Guide to the Minnesota State Capitol*. Pogo Press, Incorporated, 1994.

Oxford, June. *The Capitol That Couldn't Stay Put, The Complete Book of California's Capitols*. Fairfield, Ca.: James Stevenson, 1995.

Papanikolas, Helen Z. "Bootlegging in Zion: Making and Selling the 'Good Stuff.'" *Utah Historical Quarterly* (Utah Historical Society) 53, no. 3, (Summer 1985): 268–291.

Paul, Rodman Wilson. *Mining Frontiers of the Far West, 1848-1880*. Albuquerque, N.M.: University of New Mexico Press, revised edition 2001.

Pennsylvania Capitol Preservation Committee. *Preserving a Palace of Art, 2000-2001 Annual Report*. Harrisburg, Pennsylvania: Pennsylvania Capitol Preservation Committee, 2001.

Pickard, John. "Report of the Capitol Decoration Commission, 1917-1928." Columbia, Missouri, 1928.

Pierson, William H. Jr. *American Buildings and Their Architects*, vol. 1. Oxford: Oxford University Press, 1986.

Placzek, Adolf K., ed in chief. *Macmillan Encyclopedia of Architects*, 4 vols. New York: The Free Press, 1982.

The Political Action Handbook, 5th ed. Sacramento: California Journal Press, 1995.

Political History of Nevada, 10th ed. Carson City, Nevada, 1997.

Prindle, David F. *Petroleum and Politics: The Texas Railroad Commission*. Center for Energy Studies, The University of Texas at Austin, 1980.

Radoff, Morris I. *The State House at Annapolis*. Annapolis: The Hall of Records Commission, Department of General Services, State of Maryland, 1972.

Reith, Gerda, ed. *Gambling*. Amherst, N.Y.: Prometheus Books, 2003.

Remele, Larry, ed. *The North Dakota State Capitol: Architecture and History*. Bismarck, N.D.: State Historical Society of North Dakota, 1989.

Reps, John W. *Town Planning in Frontier America*. Columbia, Missouri: University of Missouri Press, 1980.

Rhode Island Historical Society. *"A Most Admirable Public Building" The Rhode Island State House Centennial Exhibition*. Cranston, R.I.: University of Rhode Island, Lewis Graphics, 1996.

Rhode Island State House Clippings File, Rhode Island State Archives, Providence, Rhode Island.

Rhode Island State House Restoration Society. *Most Admirable, The Rhode Island State House*. Providence, Rhode Island: Rhode Island State House Restoration Society, 2002.

Richmond, Robert W. "Kansas Builds a Capitol." *The Kansas Historical Quarterly* (The Kansas State Historical Society) 38, no. 3 (Autumn 1972).

Ritter, Harry. *Alaska's History*. Anchorage, Alaska: Alaska Northwest Books, 2003.

Robbins, Daniel. *The Vermont State House, A History & Guide*. Northlight Press, 1980.

Rockland, Michael Aaron. "For Ellis Island, a New Life." *New Jersey Monthly* 25, no. 7 (July 2000): 48.

Romero, Tom. "Uncertain Waters and Contested Lands: Excavating the Layers of Colorado's Legal Past." *University of Colorado Law Review* 73 (2002).

Roseberry, Cecil R. *Capitol Story*. Albany, New York: New York State Office of General Services, 1982.

Roth, Leland M. *A Concise History of American Architecture*. Boulder, Co.: Westview Press, 1980.

Roth, Richard, Randolph, John, and Carl Zipper. "Coal Mining Subsidence Regulation in Six Appalachian States." *Virginia Environmental Law Journal* (University of Virginia School of Law) 10, no. 2 (Spring 1991): 311–343.

Rubenstein, Bruce A., and Lawrence E. Ziewacz. *Michigan A History of the Great Lakes State*, 2nd ed. Wheeling, Ill.: Harlan Davidson, Inc., 1981.

Seale, William. *Michigan's Capitol Construction & Restoration*. Ann Arbor, Mich.: The University of Michigan Press, 1995.

Self-Guided Tour Script of South Dakota State Capitol Building, South Dakota Bureau of Administration, updated August 2003.

Shael, Herman. *The Louisiana Civil Code: A European Legacy for the United States*. New Orleans, La.: Louisiana Bar Foundation, 1993.

Shettleworth, Earle G. Jr, and Frank A. Beard. *The Maine State House, A Brief History and Guide*. Maine Historic Preservation Commission, August 1981.

Schnedlen, Jeanne H. *The Capitol*. Harrisburg, Pa.: Armstrong Printery, Inc., 2001.

Senate of West Virginia. *The West Virginia Capitol: A Commemorative History*, June 1982.

Simons, Kenneth W. *North Dakota's State Capitol*. Bismarck, N.D.: Bismarck Tribune Company, 1934.

Smith, Hubert. *A Century of Pride: The Arkansas State Capitol*. Little Rock: Arkansas State Capitol Association, 1983.

Sorensen, Mark W., ed. *Capitol Centennial Papers*. Springfield, Ill.: Illinois State Archives, 1997.

Soule, Allen, ed. *Laws of Vermont, State Papers of Vermont*, vol. 12. Brattleboro, Vt.: The Vermont Printing Company, 1964.

Southern Living 21 (January 1986): 86–89.

State Election Board v. Bayh, 521 N.E. 2d 1313 (Ind. 1988).

State of Maine, *121st Legislature, Senate and House Registers*, Augusta, Maine, 2003.

State of Oregon v. Ashcroft, 192 F Supp 2d 1077 (D. Or April 17, 2002).

Strey, Gerry. "The 'Oleo Wars' Wisconsin's Fight over the Demon Spread." *The Wisconsin Magazine of History* (Wisconsin Historical Society) (Autumn 2001).

Talcott, George N. *Building a State*. Tacoma, Wash.: Washington State Historical Society, 1940.

The Texas Capitol, A History of the Lone Star Statehouse. Research Division of the Texas Legislative Council, Austin, Texas, 2001.

"The Texas State Capitol, Selected Essays." *Southwestern Historical Quarterly* (Texas State Historical Association), 1995.

The Temporary Commission on the Restoration of the Capitol. *Capitol*. Albany, N.Y.: New York State, 1982.

Terrie, Philip G. *Forever Wild, A Cultural History of Wilderness in the Adirondacks*. Syracuse, N.Y.: Syracuse University Press, 1994.

Texas Legislative Council. *The Texas Capitol, Symbol of Accomplishment*. Austin, Texas, 1982.

Thomson, Bailey, ed. *A Century of Controversy, Constitutional Reform in Alabama*. Tuscaloosa: The University of Alabama Press, 2002.

Tung, Anthony M. *Preserving the World's Great Cities*. New York, N.Y.: Three Rivers Press, 2001.

Tuttle, Charles Richard, comp. *General History of the State of Michigan*. Detroit, Mich.: R.O.S. Tyler & Co., 1874.

University of Vermont Library, Vermont State House file.

Valley News, White River Junction, Vermont. Reports from issues January 23, 1997; February 14, 1999; April 26, 2000; December 16, 2000; January 6, 2002; April 5, 2002; and September 9, 2002.

Van Damme, Monique. "*Keystone Bituminous Coal Association v. Debenedictis*: A 'Regulatory Taking'?" *West Virginia Law Review* 89 (1986–87): 803–824.

Van West, Carroll, ed. *The Tennessee Encyclopedia of History & Culture*. Nashville, Tenn.: Rutledge Hill Press, 1998.

Verdoia, Ken, and Richard Firmage. *Utah: The Struggle for Statehood*. University of Utah Press, 1996.

Verkuil, Paul R. *Final Report of the Special Master*. Washington, D.C.: Wilson Printing Company, Inc., March 31, 1997.

Virginia Department of General Services. *The Virginia State Capitol*.

The Virginia Magazine of History and Biography (Virginia Historical Society) 104, no. 4 (Autumn 1996).

Wade, Henry F. *Ship of State on a Sea of Oil*. Oklahoma City, Okla.: The State Board of Public Affairs, Central Printing Division, 1975.

Warnock, Kae. "A Capitol Restoration and Rehibilitation." *National Conference of State Legislatures Legisbrief* 10, no. 44 (Nov/Dec 2002).

Washington State Department of Natural Resources. *State of the Trusts Report*. Olympia, Wash., October 1997.

Wickersham, James. "Full Territorial Form of Government for Alaska, Territorial Capital Building in Juneau, Alaska." Congressional Record Sixty-third Congress, Second Session, Speech of Honorable James Wickersham of Alaska in the House of Representatives, Wednesday, January 14 and 28, 1914, Washington Government Printing Office, 1914.

Wisconsin Department of Administration, Division of Buildings and Police Services, 34th ed. *Wisconsin State Capitol Guide and History*. State of Wisconsin, 2002.

"Wyoming's Superb Capitol Building." *Cheyenne Daily Leader*, (Illustrated Edition July 23, 1890), Part II, 5.

INDEX

Note: Page numbers in *italics* indicate an illustration.